Breaking the Magic Spell

Breaking
the Magic Spell

Radical Theories
of Folk and Fairy Tales

JACK ZIPES

ROUTLEDGE

NEW YORK

Published in 1979 in the United States
by the University of Texas Press.

Reprinted in 1992 by

Routledge
An imprint of Routledge, Chapman and Hall, Inc.
29 West 35 Street
New York, NY 10001

Printed in the United States of America on acid free paper.

Library of Congress Cataloging in Publication Data

Zipes, Jack David.
　Breaking the magic spell.

　Includes bibliographical references and index.
　1. Tales—History and criticism. 2. Fairy tales—
History and criticism. I. Title.
GR74.Z56　1984　　398.2′1′094　　84-1076
ISBN 0-415-90719-5 (pbk.)

For my Mother and Father

Contents

Acknowledgements

This book is largely the result of my theoretical work accomplished during the last seven years, and consequently it is also the product of the collaborative efforts of my friends and co-editors on the staff of *New German Critique*: David Bathrick, Helen Fehervary, Andreas Huyssen and Andy Rabinbach. My debt to each one of them is immeasurable. I have also benefited from the criticism and advice of Barbara Peterson and Irene Dische, who helped me revise individual chapters. Finally, I want to thank Philippa Stratton of Heinemann Educational Books Ltd and Hana Sambrook for their invaluable editorial assistance.

In the course of my work for this book, I have translated numerous poems, stories, essays and quotations. Unless otherwise indicated, all the translations which appear in the book are my own.

Chapter 2 originally appeared as 'Breaking the Magic Spell: Politics and the German Fairy Tale' in *New German Critique* (Fall 1975); Chapter 3 in *Studies in Romanticism* (Fall 1977); and Chapter 6 as a review essay in *Telos* (Summer 1977). All three essays have been substantially revised for this book.

Preface

Our lives are framed by folk and fairy tales, but in the framework we never fill in the meaning of the tales for ourselves. It remains illusive just as our own history remains illusive. From birth to death we hear and imbibe the lore of folk and fairy tales and sense that they can help us reach our destiny. They know and tell us that we want to become kings and queens, ontologically speaking to become masters of our own realms, in touch with the projects of our lives and the self-projections, to stand upright as makers of history. Folk and fairy tales illuminate the way. They anticipate the millennium. They ferret out deep-rooted wishes, needs, and wants and demonstrate how they all can be realized. In this regard folk and fairy tales present a challenge, for within the tales lies the hope of self-transformation and a better world.

Yet folk and fairy tales can be deceptive. They can lead us on a wild-goose chase and toy with our imagination if we do not learn about their history and how to evaluate their emancipatory potential. For example, what we generally refer to as a fairy tale is quite often a folk tale which has its roots in the experience and fantasy of primitive peoples who cultivated the tale in an oral tradition. And it was this oral tradition which engendered the literary fairy tale which has assumed a variety of distinct and unique forms since the late Middle Ages. To grasp the socio-historical forces which played a vast role in the transition of the oral folk tale to the literary fairy tale is crucial for understanding why both genres persist in mass-mediated forms of the culture industry today and why their 'magic' still attracts us.

The essays collected in this volume move forward historically to reflect upon present viewpoints on folk and fairy tales. Though they were all conceived independently to treat specific problems and are self-contained, they share a common concern in the evolution of the folk tale as fairy tale and often overlap. The first essay 'Once There Was a Time: An Introduction to the History and Ideology of Folk and Fairy Tales' sets forth my general ideas and terms elaborated in more detail by the studies which follow. 'Might Makes Right — The Politics of Folk and Fairy Tales' expands upon the socio-historical reasons for the transition of the folk tale to the fairy tale and focuses on the underlying power struggles which constitute the themes of the tales. 'The Revolutionary Rise of the Romantic Fairy Tale in Germany' continues this discussion on a higher theoretical level and seeks to relate the innovative aesthetics of the fairy tale to the changing conditions and spirit of the times. 'The Instrumentalization of Fantasy: Fairy Tales, the Culture Industry and Mass Media' depicts the development of folk and fairy tales as mass-mediated products in the light of critical theory and demonstrates how the culture industry predicates the reception of these works as commodities. 'The Utopian Function of Fairy Tales and Fantasy: Ernst Bloch the Marxist and J.R.R. Tolkien the Catholic' takes up Bloch's notion of utopia introduced in the previous essay and shows how popular fairy tales must be taken more seriously as indices of our relentless subjective pursuit of emancipatory ways of living. The final essay 'On the Use and Abuse of Folk and Fairy Tales with Children: Bruno Bettelheim's Moralistic Magic Wand' questions Bettelheim's theses concerning the therapeutic value and function of the tales while at the same time it argues that the tales can be actively utilized to stimulate critical and imaginative thinking.

The movement of the essays is toward a radical theory which, I hope, can provide general operative principles for approaching and using the tales in different cultural contexts. My major concern is with the reception and interpretation of the tales as part of our Western literary heritage. Since folk and fairy tales have continually influenced our attitudes toward society, I have endeavoured to dispel false notions about their own creation and historical development to comprehend the socio-psychological dynamics behind their allurement. My own approach has been strongly affected by German theoreticians and writers of fairy tales, but I have not limited the essays to German literature. Rather I have used the German cultural tradition primarily as my starting point. For the most part my remarks address general tendencies in Western societies and pertain to the instrumentalization of fantasy that threatens to void the liberating magic of all serious tales. This magic of which I speak is not etherial hocus pocus but the *real* symbolical potential of the tales to designate ways for creating what Ernst Bloch calls concrete utopias in the here and now.

The original autonomous power of the folk tales, their aura, which has been carried over into the fairy tales, was a social one, for they sought to celebrate humankind's capacity to transform the mundane into the utopian as part of a communal project. Today this fantastic projection of such utopian impulses has been cast under the magic spell of commodity production. That is, the original magic of the tales has itself been transformed to compensate for the social injustices we encounter day in and day out in a world that curtails our individual autonomy through repressive bureaucratic and administrative systems.

Only the frame of the tales remains, and we continue to search for ways to realize their meaning. Consequently, literary criticism must become more radical. This means breaking the spell of commodity production and conventional notions of literature so that we can discover our individual and communal potential for infusing our everyday reality with the utopias we glean from the tales.

The Fairy Tale in Our Time

In our time there was once a little girl who set out to find the fairy tale, for she had heard everywhere that the fairy tale had become lost. Indeed, some people said that the fairy tale had been dead for some time. Supposedly it was lying buried somewhere, perhaps in a mass grave.

But the little girl did not let herself be deterred. She simply could not believe that fairy tales no longer existed.

So she went into the forest and asked the trees, but the trees only murmured: the elves have long since left the meadows, the dwarfs have abandoned the caves, the witches the ravines.

And she asked the birds, but they said: 'Human beings fly faster than we do — tweet, tweet, there are no more human beings!'

And the deer said, ridiculous, and the rabbits laughed, and the moose refused to speak at all. The whole thing was too stupid for him.

And the cows said that they found it all foolish, and anyway one shouldn't talk about things like that in front of young calves. They shouldn't be exposed to such stupid, senseless questions. They must be prepared to be slaughtered, castrated or to give milk. Even if one should survive as bull, that was not a fairy tale. The calves must be enlightened.

An old horse stood on the street. He was going to be taken to the slaughter-house, for he had served out his purpose. The butcher sat in a bar and drank.

He won't know either, the girl thought, but I'll ask anyway since he's an old horse and must certainly know a great deal. So she asked the horse.

The horse looked at the girl and snorted with his nostrils and stamped with his hoofs. 'You're looking for the fairy tale?' he asked.

'Yes.'

'Then I don't understand,' the horse said, 'why you are still looking since this is a fairy tale already!'

And the horse blinked at the girl.

'Hmmm. It seems to me that you yourself are the fairy tale. You're looking for yourself. Yes, yes, the closer I look at you, the more I can see it. You are the fairy tale. Come, tell me a story!'

The little girl was at first greatly embarrassed. But then she began to tell a story. She told about a young horse who was very handsome and won all the prizes at the race-track. And about a horse at the grave of his master. And about wild horses who lived out in the open.

And then the old horse wept and said: 'Thank you! Yes, yes, you are the fairy tale. I knew it all along!'

The butcher came, and the horse was slaughtered.

On Sunday the little girl was at home with her parents, and they had horsemeat for dinner since they were very poor.

But the little girl would not touch anything. She thought about the horse and how he had wept.

'She doesn't eat horsemeat,' the mother said. 'Then you'll eat nothing.'

'She's a princess,' her brothers and sisters said.

And the little girl ate nothing.

But she felt no hunger.

She thought about the old horse and how he had wept, and she was full.

Yes, she was a fairy tale.

— ÖDÖN VON HORVATH[1]

Sleeping Beauty

Keep sleeping:

I'm not a prince,
I have no sword
nor have I time
to cut the hedge
to climb the wall
to give a kiss
or marry you . . .

> *Tomorrow*
I must start work early
> *(or I'll be fired)*

My dreaming must wait
> *till Sunday*

My thinking till vacation
> *time*

> *Keep sleeping*
and dream another hundred years
> *until the right one*
> *appears*

— JOSEF WITTMANN[2]

Sleeping Beauty

once upon a time
or twice upon a time
or more times and
still some more

the spell cast by the thirteenth fairy
(not invited)
and now
all the dead princes

Sleeping Beauty behind the hedge of roses
unclear voices noises
beyond that quite clearly
music: a kiss: I
write a poem and the cook
gave the kitchen boy such a smack
that he screamed

— JOCHEN JUNG[3]

Sleeping Beauty

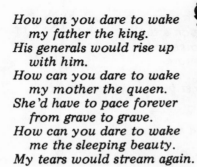

How can you dare to wake
    my father the king.
His generals would rise up
    with him.
How can you dare to wake
    my mother the queen.
She'd have to pace forever
    from grave to grave.
How can you dare to wake
    me the sleeping beauty.
My tears would stream again.

Come back in a hundred years, my prince
In a hundred years the cannons will have rusted.
    In a hundred years peace will be here.
    Come softly like the wind.
Blast open the hedge but not with hand grenades,
    don't drive tanks up to the gates.
In a hundred years the hedge will part by itself.
    Then I'll be able to love you.

— VERA FERRA-MIKURRA[4]

The Fairy Tale about Common Sense

Once upon a time there was a nice old gentleman who had the nasty habit of thinking up sensible things to do every now and then. This means that his habit actually became a nasty one only after he stopped keeping the ideas to himself but began presenting them to specialists. Since he was rich and respected in spite of his plausible ideas, the specialists had to be patient and listen to him while their ears throbbed. Certainly there is no greater torture for specialists than to listen to a sensible proposal with smiles on their faces. Everyone knows that common sense simplifies the difficult in a way which makes the difficult no longer appear uncanny to the specialists. As a consequence it appears uncanny to them. So they justifiably feel that common sense is an unlawful intrusion into their spheres of authority which they have worked hard to contrive and guard. Taking their interests into consideration, one asks what would happen to these poor people if they didn't rule and if they were replaced by common sense. What then?

One day it was announced that the nice old gentleman would speak at a conference attended by the most important statesmen on earth. According to the report, these men met to talk over ways to get rid of all the strife and want in the world. Lord almighty, they thought, who knows what the old man's planned for us now with his stupid common sense! And then they asked him to enter. He came, bowed in a somewhat old-fashioned manner and took a seat. He smiled. They smiled. Finally he began to speak.

'Gentlemen,' he said, 'I believe that I've come up with a useful idea. Its practical application has been tested. Now I'd like to make it known to people in your circles as heads of state. Please listen to me. Not for my sake but in the interest of common sense.'

The heads of state nodded, smiling through their torture, and he continued: 'You intend to provide peace and freedom for your peoples, and though your economic concerns may be very different, this meeting indicates that you are first and foremost interested in the welfare of all inhabitants of the earth from the viewpoint of common sense. Or am I incorrect on this point?'

'Heaven forbid!' they protested. 'Not at all! What do you think of us, nice old man?'

'*How wonderful!*' *he exclaimed. 'Then your problem is solved. I congratulate you and your people. Return to your homes, and bearing in mind the financial situation of your states and the laws of each constitution, grant every citizen a certain sum according to a progressive scale based on their earnings which I have figured out to the last penny and which I shall give you at the end of my talk. Here is what should happen with this sum: Each family in each one of your countries will receive as present a small pretty house with six rooms, a garden and a garage and also a car. And since the estimated sum will still not be used up after this — even this has been calculated — a new school and modern hospital will be built in each locale of the earth which has more than five thousand inhabitants. I envy you, for even though I don't believe that material things embody the highest earthly goods, I've got enough common sense to realize that peace between people depends first on the material satisfaction of human beings. If I have just said that I envy you, then I've lied. Actually I'm really happy.' The nice old gentleman took a cigar out of his breast pocket and lit it.*

The smiles on the faces of the statesmen had by now twisted. Finally the supreme head of the heads of states pulled himself together and asked in a sizzling voice: '*How high do you estimate the sum for your purposes?*'

'*For my purposes?*' responded the old gentleman, and his tone indicated that he was slightly vexed.

'*Well, are you going to tell us?*' the second highest head of state yelled unwillingly. '*How much money is necessary for this little joke?*'

'*One hundred thousand billion dollars,*' the nice old gentleman answered calmly. '*A billion has one hundred thousand million, and there are a hundred thousand billion necessary for this project. The matter concerns the figure one with twelve zeros.*' Then he puffed again on his small cigar.

'*You're completely out of your mind!*' someone yelled. Also a head of state.

The nice old gentleman sat up straight and regarded the accuser in astonishment. '*How can you possibly think that?*' he asked. '*Naturally this matter concerns a lot of money, but the last war was just as expensive according to the statistics we have.*'

At this the ministers and heads of states roared with laughter. They howled unabashed. They slapped their thighs and crowed like roosters and washed the tears of laughter from their eyes.

The nice old gentleman was puzzled and looked at them from one person to the next. '*I don't fully understand the cause of your merriment,*' he said. '*Would you be so kind as to explain to me what it is that you think so funny? If a long war costs one hundred thousand billion dollars, why shouldn't a long peace be worth exactly the same? What in all the world is so funny about this?*'

Now they all laughed even louder. It was a demonic laughter. One of the heads of states could no longer keep his seat. He jumped up, held onto his bursting ribs and yelled with the last bit of energy at his command: '*You old blockhead! A war — a war is something entirely different!*'

The heads of state, the nice old gentleman and their discussion are entirely fictitious. On the other hand, American statistics cited in the Frankfurter Neue Presse *have accurately demonstrated that the hundred thousand billion dollars spent in the last war could finance such a project as that proposed by the nice old gentleman.*

— ERICH KÄSTNER[5]

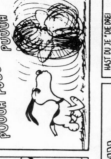

Frame 2: 'Then the wolf became very angry . . .' Frame 3: 'And he puffed and he blew the house in.'
Frame 4: 'Ridiculous! No animal could huff and puff that hard. . . .' Frame 10: 'Have you ever read "The Three Little
Pigs"? It's quite a story . . . there's this wolf, see . . .'

— *Stern* magazine, No. 77, August 24, 1978.

Mr Clean

One older sister: *Cinderella, wash the floor.*
Other older sister: *Yeah, wash it, and then re-wax it.*
   [Sisters leave for the ball.]
Cinderella: *Wash, wax, pfui.*
   [Fairy Godmother appears.]
Fairy Godmother: *Phew, ammonia. That strips wax. But use Mr Clean with no ammonia. Mr Clean gets the dirt but leaves the wax shining and you get a shine.*
Cinderella: *Wow.*
Fairy Godmother: *And now off to the ball?*
Cinderella: *Ball-schmall. Tonight's my bowling league. 'Bye.*

Police Use Cinderella Approach

In Pittsburgh, Pennsylvania, a burglar lost his shoe as he fled from the home of Mrs. M., age 43. Patrolmen arrested R.T., age 20, who was sitting shoeless in a nearby bar. Authorities said a shoe matching the one found in the M. home was discovered behind the bar.

A Fairy-Tale Story

Once upon a time there was a hawk who lived in a tree close to where a toad kept its hiding place. At the edge of a well.

The toad irritated the hawk because it continually gazed upon the world with the same expression leading the hawk to conclude that it had no idea whatsoever of how powerful and dangerous he was. So one day he swooped upon the toad, chopped it to pieces, and swallowed it.

The owner of the garden observed the scene. Now he, too, became irritated because the toad had made his well into a fairy-tale well which reminded him of his childhood, of the frog prince.

Using his rifle he was able to get rid of the source of his irritation, the hawk. Soon thereafter the neighbour's chickens dug up his garden without worrying about a thing. This led to a quarrel with the neighbour, and eventually they landed in court.

The judge went into each and every fact of the case because he wished to find the true cause of the incident. Everything ended up at the fairy-tale toad.

Then the judge pronounced the owner of the well guilty. Indeed, he said, fairy tales are not forbidden, but if you project images of them into the world, they cannot be guaranteed official protection.

— ROBERT WOLFGANG SCHNELL[6]

1 Once There was a Time

An Introduction to the History and Ideology of Folk and Fairy Tales

To begin with, a true story told in fairy-tale manner:

Once upon a time the famous physicist Albert Einstein was confronted by an overly concerned woman who sought advice on how to raise her small son to become a successful scientist. In particular she wanted to know what kinds of books she should read to her son.

'Fairy tales,' Einstein responded without hesitation.

'Fine, but what else should I read to him after that?' the mother asked.

'More fairy tales,' Einstein stated.

'And after that?'

'Even more fairy tales,' replied the great scientist, and he waved his pipe like a wizard pronouncing a happy end to a long adventure.

It now seems that the entire world has been following Einstein's advice. One of the more recent books about folk and fairy tales has declared that fairy tales are fantastically 'in'.[1] Everywhere one turns today fairy tales and fairy-tale motifs pop up like magic. Bookshops are flooded with fairy tales by Tolkien, Hesse, the Grimm Brothers, Andersen, C. S. Lewis, and scores of sumptuously illustrated fantasy works. Schools and theatres perform a wide range of spectacular fairy-tale plays for the benefit of children. Operas and musical works are based on fairy-tale themes. Famous actors make fairy-tale recordings for the radio and other mass-media outlets. Aside from the Disney vintage productions, numerous films incorporate fairy-tale motifs and plots. Even porno films make lascivious use of *Snow White and the Seven Dwarfs* and *Sleeping Beauty*. Fairy-tale scenes and figures are employed in advertisements, window decorations, TV commercials, restaurant signs, and club insignias. One can buy banners, posters, T-shirts, towels, bathing suits, stickers, ash-trays, and other household goods plastered with fairy-tale designs. Indeed, the fantastic projections of the fairy-tale world appear to have become 'in', consuming the reality of our everyday life and invading the inner sanctum of our subjective world.

Yet, one could ask whether fairy tales were ever 'out'. Have not fairy tales been with us for centuries as a necessary part of our culture? Was there ever a time when people did not tell fairy tales? Just a superficial glance back into history will tell us that fairy tales have been in existence as *oral folk tales* for thousands of years and first became what we call *literary fairy tales* toward the end of the seventeenth century.[2] Both the oral and the literary traditions continue to exist side by side today, but there is a difference in the roles they now play compared to their function in the past. This differ-ence can be seen in the manner in which they are produced, distributed and marketed. Profit mars their stories and their cultural heritage. Folk and fairy tales as products of the imagination are in danger of becoming instrumentalized and commercialized. All this has been accomplished within the framework of the modern culture industry. As Theodor Adorno has remarked:

> The culture industry fuses the old and familiar into a new quality. In all its branches, products which are tailored for consumption by masses, and which to a great extent determine the nature of that consumption, are manufactured more or less according to plan. The individual branches are similar in structure or at least fit into each other, ordering themselves into a system almost without a gap. This is made possible by contemporary technical capabilities as well as by economic and administrative concentra-tion. The culture industry intentionally integrates its consumers from above. To the detriment of both it forces together the spheres of high and low art, separated for thousands of years. The seriousness of high art is destroyed in speculation about its efficacy; the seriousness of the lower perishes with the civiliza-tional constraints imposed on the rebellious resistance inherent within it as long as social control was not yet total. Thus, although the culture industry undeniably speculates on the conscious and unconscious state of the millions towards which it is directed, the masses are not primary but secondary, they are an object of calculation; an appendage of the machinery.[3]

2

Once There Was a Time

It would be an exaggeration to argue that the culture industry in the Western world has total control over cultural production and reception, but it certainly has grown in power and has a vast influence on the consciousness of consumers through the ideology carried by its products. Thus, the emancipatory potential aesthetically conceived in the folk and fairy tales is rarely translated into social action, nor can the tales nurture sufficient discontent to make their effects reasonably certain. This is not to say that folk and fairy tales were always developed with 'revolution' or 'emancipation' in mind. But, insofar as they have tended to project other and better worlds, they have often been considered subversive, or, to put it more positively, they have provided the critical measure of how far we are from taking history into our own hands and creating more just societies. Folk and fairy tales have always spread word through their fantastic images about the feasibility of utopian alternatives, and this is exactly why the dominant social classes have been vexed by them. Beginning with the period of the Enlightenment, folk and fairy tales were regarded as useless for the bourgeois rationalization process. So it is not by chance that the culture industry has sought to tame, regulate and instrumentalize the fantastic projections of these tales.

As I have stated above, it is best not to exaggerate the hold that the culture industry has maintained over its products and our consciousness. However, it is only within the context of the culture industry that we can learn something about the history of the folk and fairy tales, or rather, why we are so little aware of the history of the folk and fairy tales. This has become more and more apparent to critics troubled about the wave of commercialization sweeping over both the folk and fairy tales. Here are two good examples of concern expressed by perceptive writers worried about the fate of the folk and fairy-tale tradition:

> Like so many folk crafts whose means of production have been expropriated by technology, the folktale in most of its traditional genres has become a marketable commodity, ripped untimely from the socio-cultural setting in which it once flourished. And, to complete the process, what is left of the tales returns to contribute to the epidemic self-depreciation infecting the modern conscience. Children subjected to the biases of standardized schooling and mass modes of entertainment no longer want to be 'told' stories that might depart from the 'correct' versions printed in books or on film. And their educators, wary of offending the

complex psychology of the child's development, learn to trust modernized editions of folktales, if indeed they tell them at all. The stories grow too heavy to be sung. They lose the right to roam about from mouth to mouth and be transformed each time they come to rest in a storyteller's heart.[4]

In this century at least, so many people know fairy tales only through badly truncated and modernized versions that it is no longer really fairy tales they know.

The enemy, thus, is historical provincialism, the attitude that pretends one's native latter-day eyes and instincts are bound to be enough to gain an understanding of fairy-tale literature. Of course our eyes and instincts are all we have to work with, but they can become more alert and better attuned just by reading many fairy tales, from many different places, with as much slowness and patience as can be mustered. Some sense of historical change can help here.[5]

Over the last three centuries our historical reception of folk and fairy tales has been so negatively twisted by aesthetic norms, educational standards and market conditions that we can no longer distinguish folk tales from fairy tales nor recognize that the impact of these works stems from their imaginative grasp and symbolic depiction of social *realities*. Folk and fairy tales are generally confused with one another and taken as make-believe stories with no direct reference to a particular community or historical tradition. Their own specific ideology and aesthetics are rarely seen in the light of a diachronic historical development which has great bearing on our cultural self-understanding.

Once there was a time when this was not the case. Once there was a time when folk tales were part of communal property and told with original and fantastic insights by gifted storytellers who gave vent to the frustration of the common people and embodied their needs and wishes in the folk narratives. Not only did the tales serve to unite the people of a community and help bridge a gap in their understanding of social problems in a language and narrative mode familiar to the listeners' experiences, but their aura illuminated the possible fulfilment of utopian longings and wishes which did not preclude social integration. According to Walter Benjamin, the aura of a work of art consists of those symbolical properties which constitute its autonomy.[6] In fact, folk tales were autonomous reflectors of actual and possible normative behaviour which could strengthen social bonds or

4

create more viable ones. Their aura depended on the degree to which they could express the needs of the group of people who cultivated them and transformed them through imaginative symbolical composition. In many respects the aura of the folk tale was linked to a community of interests which has long since disintegrated in the Western world. Today the folk tale as an oral art form has lost its aura and given way to the literary fairy tale and other mass-mediated forms.

Very little has been written about the transition of the folk tale to the fairy tale, why this occurred, and how. Since the development is so complex and has its unique tradition in different countries, I shall limit myself in this introduction to broad remarks about the general history and ideology of folk and fairy tales in the Western world. The theses introduced here should not be considered definitive but are intended more to stimulate further thought about the subject and to provide a framework from which more thorough historical accounts of the transition of the folk tale to the fairy tale may be written. The essays which follow this introduction will substantiate my general arguments and focus on specific topics which have a direct bearing on how we read the tales today.

Originally the folk tale was (and still is to a certain degree) an oral narrative form cultivated by the common people to express the manner in which they perceived nature and their social order and their wish to satisfy their needs and wants. Historical, sociological and anthropological studies have shown that the folk tale originated as far back as the Megalithic period and that common people have been the carriers and transformers of the tales. As August Nitschke has demonstrated, the tales are reflections of the social order in a given historical epoch, and, as such, they symbolize the aspirations, needs, dreams and wishes of the people, either affirming the dominant social values and norms or revealing the necessity to change them.[7] According to the evidence we have, gifted narrators told the tales to audiences who actively participated in their transmission by posing questions, suggesting changes and circulating the tales among themselves. The key to comprehending the folk tale and its volatile quality is an understanding of the audience and reception aesthetics.

Gerhard Kahlo has shown that most of the folk-tale motifs can be traced back to rituals, habits, customs and laws of primitive or pre-capitalist societies. Just a knowledge of the etymology of the words 'king' and 'queen' can help us grasp how the folk tales were directly representative of familial relations and tribal rites. 'The kings in the ancient folk tales were the oldest of the clan according to the genuine, original meaning of the word, nothing else. The word *König*, Old High German *kunig*, comes from *kuni*-race, which corresponds to the Latin *gens* and designates the head of the primordial family.'[8] This is also true of the word queen or *Königin*, who was the dominant figure in matriarchal societies. Moreoever, such acts which occur in folk tales as cannibalism, human sacrifices, favourization of the first-born, the stealing and selling of a bride, the banishment of a young princess or prince, the transformation of people into animals and plants, the intervention of beasts and strange figures were all based on the social reality and beliefs of different primitive societies. Characters, too, such as water nymphs, elves, fairies, giants, dwarfs, ghosts were real in the minds of primitive peoples and had a direct bearing on social behaviour, world views, and legal codification.

Each historical epoch and each community altered the original folk tales according to its needs as they were handed down over the centuries. By the time they were recorded in the late eighteenth and early nineteenth centuries as literary texts, they contained many primitive motifs but essentially reflected late feudal conditions in their aesthetic composition and symbolic referential system. The folk tales collected by the Grimm Brothers can serve as an example here. The initial ontological situations of the tales generally deal with exploitation, hunger and injustice familiar to the lower classes in pre-capitalist societies. And the magic of the tales can be equated to the wish-fulfilment and utopian projections of the people, i.e., of the folk, who guarded and cultivated these tales. Here the notion of *the folk* should not be glamorized or mystified as an abstract concept representing goodness or revolutionary forces. Sociologically speaking the folk were the great majority of people, generally agrarian workers, who were illiterate and nurtured their own forms of culture in opposition to that of the ruling classes and yet often reflecting the same ideology, even if from a different class perspective. If we take some of the folk tales gathered by the Grimm Brothers such as *Rapunzel, Rumpelstiltskin, The Bremen Town Musicians, Snow White, Mother Holle, The Seven Ravens*, it can be demonstrated that each narrative begins with a seemingly hopeless situation and that the narrative perspective is that of the folk in sympathy with the exploited protagonist of the tale. This aspect has been elaborated by Dieter Richter and Johannes Merkel: 'The basic structure of most folk tales is connected to the social situation of the agrarian lower classes. By this we mean that the passivity of the hero is to be seen in relation to the objectively hopeless situation of the folk-tale audiences. These classes had practically no opportunity to resist the increasing exploitation since they were isolated in their work, geographically spread out, and always stood as mere individuals in opposition to their lords and exploiters. *Thus they could only conceive a utopian image of a better life for themselves.* This historical meaning of folk tales becomes even more evident if one compares the folk tales with the stories of the urban lower classes at the beginning of this new epoch. These stories were incorporated like the folk tales into bourgeois children's literature and were placed side by side with the folk tales in the Grimms' collection.'[9] As short farcical tales (*Schwank-Märchen*), these narratives reveal a more optimistic point of view in keeping with the more active journeymen and[1] workers who told them and altered older versions to fit their own experiences. Clearly all folk tales have taken their departure from a point in history which it is necessary to relocate if we are to grasp their unusual power in the present and their unique influence at all levels of culture and art.

When we look at more refined and subtle forms of cultural expression, it becomes obvious that folk tales and folk-tale motifs have played a major role in their development. For example, Shakespeare's plays were enriched by folk tales,[10] and one could return to Homer and the Greek dramatists to trace the importance of folk-tale motifs in the formation of enduring cultural creations. However, what is most interesting about the historical development of the folk tale is the manner in which it was appropriated in its entirety by the aristocratic and bourgeois writers in the sixteenth, seventeenth and eighteenth centuries with the expansion of publishing to become a new literary genre which one could rightly call the fairy tale (*Kunstmärchen*). As a *literary* text which experimented with and expanded upon the stock motifs, figures and plots of the folk tale, the fairy tale reflected a change in values and ideological conflicts in the transitional period from feudalism to early capitalism. All the early anthologies, *Le piacevoli notti (Delightful Nights*, 1550) by Giovanni Francesco Straparola, *Pentamerone* (1634-36) by Giambattista Basile, and *Histoires ou Contes du Temps Passé*

7

(*Stories of the Past*, 1696-97) by Charles Perrault, demonstrate a shift in the narrative perspective and style which not only obliterated the original folk perspective and reinterpreted the experience of the people for them but also endowed the contents with a new ideology. This was most apparent in France during the eighteenth century when there was a craze for fairy tales written by such aristocratic ladies as Countess d'Aulnoy, Madame de Villeneuve, Madame de Beaumont, Mademoiselle de Héritier, and Madame de Murat.[11]

A good example of the drastic change of the folk tale for aristocratic and bourgeois audiences is *Beauty and the Beast.*[12] The transformation of an ugly beast into a saviour as a motif in folklore can be traced to primitive fertility rites in which virgins and youths were sacrificed to appease the appetite and win the favour of a drought dragon or serpent. Parallels can be found in other tales and wall paintings during the Ice Age when people worshipped animals as protectors and providers of society. It was also believed that human beings were reincarnated after death as animals or plants and could intercede for the maintenance of a social order. Their magic power provided balance and sustenance for people opposed to forces which they could not comprehend. In 1740 Madame Gabrielle-Suzanne de Villeneuve published her version of *Beauty and the Beast* in *Les Contes Marins*. It was 362 pages long. In 1756, Madame Le Prince de Beaumont published her shorter but similar version in *Magasin de enfans, ou dialogues entre une sage gouvernante et plusieurs de ses elèves* which has served as the basis for the numerous popular English translations widely circulated right up to our times.[13] Both versions are didactic stories which totally corrupt the original meanings of the folk-tale motifs and seek to legitimize the aristocratic standard of living in contrast to the allegedly crass, vulgar values of the emerging bourgeoisie. The theme of this aristocratic tale involves 'putting the bourgeoisie in their place'. If we can historically recall — and this means suppressing our Walt Disney consciousness — the tale concerns a very rich merchant whose children become arrogant because of the family's acquired wealth. Indeed, with the exception of Belle, all the children aspire beyond their class. Hence, the family must be punished. The merchant loses his money and social prestige, and the children are humiliated. Yet, they remain haughty and refuse to help the father overcome his loss, particularly the two older daughters. Only Belle, the youngest, exhibits modesty and self-sacrificial tendencies, and only she can save her father when he is in danger of losing his life for transgressing against the beast, i.e., the nobility. As a model of industry, obedience, humility and chastity, Belle saves her father by agreeing to live with the beast. Later, impressed by the noble nature of the beast (appearances are obviously deceiving, i.e., aristocrats may act like beasts, but they have gentle hearts and kind manners), she consents to give him a kiss and marry him. Suddenly he is transformed into a handsome prince and explains that he had been condemned to remain a beast until a beautiful virgin should agree to marry him. So, the good fairy now intercedes and rewards Belle because she has preferred virtue above either wit or beauty while her sisters are to be punished because of their pride, anger, gluttony and idleness. They are to be turned into statues and placed in front of their sister's palace. Surely, this was a warning to all those bourgeois upstarts who forgot their place in society and could not control their ambition.

The lesson to be learned from this tale involves the instrumentalization of fantasy. As Jessica Benjamin has pointed out, 'an instrumental orientation implies a relation to objects and to one's actions which uses them purely as a means to an end'.[14] If 'social activity is reduced to an orientation toward calculable and formal processes, which, in turn, eliminate the question of social intentions and implications of human action,'[15] then the projections of the imagination can only be turned in against themselves and repressively desublimated. Concretely speaking, this means that products of the imagination are set in a socio-economic context and are used ultimately to impose limitations on the imagination of the producers and receivers. The mediation between the imagination of the producer and audience becomes instrumental in standardizing forms and images of the fantasy in that it seeks to govern the independent resistance of the imagination to such instrumentalization.

Fantasy in its split sense — as the word fantasy is generally used in everyday speech — was a product of the bourgeoisie. In this regard the word did not designate the conceptual and intellectual productive power which has a unified and specific labour process with its own laws of motion at its basis. *This productive power was first schematized much more by extraneous rules — those of the capitalist utilization process. Thus, what was later to be called fantasy was primarily the result of separation and confinement.* From the viewpoint of utilization, all that which appeared to be especially difficult to control — the raw work, the leftover potential of undeveloped wishes, conceptions, the brain's own laws of motion which could not be placed in bourgeois categories — was represented as fantasy, as the gypsy, as the unemployed among the intellectual faculties. *In truth, this fantasy is a specific means of production which is needed for a labour process that does not take into view the capitalist utilization process but seeks the transformation of human beings' relationships to one another, to nature, and the reappropriation of the dead work of human beings bound by history.* That is, fantasy is not a certain substance as one says 'he has too much imagination,' but rather it is the organizer of the mediation, i.e., of the special labour process through which human drives, consciousness, and the outside world connect themselves. If this productive power of the brain is split in such a way that it cannot follow the laws of motion of its own labour process, then this leads to a crucial hindrance of any kind of emancipatory praxis.[16]

The splitting of the fantasy is at the core of the instrumentalization process. The ways in which the fantasy and products of the fantasy have been instrumentalized by the capitalist culture industry are fully illustrated in Oskar Negt and Alexander Kluge's work *Öffentlichkeit und Erfahrung*, and I shall deal with this problem in relation to the folk and fairy tale more fully in another essay. What is important to consider here is that there were already definite tendencies to utilize the fantastic images of literature in the seventeenth century in an instrumental way and that folk tales were subjected to a controlled process of reutilization that belied the original social function of the tales.

In the case of *Beauty and the Beast*, not only was a folktale motif transformed and adorned with baroque features by the imagination of the writer, but the literary mediation controlled the production, distribution and reception of the tale. As a written, innovative, privately designed text which depended on the technological development of printing and the publishing industry, the fairy tale in the eighteenth century excluded the common people and addressed the concerns of the upper classes. It was enlarged, ornamented, and filled with figures and themes which would appeal to and further the aesthetic tastes of an élite class. Moreover, the new class perspective began to establish new rules for the transformed genre: the action and content of the fairy tale subscribed to an ideology of conservatism which informed the socialization process functioning on behalf of the aristocratic class. The fantasy of the individual writer coated the ideological message with personal ingredients. But it was European absolutism of the seventeenth and eighteenth centuries which determined the structure and mediation of the fairy tales.

The example or lesson of *Beauty and the Beast* is an extreme one and must be further studied in relation to the French tradition. I purposely selected it to demonstrate the most obvious way in which the folk tale was 'mass-mediated' and changed by technology to serve the interests of the ruling class in French society of the eighteenth century. Not all writing of fairy tales was as one-dimensional and class-biased as *Beauty and the Beast*. However, the transformation of the oral tale into the literary fairy tale does mark a significant historical turning point in the arts, for with the rise of such technology as the printing press the possibility to instrument-alize products of the fantasy and govern their effect on the masses was made manifest. To clarify this point, let us look at the characteristics distinguishing folklore from literature:

Folklore	*Literature*
Oral	Written
Performance	Text
Face-to-face Communication	Indirect Communication
Ephemeral	Permanent
Communal (Event)	Individual (Event)
Re-creation	Creation
Variation	Revision
Tradition	Innovation
Unconscious Structure	Conscious Design
Collective Representations	Selective Representations
Public (Ownership)	Private (Ownership)
Diffusion	Distribution
Memory (Recollection)	Re-reading (Recollection)[17]

In studying the lists, it becomes clear that folklore thrives on the collective, active participation of the people who control their own expressions. Literature as the printed form of individual and collective products of the fantasy brings an entirely new dimension to the way people relate to their own cultural expressions. The technology of printing by itself is not the decisive factor in analysing the development of the fairy tale in relation to the culture industry but rather the formation of a new group of middle-class readers, the growth of literacy among the people of this class, and its creation of a public sphere which began organizing and exercising control over all forms of cultural expression. Consequently, folk art when appropriated by middle-class writers and publishers underwent drastic changes in its printed mass-mediated form.

Of course, one should not forget the dialectics of the situation: mass production and distribution of the texts helped people increase contact among themselves, exchange ideas and imaginative projects, and organize around their interests. Yet, who could read in the eighteenth century? Who controlled the printing and distribution of the texts? Once the folk tale began to be interpreted and transmitted through literary texts its original ideology and narrative perspective were diminished, lost or replaced. Its audience was abandoned. As text, the fairy tale did not encourage live interaction and performance but passivity. The perspective became that of the individual author who either criticized or affirmed the existing social conditions. No matter what the viewpoint was, there was a switch in class emphasis to either the aristocratic or the bourgeois. Upper-class taste and control of publishing influenced the narrative perspective as well. The distribution was exclusive due to the controls over production and the limited reading audience. Social experiences of all classes and groups of people were becoming more and more mediated through the socialization process and technological changes in production and distribution.

The rise of the fairy tale in the Western world as the mass-mediated cultural form of the folk tale coincided with the decline of feudalism and the formation of the bourgeois public sphere. Therefore, it quickly lost its function of affirming absolutist ideology and experienced a curious development at the end of the eighteenth century and throughout the nineteenth century. On the one hand, the dominant, conservative bourgeois groups began to consider the folk and fairy tales amoral because they did not rejoice in the virtues of order, discipline, industry, modesty, cleanliness, etc. In particular, they were regarded as harmful for children since their imaginative components might give young ones 'crazy ideas', i.e., suggest ways to rebel against authoritarian and patriarchal rule in the family. So the writing and printing of folk and fairy tales were opposed by the majority of the middle class who preferred didactic tales, homilies, family romances and the like. On the other hand, within the bourgeoisie itself there were progressive writers, an avant-

12

garde, who developed the fairy tale as a form of protest against the vulgar utilitarian ideas of the Enlightenment. If we recall Max Horkheimer and Theodor Adorno's study of the *Dialectic of the Enlightenment*,[18] we can see that the struggle against what they called the instrumentalization of reason had great significance for the rise of the innovative fairy tale of the romantics, particularly in Germany. Even in the United States, the lines of opposition in the ranks of the bourgeoisie regarding the instrumentalization of reason *and* fantasy can be seen in the differing attitudes toward the fairy tale and imagination. While championing the cause of the creative individual in his fairy tales, Hawthorne ranted against the female writers of moralizing fairy tales, and Poe sought to frighten rationalistic bourgeois audiences with his fantastic tales that chilled a Victorian mentality. In England the battle over the moral worth of the fairy tale was especially fierce. As Michael C. Kotzin has pointed out in his book *Dickens and the Fairy Tale*:

> The cause for which the Romantics spoke came to have greater urgency as the conditions which provoked them to defend the fairy tale intensified during the Victorian period. Earnest, artless, middle-class Evangelicalism increased its influence; the educational theories of the Enlightenment were succeeded by those of its even less imaginative descendant. Utilitarianism, and the age of the city, industrialism, and science came fully into being. These conditions of England were objected to by Carlyle and by such followers and admirers of his as Ruskin and Kingsley. In discussing the fairy tale these men followed the Romantics by stressing its imaginative value in the new world. But they also reverted a bit to the position of the enemy: the educational values they pointed to in the tales, while not usually as simply and exclusively instructional as those the Enlightenment advocated, are more conventionally moral than those which had been defended by Wordsworth and Coleridge. With their statements in defense of the fairy tale (made more publicly than those of the Romantics had been), the Victorian men of letters probably contributed to its new status. In those statements and elsewhere, they reveal the synthesis of appreciation of the imagination and moral posture which characterizes the Victorian acceptance of the fairy tale.[19]

Kotzin's remarks on the historical development of the fairy tale in nineteenth-century England are significant because they outline how the bourgeois public gradually accommodated and instrumentalized fantastic art production

to compensate for some of the ill effects of capitalist regulation and rationalization. This development in England had its
parallels in most of the advanced industrial countries of the
Western world. The resistance at first to the fairy tale during
the Enlightenment stemmed from the tales' implicit and
explicit critique of utilitarianism. The emphasis on play,
alternative forms of living, pursuing dreams and daydreams,
experimentation, striving for the golden age — this stuff of
which fairy tales were (and are) made challenged the rationalistic purpose and regimentation of life to produce for profit
and expansion of capitalist industry. Therefore, the bourgeois
establishment had to make it seem that the fairy tales were
immoral, trivial, useless and harmful if an affirmative culture
of commodity values supportive of élite interests were to
take root in the public sphere. In the early stages of capitalism, the imagination had to be fought and curbed on all
cultural levels, but toward the latter part of the nineteenth
century, when capitalism had firmly established its dominant
norms, the fairy tales did not have to be as furiously opposed
as in the initial stages of the Enlightenment. They could be
instrumentalized in more subtle and refined ways as the
technological power for manipulating cultural products in
the bourgeois public sphere became stronger. Consequently,
the aesthetic standards and social norms became more
tolerant in a repressive sense. Either fairy tales themselves
were rewritten and watered down with moralistic ,endings,
or they began to serve a compensatory cultural function.
'Beset by a changing world, the Victorian could find stability
in the ordered, formulary structure of fairy tales. He could
be called from his time and place to a soothing other world
by the faintly blowing horns of Elfland. He could be taken
from the corruptions of adulthood back to the innocence of
childhood; from the ugly, competitive city to beautiful,
sympathetic nature; from complex morality to the simple
issue of good versus evil; from a different reality to a comfort-
ing world of imagination.'[20] In other words, the tremendous
increase in the regulation of daily life as a result of capitalist
rationalization began to atomize and alienate people to such
an intense degree that amusement in the sense of distraction
had to be promoted to alleviate the tensions at work and in
the home. The development of a culture industry which
could instrumentalize products of the fantasy for increased
production and profit and also for softening the drudgery of
the work-day, disciplined schooling and dull home routines

began to assume firm contours in the nineteenth century. In particular the fairy tale offered an escape and refuge from the brutalizing effects of socialized and working reality administered by laws and norms of a bourgeois public sphere which had already become perverted to outlaw what it once tried to promote as democratic decision-making and rational discourse.

This is not to argue that the fairy tale was totally absorbed and manipulated by the growing capitalist culture industry. In the first place, the folk tale was still the dominant art form among the common people in the nineteenth century. But, with urbanization and the expansion of the publishing industry the mediation and transformation of the folk tale as fairy tale took on greater proportions and has affected the general public's view of the folk tales in the twentieth century. If we were to look back at the more significant tendencies in the nineteenth century, we could note the following:

1. After the Grimm Brothers made their first collection in 1812, folk tales were gathered, transcribed and printed for the purpose of establishing authentic versions. This was usually done by trained professionals who often stylized the tales, changed them, or were highly selective. Once gathered, the printed tales were rarely read and circulated among the original audiences.

2. Folk tales were rewritten and made into didactic fairy tales for children so that they would not be harmed by the violence, crudity and fantastic exaggeration of the originals. Essentially the contents and structure of these saccharine tales upheld the Victorian values of the *status quo*.

3. Folk tales were transformed into trivial tales, and new fairy tales were composed to amuse and distract audiences and make money. Fairy-tale plays became fashionable, especially fantasy plays for children by the end of the nineteenth century.[21]

4. Serious artists created new fairy tales from folk motifs and basic plot situations. They sought to use fantasy as a means for criticizing social conditions and expressing the need to develop alternative models to the established social orders.

5. As new technological means of the mass media were invented, they incorporated the fairy tale as a cultural product to foster the growth of commercial entertainment or to explore manifold ways in which fantasy could enhance the technology of communication, and how the effects of

fantasy could be heightened through technology.

All the above tendencies have been operative in different forms of mass-mediated culture in the twentieth century. If we were to take the dates of key technological inventions such as photography (1839), telegraph (1844), telephone (1876), phonograph (1877), motion pictures (1891), radio (1906), television (1923) and sound motion pictures (1927), we could trace how each new invention enabled the mass media to utilize the fairy tale along two broad dominant lines: (1) for the negative purpose of affirming the interests of the culture industry to curtail active social interchange and make audiences into passive consumers; (2) for the positive purpose of communicating and unifying cultural products of fantasy necessary for developing a more humanistic society and for stimulating audiences to play an active role in determining the destiny of their lives. Needless to say, the instrumentalization of the fairy tale and fantasy via the mass media has evolved commensurately with the power and growth of effective controls in the interests of the culture industry. As Richard M. Dorson has stated:

> Only in hidden pockets of our civilization, deep in mountain hollows, out on scrub country flats, or among extreme orthodox sects like the Amish and Hasidim, impervious to modern ways, do the undefiled word-of-mouth tradition and face-to-face audience still persist. The enemy of folklore is the media that blankets mass culture: the large circulation newspapers and magazines we read, the movie and television screens we watch, the recording industry whose disks we listen to. So runs the lament. What is distributed to the millions, after an elaborate, expensive packaging process, does seem the antithesis of the slow drip of invisible tradition.[22]

What Dorson calls the 'invisible tradition' is the actual common people's cultural version of their own history without the mediation of the culture industry which intercedes and interprets the experience of the people according to its marketability. The major accomplishment of the mass media in the twentieth century in regard to the instrumentalization of the folk and fairy tale resides in their power to make it seem (unlike publishing) that the voice and narrative perspective of folklore emanate from the people's own voice of cultural expression and heritage. The mass-produced books, magazines, comics and newspapers were not able to accomplish this. It was the radio, then movies, and

16

ultimately TV which were able to draw together large groups
of people as the original folk-tale narrators did and to relate
tales as though they were derived from the point of view of
the people themselves. Mass-mediated fairy tales have a
technologically produced universal voice and image which
impose themselves on the imagination of passive audiences.
The fragmented experiences of atomized and alienated
people are ordered and harmonized by turning the electric
magic switch of the radio or TV or by paying admittance to
the inner sanctum of a movie theatre. Whereas the original
folk tale was cultivated by a narrator *and* the audience to
clarify and interpret phenomena in a way that would
strengthen meaningful social bonds, the narrative perspective
of a mass-mediated fairy tale has endeavoured to endow
reality with a total meaning except that the totality has
assumed totalitarian shapes and hues because the narrative
voice is no longer responsive to an active audience but
manipulates it according to the vested interests of the state
and private industry. The manipulation of fairy-tale images
and plots should not be considered as some kind of a sinister
conspiracy on the part of big business and government. As
Herbert Schiller has pointed out: 'The process is much more
elusive and far more effective since it generally runs without
central direction. It is embedded in the unquestioned but
fundamental socio-economic arrangements that first determine, and then are reinforced by property ownership,
division of labor, sex roles, the organization of production,
and the distribution of income. These arrangements, established and legitimized over a very long time, have their own
dynamics and produce their own "inevitabilities".'[23] As a
consequence, the inevitable outcome of most mass-mediated
fairy tales is a happy reaffirmation of the system which
produces them.

It is now time again to return to questions raised at the
beginning of this essay: Have we reached a point in the
history of the folk and fairy tale where the emancipatory
potential of the tales will be totally curtailed by the technology of the culture industry? Can the fantastic symbols
be brought fully under control and instrumentalized in the
service of bureaucratized socio-economic systems in both
West and East? To answer these questions, we must bear in
mind that folk and fairy tales *per se* have no actual emancipatory power unless they are used actively to build a

social bond through oral communication, social interaction, dramatic adaptation, agitatorial cultural work, etc. To the extent that the folk and fairy tales of old as well as the new ones form alternative configurations in a critical and imaginative reflection of the dominant social norms and ideas, they contain an emancipatory *potential* which can never be completely controlled or depleted unless human subjectivity itself is fully computerized and rendered impotent. Even the mass-mediated fairy tales which reaffirm the goodness of the culture industry that produces them are not without their contradictory and liberating aspects. Many of them raise the question of individual autonomy versus state domination, creativity versus repression, and just the raising of this question is enough to stimulate critical and free thinking. The end result is not an explosion or revolution. Literature and art have never been capable of doing this and never will be. But they can harbour and cultivate the germs of subversion and offer people hope in their resistance to all forms of oppression and in their pursuit of more meaningful modes of life and communication.

The ultimate cultural value of folk and fairy tales today depends on how we convert technology to give us a stronger sense of history and of our own powers to create more just and equitable social orders. Technology itself is not the enemy of folk and fairy tales. On the contrary, it can actually help liberate and fulfil the imaginative projections of better worlds which are contained in folk and fairy tales. As we shall see, the best of folk and fairy tales chart ways for us to become masters of history and of our own destinies. To become a human being, according to Novalis, one of the great German fairy-tale writers, is an art, and the fantastic and artistic designs of folk and fairy tales reflect the social configurations which lead to conflict, solidarity or change in the name of humanity. Paradoxically the magic power of folk and fairy tales stems from the fact that they do not pretend to be anything but folk and fairy tales, that is, they make no claims to be anything but artistic projections of fantasy. And in this non-pretension they give us the freedom to see what path we must take to become self-fulfilled. They respect our autonomy and leave the decisions of reality up to us while at the same time they provoke us to think about the way we live. Einstein saw this, and it is no wonder that he had such a high regard for folk and fairy tales. Like his theory of relativity, they transform time into relative elements and offer us the hope and possibility to take history into our hands.

2 Might Makes Right — The Politics of Folk and Fairy Tales

Politics and the fairy tale. Power struggles and magic. One is tempted to ask what all those enchanting, lovable tales about fairies, elves, giants, kings, queens, princes, princesses, dwarfs, witches, peasants, soldiers, beasts and dragons have to do with politics. One is tempted by the magic spell of the tales, so it would seem, to obliterate their real historical and social basis and to abandon oneself to a wondrous realm where class conflict does not exist and where harmony reigns supreme. Yet, if we reread some of the tales with history in mind, and if we reflect for a moment about the issues at stake, it becomes apparent that these enchanting, lovable tales are filled with all sorts of power struggles over kingdoms, rightful rule, money, women, children and land, and that their real 'enchantment' emanates from these dramatic conflicts whose resolutions allow us to glean the possibility of making the world, that is, shaping the world in accord with our needs and desires. In essence, the meaning of the fairy tales can only be fully grasped if the magic spell of commodity production is broken and if the politics and utopian impulse of the narratives are related to the socio-historical forces which distinguished them first as a pre-capitalist folk form (*Volksmärchen*) in an oral tradition and which then gave rise in Germany at the end of the eighteenth century to a bourgeois art form (*Kunstmärchen*) that has its own modern literary tradition.

Since we lack an adequate history of the transitional period between the folk and fairy tales, and since they have had unique national and cultural developments, I want to limit my discussion to the politics of the tales in Germany during the eighteenth and the early nineteenth centuries with the intention of dispelling false notions about both narrative forms. Needless to say, understanding the politics is not the only approach one can take to folk and fairy tales. Yet, such a perspective is vital because of its double function: it allows us to gain greater insight into the historical forces which influenced the formation of these genres, and it provides us with a basis to review theories of the folk and fairy tale which have not considered their own premises in terms of politics. The politics in the folk and fairy tales is integrally tied to their reception in the 'once upon a time ago' and in the here and now.

Heretofore, critics have not been concerned with explaining the socio-political connection between the folk and fairy tale. Most of the research has been conducted in the area of the folk tale with heavy emphasis on anthropological, sociological, psychological, philological and literary methods.[1] The anthropological and sociological studies reveal divergent tendencies which often complement one another: the so-called Finnish School, best exemplified in America by the work of Stith Thompson,[2] seeks to reconstruct the history of a tale by tracing, collecting and categorizing all its variants; the receptionist-biographical approach focuses largely on the specific input folk narrators make in retelling the tales and how they are influenced by their communities;[3] the ethnological-comparative research centres around isolating and examining national characteristics in the tales by comparing variants of different countries.[4] Psychological interpretations always depend on the adherence to a particular discipline and school of thought.[5] Obviously the Jungians and Freudians have been among the most active in this field: Jungians have diagnosed the patterns and figures of the tales in relation to the archetypes of the collective unconscious, following Jung's lead in his famous essay 'The Phenomenology of the Spirit in the Fairy Tales', while Freudians and neo-Freudians have made exhaustive studies of the tales in connection with sexual drives, dream symbolism and phases of sexual development and maturation. The philological school has concentrated mainly on providing correct texts, documents and thorough explications of the original tales. An offshoot of the philological school is the formalist. Here the work of Vladimir Propp in the 1920s has been most influential in that he was the first to show the morphological patterns and structures of the tales as though their genetic development were bound by their own aesthetic laws.[6] Structuralists and literary scholars have moved from this purely formalist

approach to include the folk tale in a larger cultural development, and here the work of Max Lüthi has had great impact.[7]
He has studied the historical development and relation of
the folk tale to other genres and explained how folk motifs
play a role in other forms of literature. With the exception of
the remarkable work by Linda Dégh,[8] who tends perhaps to
overemphasize the importance of the storyteller, very few
scholars have tried to place the folk tale in the broader
context of a socio-cultural development, and even in Dégh's
book, not enough attention is paid to the politics of the
tales. In this regard, despite its immense contribution, the
scholarship in this field has simultaneously played a part in
casting a magic spell over the vital quality of the tales,
diluting their socio-historical import and often obscuring
problems with extraneous material. By focusing on the
politics of *both* the folk and fairy tales from the middle of
the eighteenth century to the beginning of the nineteenth,
I want to indicate how these approaches are themselves
part of 'a socio-historical context and could consequently
serve to disenchant the tales when used to clarify the
underlying forces which constitute their own epistemological telos. Only through such disenchantment can the
nature of their structure and contents be fully comprehended.

Over the centuries the influence of folk and fairy tales has
not diminished. On the contrary, they continue to exercise
an extraordinary hold over our real and imaginative lives
from childhood to adulthood. The enormous amount of
scholarship testifies to this as does the constant use and
transformation of this material in novels, poetry, films,
theatre, TV, comics, jokes and everyday conversation.
Recently the thriving pornographic industry has sought to
capitalize on the general appeal of folk-tale motifs by publishing volumes of sexy fairy tales. The motifs and stories appear
to be so well known and so much part of our lives that mere
allusion is all that is necessary to provide pleasure and stimulate interest. Yet, in fact, our comprehension of the folk and
fairy tales remains limited and has been coloured perversely
by a culture industry which has not only begotten a Walt
Disney monopoly of this material but which also fogs the
underlying reasons for our attraction to the tales. By relocat-
ing the historical origins of the folk and fairy tales in politics
and class struggle, the essence of their durability and vitality
will become more clear, and their magic will be seen as part
of humankind's own imaginative *and* rational drive to create

new worlds that allow for total autonomous development of
human qualities. The utopian impulse has its concrete base.
'The magic in the tales (if magic is what it is) lies in people
and creatures being shown what they really are,'[9] and one
could add, in being shown what they are really and realistically capable of accomplishing.

The term *Märchen* stems from the Old High German *mâri*,
Gothic *mêrs*, and Middle High German *Märe*, and it originally
meant news or gossip. *Märchen* is the diminutive form of
Märe, and the common term *Volksmärchen* or folk tale (of
medieval origins) clearly signifies that the people were the
carriers of the tales. In English, the term 'fairy tale' does not
emanate from the German *Volksmärchen* but from the
French *conte de fées* and is comparatively speaking of
modern usage. According to the *Oxford English Dictionary*,
the first reference to the term fairy tale was in 1750.[10] Most
likely the term was derived from Countess D'Aulnoy's book
Contes de fées, published in 1698 and translated the following year in London as *Tales of the Fairys*.[11] It is extremely
important to understand the social connotations of the
historical origins of the English term fairy tale, which was
applied to all folk tales recorded by the Brothers Grimm in
1812 and practically all the *Volksmärchen* that have been
collected and translated into English, a good example being
Andrew Lang's nineteenth-century collections of the Green,
Violet, Yellow Fairy books, etc. However, the term fairy tale,
when used for *Volksmärchen*, is a misnomer. Clearly, fairy
tale refers to the *literary* production of tales *adapted* by
bourgeois or aristocratic writers in the seventeenth and
eighteenth centuries such as Basile, Perrault, Countess
D'Aulnoy, Madame de Beaumont, Musäus and others, who
wrote for educated audiences, and the nature of the author's
social class, which must be studied in detail, added a new
dimension to the folk tale as it was transformed into the fairy
tale. Secondly, the term fairy tale came into the language at
a particular historical juncture and gradually eclipsed the
more explicit term folk tale. Since fairies were associated
with the supernatural and make-believe and since the upper-
class recorders of the tale shifted the emphasis of the stories,
the original material basis of the tales became obfuscated,
and it appeared that their contents and meaning were derived
from bizarre occurrences and irrational minds and not from
actual social and political conditions. In other words, it is not

by chance that the terms fairy tale and *conte de fées* enter
the English and French languages during the seventeenth and
eighteenth centuries to indicate the ideological separation of
'high' and 'low' culture and discrimination against fantasy.
In feudalism, 'the reigning classes accepted storytelling to
distract them, entertain them, and lull them to sleep. Storytelling in these circles was considered not an art but a service
to be expected from the serf and from the entertainer, and
it was valued as such. . . . While the folktale was the best-
loved entertainment at ducal banquets and in the bedrooms
of the big landowners, the tales circulating among the people
were branded by both the clerical and the secular powers as
damnable and inspired by the devil'.[12] Since the imaginative
motifs and symbolical elements of class conflict and rebellion
in the pre-capitalist folk tales ran counter to the principles of
rationalism and utilitarianism developed by a bourgeois class,
they had to be suppressed or made to appear irrelevant.

The development in Germany makes for an interesting case
study. Given the spirit of the *Aufklärung*, which sought to
promote an educational revolution, the suppression and
deprecation of the folk tale might seem to be inconsistent
with the aims of the bourgeoisie. Yet, 'the idea of education
for the people (*Volksbildung*) in the eighteenth and nineteenth centuries was a contradictory matter. And this
contradiction became even more pronounced when the
bourgeoisie, which had at first made itself the champion of
education for the people, had to recognize that the interests
of the "people", i.e., the peasant, plebeian and proletarian
strata, were not (any longer) identical with the bourgeois
interests of domination. The "educators of the people" in the
eighteenth and nineteenth centuries (increasingly supported
by the courts of political rule, which put through bans on
reading and education, for instance, through censorship)
sought to solve this contradiction by arguing for the concept
of a "limited enlightenment". To be sure, the people should
be educated and learn how to read — but the contents of this
education and reading was to remain controlled.'[13]

The controls were not only placed on the folk tales but on
all literary forms which appealed to the imagination and
might stir rebellious impulses.[14] In regard to the folk tales,
they were predominantly censored in two ways: (1) they
were not published and circulated in their original form as
told by the lower-class storytellers — the Brothers Grimm
made the first attempt along these lines in the early nine-

teenth century, and even here, they stylized the tales to improve their quality; (2) instead of folk tales, the newspapers, weeklies, yearbooks and anthologies were filled with, and flooded the market with, didactic stories, fables, anecdotes, homilies and sermons which were intended to sanctify the interests of the emerging middle class.[15] As Leo Balet and E. Gerhard remark, the eighteenth century was the unique era of moralism and was insistent on preaching about the perfectibility of mankind.[16] However, the morals proved themselves to have a class bias which excluded the 'imperfect' lower-class elements of society and their cultural forms as well. Thus, the folk tale as a pre-capitalist art form continued to be preserved and cultivated mainly by the common people in Germany throughout the eighteenth and nineteenth centuries. As Linda Dégh points out:

> With the spread of literacy, the growth of urban life, and the development of cultural and educational class distinctions, the European folktale became one of the most important means of artistic expression for the lowest strata of society, since education of the people progressed only very slowly as a result of increasingly stronger distinctions among the educational élite. The fundamental feudal aspect of the folktale did not change, or changed only slightly. Though elements of modern technology penetrated the folktale, they did not essentially transform it. The uneven industrial and urban development in Europe had its effect upon the existence of the folktale: the mighty industrial evolution in Western Europe made peasants into a middle class. The folktale remained within the lower middle class and retired to the nursery.[17]

As the bourgeoisie gradually solidified itself into a class in Germany, the folk tale began to be regarded with suspicion and was labelled inferior art because of its supposed vulgarity and lack of morals, i.e., it belonged to the illiterate lower classes and did not contain a bourgeois ethos.[18] In its place bourgeois writers industriously produced didactic tales which preached how one was to conduct oneself in conformity with laws of one's social class and state — among the best known of these writings are those of Joachim Heinrich Campe[19] and Christian Friedrich Nicolai[20] published toward the end of the eighteenth century. However, there were certain writers from the bourgeois class such as Wieland (*Der goldene Spiegel*, 1772), Musäus (*Volksmärchen der Deutschen*, 1782-6) and Mozart (*Die Zauberflöte*, 1792), who saw the folk tale as part of a national heritage which had to be recovered if a native German art of high quality were to be developed. These authors as well as the *Sturm und Drang* writers, who followed more in the tradition of Herder, borrowed heavily from folklore and used it in order to try to forge a sense of unity among the German people. A second wave of German bourgeois writers, the romantics, went a step further at the end of the 1790s by radically utilizing the folk tradition in a heavily symbolical literature to criticize the restraints and hypocrisy of bourgeois codes which were gradually being instituted in public spheres of interest. In sum, the end of the eighteenth century saw the following development: (1) the gradual designation of the folk tale as inferior art (*Trivialliteratur*) by rapidly growing bourgeois reading audiences who were 'cultivating' themselves with didactic tales, novels and plays which espoused a bourgeois ethos; (2) a radical transformation of the folk tale by the romantics, who opposed not only the crude manner in which the folk tradition was being discarded by their own class but who also sought to 'revolutionize' the folk motifs so that they could serve as a new art form to expose and criticize the growing alienation and banality of everyday life which was slowly becoming dominated by a bureaucratized and industrialized market economy. It should be stressed that, while the romantics assumed a positive attitude toward the folk tale and its tradition, these writers represented a minority position. In essence, bourgeois audiences began to thrive on rationalistic and moralistic stories and novels published by Nicolai and other entrepreneurs and light didactic plays sanctifying the bourgeois order written by Iffland and Kotzebue. The folk tale, though it continued to exist, was downgraded, as though it were but a figment of people's imagination. By dispensing with the folk tale and establishing their own literary market and art forms which tended to legitimize their interests (and which in part also contained the minority protest of the romantics), the bourgeoisie could effectively minimize and control the utopian impulse of the imaginative elements in the folk tales, dismissing them as nonsensical, irrational and trivial.

Though the term *Volksmärchen* was retained, the nineteenth century saw the creation of a new term *Kunstmärchen* and the relegation of the *Volksmärchen* to the lower classes and the domain of the household and children. While the term fairy tale is not the 'correct' translation and definition of *Kunstmärchen*, I shall be using it as such since it serves to make a clear *historical* distinction *vis-à-vis* the *Volksmärchen*. The folk tale is part of a *pre-capitalist people's oral tradition* which expresses their wishes to attain better living conditions through a depiction of their struggles and contradictions. The term fairy tale is of *bourgeois coinage* and indicates the advent of a new literary form which appropriates elements of folklore to address and criticize the aspirations and needs of an emerging bourgeois audience.

In discussing the connection between the *Volksmärchen* and *Kunstmärchen*, it is vital that a further distinction be made between those bourgeois writers such as the romantics who 'revolutionized' the folk tale at the end of the eighteenth century by endowing it with new forms and meanings in keeping with social and political changes, and the larger bourgeois audience which tended to negate the original utopian potential in the folk tales that was grounded in the common people's drive to realize their goals in conflict with their oppressors. This important distinction has been thoroughly investigated in the historical study of the folk tale's reception in Germany by Dieter Richter and Johannes Merkel. Their book, *Märchen, Phantasie und soziales Lernen*, is concerned for the most part with the imaginative elements in folk tales, and they begin by taking the Freudian notion of the imagination and redefining it in a socio-historical context: imagination is not only the necessary product of an individual's unfulfilled needs which are bound by static infantile sexual wishes for gratification, but it is socially and historically conditioned and embraces more than sexual desires. According to Richter and Merkel: 'Imagination is the organizer of mediation, in other words, the [mental] labour process through which natural drives, consciousness and the outer world are connected with one another.'[21] Hence, imagination is historical and changes; it can be used not only to compensate for what is lacking in reality but can be used *in reality* to supply practical criticism of oppressive conditions and the hope for surmounting them.

Richter and Merkel argue that the domination of the bourgeoisie and the socialization process which developed since the eighteenth century contributed to organizing and controlling the imagination of all segments of society, thereby preventing its emancipatory potential from being realized whether in action or in art forms. To illustrate this point, they study the function of imaginative elements in the folk tale and show how they underwent a decisive change when the bourgeoisie began consciously to control their transmission in books and magazines. As we know, the folk tales were oral narratives and contained popular motifs which were thousands of years old. In each historical epoch they were generally transformed by the narrator *and* audience in an active manner through improvisation and interchange to produce a version which would relate to the social conditions of the time. These tales did not spring from a supernatural realm, nor were they conceived for children. The basic nature of the folk tale was connected to the objective ontological situation and dreams of the narrators and their audiences in all age groups. In their close study of the Grimms' collection of folk tales, Richter and Merkel show that these narratives, even though marked by bourgeois stylization, all retain hope for improving conditions of life and that the fantastic elements (miracles, magic) function to bring about a *real* fulfilment of the desires of the protagonists who were often underdogs or victims of social injustice.

To the extent that Richter and Merkel show how liberating fantasy can be and how it has been curbed in bourgeois society, their book is an immensely valuable contribution to the theoretical study of folk and fairy tales. However, there is one significant problem with their work: they do not investigate *the contradictory* aspects of the fantastic and emancipatory elements in the folk tale.[22] Whereas it is true that change is realized in the tales, this change reflects the desire of the lower classes to move up in the world and seize power *as monarchs*, not necessarily the desire to alter social relations. The endings of almost all folk tales are not solely emancipatory, but actually depict the limits of social mobility and the confines of the imagination. Still, the tales are vivid images of the contradictions of that period, and they glimpse the need and possibility for limited change.

The *Märchen, as we know it today*, is a folk form of art which stems largely from late feudalism and early capitalism. This was the period in Germany when the tales became of general interest, were collected and recorded. Therefore, in analysing a particular tale it is necessary to take into account where and when it was recorded, what possible changes were made in the tale which might have originated thousands of years ago, and what unique contribution the storyteller may have made in light of communal conditions. Often it is difficult to be exact in demonstrating where definite changes were made in a particular version of a tale. However, we do know from the historical evidence and different versions gathered by the Finnish School that in the active telling of the tales the contents were easily made applicable to the conditions of late feudalism and early capitalism. Thus the folk tale as an art form that was changed constantly by its carriers can be said to be stamped by the uneven historical transition from late feudalism to early capitalism in Germany. To this extent the fairy tale (*Kunstmärchen*) is the bourgeoisification of this pre-capitalist folk form arising in Germany largely because of the social changes and upheavals in the eighteenth century.

As pre-capitalist art form, the folk tale presents, in its partiality for everything metallic and mineral, a set and solid, imperishable world.[23] This imperishable world can be linked to concepts of medieval patriarchalism, monarchy and absolutism, particularly in the seventeenth and eighteenth centuries in Germany. The world of the folk tale is inhabited largely by kings, queens, princes, princesses, soldiers, peasants, animals and supernatural creatures, rarely by members of the bourgeoisie. Nor are there machines and signs of industrialization. In other words, the main characters and concerns of a monarchistic and feudal society are presented, and the focus is on class struggle and competition for power among the aristocrats themselves and between the peasantry and aristocracy. Hence the central theme of all folk tales: 'might makes right'. He who has power can exercise his will, right wrongs, become ennobled, amass money and land, win women as prizes. This is why the people (*das Volk*) were the carriers of the tales: the *Märchen* catered for their aspirations and allowed them to believe that anyone could become a knight in shining armour or a lovely princess, and they also presented the stark realities of power politics without disguising the violence and brutality of everyday life. The manner of portrayal, as Max Lüthi has shown,[24] is direct, clear, paratactical and one-dimensional in its narrative perspective, and this narrative position reflects the limitations of feudal life where alternatives to one's situation were extremely limited. So it is in the folk tale. There is no mention of another world. Only one side of characters and living conditions is described. Everything is *confined to a realm without morals*, where class and power determine social relations. Hence, the magic and miraculous serve to rupture the feudal confines and represent metaphorically the conscious and unconscious desires of the lower classes. In the process,

29

power takes on a moral quality. 'A world inverted, an exemplary world, fairyland is a criticism of ossified reality. It does not remain side by side with the latter; it reacts upon it; it suggests that we transform it, that we reinstate what is out of place.'[25] This statement by Michel Butor about French fairy tales is applicable to the folk tale as well and points to the social critique latent in the imaginative elements. The fact that the people as carriers of the tales do not explicitly seek a total revolution of social relations does not minimize the revolutionary and utopian aspect in the imaginative portrayal of class conflict. Whatever the outcomes of the tales are — and for the most part, they are happy ends and 'exemplary' in that they affirm a more just feudal order with democratizing elements — the impulse and critique of the 'magic' are rooted in a historically explicable desire to overcome oppression and change society.

Perhaps the best-known and most widely circulated collection of folk tales is that of the Brothers Grimm. These *Märchen* were recorded during the first decade of the nineteenth century in the Rhineland. They were told in dialect, largely by servants, housewives, a watchman and inhabitants from towns and small cities and were stylized and transcribed into High German by the Grimms.[26] Consequently, a thorough analysis of the tales must take into account the background of the narrators and their communities, the social upheavals of the times caused by the Napoleonic Wars, the advent of mercantilism and the perspective of the Grimms, including their reasons for choosing certain folk tales for their collection. In dealing with the politics of the tales I want to limit my discussion to an analysis of the socio-historical conditions as reflected in two tales, *How Six Travelled through the World* and *Hansel and Gretel*, to demonstrate how links might be established with the actual struggles of that period. In the first, *How Six Travelled through the World*, the elements of class struggle are most apparent, and the entire feudal system is placed in question. In the second, *Hansel and Gretel*, which is more widely known and has been watered down in modern versions, the social references are at first not as clear. For audiences of the eighteenth and early nineteenth centuries, particularly for the peasantry, the social and political signs were unmistakable.

How Six Travelled through the World concerns a man, who 'was well-versed in all kinds of skills',[27] served a king valiantly during a war, but was miserably paid and dismissed by the

king when the war ended. The soldier swears that he
will avenge himself if he can find the right people to help him.
Indeed, he encounters five peasants who possess extraordinary
powers and agree to assist him. The soldier seeks out the king,
who has declared in the meantime that anyone who can defeat
his daughter in a foot race can marry her. If she happens to
win, death is the reward. With the help of his friends and
their supernatural gifts, the soldier wins the race. However,
the king is annoyed, and his daughter even more so, that such
a common soldier formerly in his employ should win the
wager. The king plots to kill the soldier and his friends, but
they outsmart him. The king promises the soldier all the gold
he can carry if he renounces his claim to the princess. The
soldier agrees and has one of his friends, who has enormous
strength, to carry away the entire wealth of the kingdom.
The king sends the royal army after the soldier and his friends
to retrieve the gold. Of course, they easily defeat the army,
divide the gold amongst themselves, and live happily ever
after.

It is obvious that this tale treats a social problem of utmost
concern to the lower classes. In the eighteenth century it was
customary for the state to recruit soldiers for standing armies,
treat them shabbily and abandon them when there was no
more use for them. Here the perspective of the story is clearly
that of the people, and though its origins are pre-capitalist,
the narrator and the Grimms were probably attracted to its
theme because of its relation to the Napoleonic Wars and
perhaps even the Napoleonic Code (instituted in the Rhineland). Common soldiers were indeed treated miserably during
these wars; yet, the Code gave rise to hopes for greater demo-
cratization. In this tale a common man shows himself to be
the equal of a king if not better. The miraculous talents —
the magic — are symbolic of the real hidden qualities which
he himself possesses, or they might represent the collective
energies of small people, the power they actually possess.
When these talents are used properly, that is, when they are
used to attain due justice and recompense, the people are
invincible, a theme common to many other folk tales such as
The Bremen Town Musicians. Thus, the imaginative elements
have a real reference to history and society, for the peasant
uprisings and the French Revolution in the eighteenth
century were demonstrations of how the oppressed people
could achieve limited victories against the nobility. To be
sure, these victories were often of short duration, and the

peasants and lower estates could be divided or pacified with money as is the case in this tale, where the social relations are not changed. Still, it is important that the tale does *illustrate* how common people can work together, assert themselves *actively* and achieve clear-cut goals, using their skills and imagination.

The story of Hansel and Gretel is also a story of hope and victory. Again the perspective is plebeian. A woodcutter does not have enough food to feed his family. His wife, the step-mother of his children, convinces him that they must abandon *his* children in the woods in order to survive. The children are almost devoured by a witch, but they use their ingenuity to trick and kill her. No fooling around here. Then Hansel and Gretel return home with jewels and embrace their father.

The struggle depicted in this tale is against poverty and against witches who have houses of food and hidden treasures.[28] Here again the imaginative and magic elements of the tale had specific meanings for a peasant and lower-class audience at the end of the eighteenth century. The wars of this period often brought with them widespread famine and poverty which were also leading to the breakdown of the feudal patronage system. Consequently, peasants were often left to shift on their own and forced to go to extremes to survive. These extremes involved banditry, migration or abandonment of children. The witch (as parasite) could be interpreted here to symbolize the entire feudal system or the greed and brutality of the aristocracy, responsible for the difficult conditions. The killing of the witch is symbolically the realization of the hatred which the peasantry felt for the aristocracy as hoarders and oppressors. It is important to note that the children do not turn against their father or stepmother as one might think they would. On the contrary, they reluctantly comprehend the situation which forces their parents to act as they do. That is, they under-stand the social forces as being responsible for their plight and do not personalize them by viewing their parents as their enemies. The objectification of the tale is significant, for it helps explain the tolerant attitude toward the stepmother (which is not always the case). It must be remembered that women died young due to frequent child-bearing and insanitary conditions. Thus, stepmothers were common in households, and this often led to difficulties with the children by former wives. In this respect, the tale reflects the strained relations but sees them more as a result of social forces. The stepmother is not condemned, either by the narrator or the children. They return home, unaware that she is dead. They return home with hope and jewels to put an end to *all* their problems.

In both these tales class conflict is portrayed in the light of pre-capitalist social conditions which were common in the late eighteenth and early nineteenth centuries in Germany. In neither tale is there a political revolution. What is important is that the contradictions are depicted, whereby the prejudices and injustices of feudal ideology are exposed. The magic and fantastic elements are closely tied to the real possibilities for the peasantry to change conditions, albeit in a limited way. The emphasis is on hope and action. The soldier and his friends *act* and *defeat* the king whenever they are tested. Hansel and Gretel *act* and *kill* the witch. The form of the tale, its closed, compact nature, is shaped by the individual carriers who distribute the stories and allow the common people to learn how they might survive in an unjust society and struggle with hope. Whatever symbols and magic are used can clearly be understood when placed in the historical context of the transition from feudalism to early capitalism.

Naturally it could be argued that the folk tale has nothing to do with the socio-political conditions of feudalism. That is, the folk tale originated thousands of years ago, and we cannot be entirely certain about the conditions which gave rise to them. But we do know that it was cultivated in an oral tradition by the people and passed on from generation to generation in essentially 35 different basic patterns which have been kept intact over thousands of years. As Vladimir Propp has shown, there have been transformations of elements within the patterns, and these changes depend on the social realities of the period in which the tales are told.[29] Linda Dégh clarifies this point in her thorough examination of the social function of the storyteller in a Hungarian peasant community: 'Our knowledge of European folktale material stems from two sources: literary works and oral tradition. The most striking characteristic of the traditional tale lies in the fact that the social institutions and concepts which we discover in it reflect the age of feudalism. Thus the question of the origin of the folktale coincides with that of the origin of literature in general.'[30] Clearly the folk tales collected in the seventeenth, eighteenth and nineteenth centuries, though they preserved aesthetic patterns derived from pre-capitalist societies, did so because these patterns plus the transformed elements and motifs continued to reflect and speak to the conditions of the people and the dominant ideology of the times to a great degree. Though primitive in origin, the folk tale in Germany, as told in the late eighteenth century and collected by the Grimms in the early nineteenth, related to and was shaped by feudal conditions.

During the transitional period from feudalism to capitalism in Germany when the aspirations of the emerging middle class became more pronounced, when a trend toward unification of the different principalities increased the chances for expanded trade and manufacturing, when growing public education led to greater literacy of the people, another art form, the *Kunstmärchen*, which owed its origins to the folk tale, began to develop. This fairy tale can be called the bourgeoisification of the folk tale both as short narrative and drama. From the very beginning, if we examine the works of Wieland, Musäus, Klinger, Jung-Stilling and others toward the end of the eighteenth century, we can see that the fairy tale derived its perspective from the socio-political concerns of the respective authors. The folk tale as a popular narrative and dramatic form which addressed the needs and dreams of the masses during feudalism was gradually appropriated and reutilized by bourgeois writers who sought to express the interests and conflicts of the rising middle classes during the early capitalist period.

At first the fairy tale was hampered by too much dependence on the original folk tale and feudal ideology. It was not until the 1790s when Goethe with his programmatic *Das Märchen*, which concerns the French Revolution and the formation of a new society based on ideas of social reformism and classicism,[31] and the romantics first with the tales of Wackenroder, Tieck and Novalis and later with those of Brentano, Eichendorff, Fouqué, Chamisso, Hoffmann and others, were drawn to this form that its real 'revolutionary' potential could be demonstrated. Characteristic of the tale is the emphasis on class conflict involving progressive segments of the bourgeoisie against more conservative elements. The new hero is no longer a prince or peasant, but a bourgeois protagonist, generally speaking an artist, the creative individual, who has numerous adventures and encounters with the supernatural in pursuit of a 'new world' where he will be able to develop and enjoy his talents. The quest is no longer for wealth and social status (though class struggle is involved) but for a change in social relations and a millennium, and this is significant, for it reflected the influence of the American and French Revolutions and other revolutionary movements at the end of the eighteenth century. Whereas the folk-tale world of absolutism always remains intact, the fairy tale records the breakdown of an old world structure, chaos, confusion, and the striving to attain a new world which might allow for more humane conduct. In its form, the fairy tale is multi-dimensional, hypotactical not paratactical, and open-ended. Often it is difficult to distinguish between the unreal and the real in the tale. This complex mode of portrayal again reflects a change in society where new perspectives and styles of life were more accessible to and were appropriated by the middle classes and where everything associated with the feudal world and the Judaeo-Christian tradition was brought into question.

As an expression of the progressive elements of the bour- geoisie in early capitalism, the fairy tale at first, both in form and content, places a high regard on the freedom of the creative individual, opposes the growing mechanization of life and the alienation caused by capitalism, and implies that human beings must master both their own talents and time to create a new world where humanism reigns, not harmony. In contrast to the one-dimensional world of the folk tale, the world of the fairy tale has a broader spectrum of social types. Ideological elements associated with free enterprise, wage labour, accumulation and profit are added, questioned and evaluated. Anti-capitalist attitudes are frequent (for different reasons, of course) in the fairy tales of Brentano (*Gockel, Hinkel und Gackeleia*), Eichendorff (*Libertas und ihre Freier*), Chamisso (*Peter Schlemihl*) and Hoffmann (*Klein Zaches* and *Meister Floh*) and become more pronounced by the end of the nineteenth century in Hofmannsthal's *Geschichte des Kaufmannsohnes und seiner vier Diener* and during the twentieth century in Horváth's *Sportmärchen* and Döblin's *Märchen vom Materialismus*. Machines, inventions, auto- matons and cities become standard parts of the settings as Marianne Thalmann has demonstrated in *Romantiker ent- decken die Stadt*.[32] Subjectivity assumes a more important role. The tale is now part of a *literary tradition*, and the language is more subtle and metaphorical. The action, ideas and forms depend on the author's socio-political stance. In fact, it was through the fairy tale as narrative and drama that bourgeois artists presented the need for social change by purposely reutilizing folk motifs, elements and plots. One could possibly argue that German bourgeois artists were particularly attracted to the fairy tale since they could write their social and political protests in a type of 'slave language'. Given the censors during the Napoleonic Wars and early Metternich period and the restraints placed on their energies and progressive ideas, German writers and intellectuals became prone to a metaphysical drive to interiorize. 'Since the aristocracy prevented the free-lance writer from participating in the decision-making process, and thereby, at the same time excluded him from that social situation in which he could have fully developed his bourgeois personality, there remained only the way of resignation. This led to different types of inwardness (*Innerlichkeit*) in which the free-lance writer — estranged from his literary-political possibilities — was left no other recourse but to make the politically homeless members of the "middle strata", i.e., the bourgeois "class", appear noble in an aesthetic sense.'[33] To a certain degree, the fairy tale provided a suitable metaphorical mode for the bourgeois free-lance writers to express their unfulfilled wishes for greater social and cultural freedom. Though some writers took an élitist position and portrayed the artist as saviour of society, they all recognized that a new world had to be formed out of chaos, and this world can be likened to a world of Eros, ideologically and aesthetically projected as a world where the creative nature of all human beings is allowed full development and where differences between people are cultivated and respected. No matter what has become of the fairy tale, its main impulse was at first revolutionary and progressive, not escapist, as has too often been suggested. The realm of that fairy tale contains a symbolical reflection of real socio-political issues and conflicts.

In the early phase of romanticism, Wackenroder, Tieck and Novalis wrote fairy tales of protest which drew upon their resentment of the rationalist utilitarian principles being institutionalized by the bourgeoisie and the states in which they lived. Wackenroder's *Ein wunderbares morgendländisches Märchen von einem nackten Heiligen* (A Wonderful Oriental Tale about a Naked Saint) uses the wheel of time as a symbol of bourgeois strict regulation of work ('time is money') to demonstrate how humankind and the imagination can be depleted of their vital essence in such a process. In Tieck's *Der Runenberg*, Christian seeks to escape the orderly life of town and garden since he finds such respectability suffocating. Eventually he goes insane because there are no options for the imagination within bourgeois confines. In his *Klingsohrs Märchen*, Novalis has *der Schreiber* (the scribe), representing utilitarian rationalism, pose a threat to the creation of a new realm which is to be composed of love (Eros) and peace (Freya). After the *Schreiber* is defeated, wisdom and imagination give rise to the new realm — obviously a counter model to the real German states which held creative forces in check. In each one of these fairy tales there is a socio-political statement about existing conditions along with an expression of hope that humankind can create non-repressive societies.

Wackenroder, Tieck and Novalis were only the inaugurators of the radical romantic fairy tale. E. T. A. Hoffmann, who came after them, is perhaps the best example for demonstrating how revolutionary and utopian the fairy tale could become. Not only was Hoffmann the culminator of the romantic movement, but he was the most original and ingenious in exploring the aesthetic and political possibilities of the fairy tale. Here with *Der goldene Topf* (*The Golden Pot*, 1814), conceived at the end of the Napoleonic Wars, at a time when he was experiencing personal difficulties regarding what professional career he should pursue (musician, writer or lawyer?) and at a time when early capitalist market conditions in publishing and the absence of copyright made the process of writing for unknown audiences all the more alienating, Hoffmann consciously uses the fairy tale to make a socio-political statement. Subtitled 'Ein Märchen aus der neuen Zeit',[34] Hoffmann's story is divided into twelve vigils, two of which recount the myth of the lost paradise Atlantis. The plot concerns the young student Anselmus, who is being groomed to become a privy councillor, but who has a mysterious encounter with the beautiful blue-eyed snake Serpentina, daughter of the archivist Lindhorst. We are informed that Lindhorst was actually banished from Atlantis because he had violated the erotic principles of this paradise. His return is predicated on how he defends these principles on earth and whether he can find suitable husbands for his three daughters — young men who believe in the powers of the imagination and love. After Anselmus falls in love with Serpentina, he takes a position with Lindhorst as *scribe*, and discovers his unusual creative powers as writer. This position as *writer* brings him into conflict with the dean Paulmann and registrar Heerbrand, who want him to marry the prim and proper Veronika, settle down as councillor, and lead an orderly, useful bourgeois life. A series of conflicts which involve drunkenness, missed appointments, dream adventures and psychological torment culminate in a major battle between the forces of rationalism, utilitarianism and repression (represented by a witch) and the forces of creativity, imagination and freedom (represented by Lindhorst). Naturally, Lindhorst wins, and in the end, Anselmus arrives in Atlantis where he can realize his love for Serpentine and give full reign to his gifts as artist, unharassed by the constraining forces of the functionaries, who want to mould him in their own image.

Obviously there are many levels to this tale, and this short resumé, which focuses on the socio-political implications, does not do justice to the remarkable ironic manner in which Hoffmann subtly weaves dreams, visions, myths and reality to form what Baudelaire has termed a *paradis artificiel*.[35] The artificial paradise of this fairy tale is a real composite picture of the social struggles which Hoffmann and other bourgeois artists of that time were experiencing. Anselmus as a young writer (or as a member of the intelligentsia) seeks to avoid the manipulations of civil servants who want to make him into a mere tool of the state. He senses his potential as a creative human being and seeks to liberate himself from forces (Paulmann, Heerbrand) that seek to chain him to a life of drudgery — forces symbolical of social rationalization, civil service conformity and market conditions. The movement in the tale is dialectical: Anselmus swings between two poles, rationalism and idealism, seeking to incorporate the best of both in order to achieve his paradise. His instinctive rebellion (begun in a moment of intoxication) becomes more and more a conscious one during the course of the struggle, and the struggle is clearly against a socialization process which wants to drain the individual of his or her creative and critical qualities for the profit of a ruling class. The very beginning of the tale involves Anselmus knocking over a basket of apples and cakes set out for sale by the witch. This clash, described as accidental, turns out to be the major dramatic conflict of the story: market versus human values. As we know from Hoffmann's other tales like *Der Sandmann* and *Die Automate*, he was very much disturbed by tendencies of early capitalism which caused humans and human relations to assume the properties of things and machines while the real productive power and quality of human beings became distorted and obscured. Therefore, he endeavoured to expose this dehumanization in his writings, and in *Der goldene Topf*, he argues that intellectuals and artists from the bourgeois class itself must *refuse* to participate in such a demeaning and demented socio-economic process and must take a stand for another world. This world is not just one of flight, but it is also *an imaginative projection of real possibilities for changing human and productive relations.*

The romantics and their fairy tales have too often been misread and misinterpreted, particularly by Georg Lukács,[36] as having initiated irrationalism and a literature of flight and fancy in the German tradition. Nobody can deny the idealistic and imaginative features of romantic literature. However, it is not important to ascertain and judge whether the romantics were consequently decadent and irrational, but to comprehend why and how they reacted to those disruptive and unsettling social forces during the transition from feudalism to early capitalism. By developing the fairy tale, they were actually continuing a folk tradition which they wanted to endow with their own class aspirations and interests. Specifically they all wanted at different stages to project the possibilities for realizing greater freedom in civic life and the body politic which were undergoing great upheavals. The fairy tale changes and questions the limits of change in a conservative society. It does not present happy-end solutions because there were none in reality (except for Metternich's 'happy' Holy Alliance) at the beginning of the nineteenth century. In its candour and its imaginative use of folklore, the fairy tale proves itself to be a characteristic national form, expressing the need for greater justice and more rational alternatives in opposition to arbitrary socio-political repression. Thus it is not by chance that almost all the established and reputable writers of the nineteenth and twentieth centuries (Mörike, Stifter, Keller, Heine, Raimund, Nestroy, Büchner, Storm, Gotthelf, Raabe, Hofmannsthal, Hesse, T. Mann, Rilke, Brecht, Kafka, up to Böll and Lenz) have turned to the fairy tale not only to seek refuge from the German *misère* but to comment on it and suggest that the *misère* need not be, that change is possible in reality. Naturally, the fairy realms of each one of these authors must be explored carefully in relation to the peculiar attitudes and philosophies of each author, for many of these writers have also used the fairy tale to delude themselves and their audiences about social conditions. Still, at their symbolical best, the German fairy tales include historical and political references which reveal the imagination actively serving the general struggle for greater clarity and freedom in society. Indeed, in transcending the limits and springing the confines of their own society with magic, fairy tales provide insight on how the rationalization process of exploitative socio-economic systems needs to be and can be humanized. Hence, the reason for the continual attraction of folk and fairy tales: breaking the magic spell in fairy realms means breaking the magic hold which oppressors and machines seem to have over us in our everyday reality.

3 The Revolutionary Rise of the Romantic Fairy Tale in Germany

Most studies of the romantic fairy tale (*Kuntsmärchen*)[1] usually agree that its development marked the beginnings of a new form which broke radically with the traditional folk tale (*Volksmärchen*) and contained the essence of romantic aesthetic and philosophical theories.[2] Generally speaking these studies have focused on the formal experiments of the romantics and have made careful distinctions between the different kinds of fairy tales. Though this scholarly research has provided valuable insights into the particular intentions and designs of romantic authors, the underlying socio-historical forces which governed the rise of the fairy tale in the late eighteenth century have not been sufficiently studied, and misconceptions still exist about the meaning and rise of the fairy tale.[3] Whatever approach has been assumed, there has been a tendency to stamp the fairy tale either as an idealist expression of a given writer's *Weltanschauung* or as an escapist, imaginative projection of a writer mired in an art-for-art's sake movement. The profound socio-political impulse behind the creation of the *new* fairy tales has rarely been accorded its due, and, therefore, most attempts to develop a theory of the romantic fairy tale have remained on a formalist descriptive level or have surveyed the idiosyncrasies of a romantic writer and his fairy tales in sketchy chronological order. It is true that there have also been Jungian and Freudian 'plunges'[4] into the mysterious depths of the tales. But these research expeditions have been deceptive. In fact, it is almost meaningless to describe them as 'research' since they only fish for what their psychological premises dictate. The over-all lack of a general theoretical base appropriate to the historical rise of the fairy tale has been evident, and this has been unfortunate since the romantics' contribution to German culture was truly revolutionary in both an aesthetic and

41

political sense.

Revolutionary in form, revolutionary in statement. Here we have the basis for comprehending the rise of the romantic fairy tale in Germany. This does not mean that all fairy tales preached revolution nor that the romantics were all political revolutionaries in disguise. However, this premise does assume that the romantics were consciously aware of revolutionizing an older form of art under new socio-economic conditions which they perceived to be problematic. No matter what the individual political or aesthetic bias of a romantic writer was, all the romantics sought to contain, comprehend and comment on the essence of the changing times in and through the fairy tale, and this common goal has stamped the contours of the fairy tale up to the present.

To understand the historical rise of the romantic fairy tale and its implications for the present, it is necessary to begin by developing an adequate theory which would account for the socio-political aspects in relation to the aesthetics of the tales. Such a task cannot be accomplished in a short essay, and, therefore, the ideas I want to develop in this chapter will be confined to two areas. First, I want to discuss the significance of August Nitschke's *Soziale Ordnungen im Spiegel der Märchen*[5] and Ferenc Fehér's 'Is the Novel Problematic?'[6] for a theoretical comprehension of the revolutionary nature of the German romantic fairy tale, in comparison to other pertinent research. Second, I want to synthesize and apply the findings of these studies to several romantic fairy tales in order to test the validity of my own premises. Neither Nitschke's book nor Fehér's essay deals explicitly with the fairy tale. However, their methodological approaches and findings have great relevance for developing a theory about the German romantic fairy tale. Both are innovative studies about genres related to the fairy tale and provide useful insights for grasping the revolutionizing forms and radical implications of this genre.

I

The difficulty with most genetic studies of the German fairy tale is that they do not deal adequately enough with the folk tale. Yet, without a thorough historical grasp of the aesthetics and social significance of the folk tale, it is impossible to develop a theory about the origins and meaning of the fairy tale. This becomes abundantly clear if one reviews the most recent study of the German fairy tale, *Narziss an der Quelle*, by Hans Schuhmacher.[7] There are only eight pages devoted to the pre-history of the fairy tale, and they are limited to a discussion of the French *contes des fées* and the literary debates about aesthetics in Germany during the eighteenth century.[8] Schuhmacher sees these antecedents as important for the romantic notion of allegories and myths and comes to the following conclusion:

> While the folk tale is a natural form, lives in a veiled symbolism, neither self-explanatory nor self-conscious, and not only intro-duces secrets but is a secret unto itself, the romantic fairy tale is in no way a secret unto itself. It only reflects upon such a secret and would like to become one. In other words, it is the product of a certain ideology which bases itself upon and harks back to forgotten, sunken, repressed and misunderstood trad-itions. This results from the fact that it seeks to interpret and reevaluate them in a positive new way within the framework of a new future vision of human society. However, since it is, as already stated, a product of art, since it is reflected myth, it loses the binding force of Herder's postulation of the mythical and becomes much more akin to the concept of aesthetic play developed by Kant and Schiller.[9]

These remarks serve as the theoretical apparatus for categorically interpreting the romantic fairy tales in some vague chronological order, and as a consequence their inter-connections are entirely lost because their origins and impact are reduced to a literary tradition. The socio-historical context is ignored, and art forms are shown to have thrived apparently solely upon themselves. In fact, the folk tale was never a secret unto itself, and the fairy tale never sought to become such a secret. Folk tales were consciously created to expound upon natural occurrences and social behaviour in an oral tradition that involved participation by the audience who sought clarification of social and natural processes. The meanings of the folk tales were eminently clear to the original audiences. The symbols were significations, and only later did they become 'secrets' which remained unsolved until anthropologists and literary scholars of the nineteenth and twentieth centuries began unveiling how they related directly to the experiences of primitive peoples who had conceived and cared for them. This change came about as the cultural needs of society changed in the transition from feudalism to capitalism. Thus, the socio-cultural basis of the fairy tale is intricately linked to that of the folk tale which must first be defined if a theory about the origins of the fairy tale is to have any substantial worth.

Numerous scholars have endeavoured to place and clarify the origins of the folk tale,[10] but August Nitschke has developed the most convincing method not only for dating the origins of the folk tales but also for defining their socio-historical context. The over-all aim of his two-volume study is to demonstrate how the reflections of social orders in the folk tales from the Ice Age to the twentieth century can help us to form prognostications about the capacity of different societies to adjust to the demands of industrialization. Neither his prognostications nor the application of his method are of major concern here. What is significant for our understanding of the fairy tale's rise is that Nitschke provides ample evidence to show that (1) the folk tales were part of a socio-historical process and reflected symbolically upon this process revealing how social behaviour changed from one historical epoch to the next; (2) these reflections also demonstrated that substantive and constitutional changes in society did not occur only because there was a change in the mode of production, but that changes in perception, attitude, and behaviour could lead to the rise of a new social order; (3) the German folk tale evinced certain characteristics indicative of cultural attitudes which were rejected by the romantics. By establishing the manner in which the folk tale evolved in relation to social attitudes and behaviour, Nitschke enables us to grasp why there was a gradual shift from the oral folk tale to the literary fairy tale in eighteenth-century Germany. Moreover, it becomes apparent from the evidence he presents that the fairy tale's radical departure from the folk tale cannot be simply considered a literary phenomenon but is based on a historical transformation of social attitudes and behaviour. Since these findings have great import for a theory of the fairy tale, they need further explication. Here only those ideas will be explored which help us understand what the relationship of the folk tale was to the transformation of social behaviour and why the folk tale began to yield to the literary fairy tale in the period of transition from feudalism to capitalism.

Nitschke borrows research principles from biology, physics and anthropology to develop his own method of historical epoch research. Production for him is not the key to societal change. In fact, the purpose of the first volume of his study is to go beyond the traditional Marxist theory of value and base-superstructure analyses in order to seek other historical-sociological factors which may be just as significant in contributing to change in the social order of things as the relations of production. Thus, he uses the discoveries of biologists to demonstrate that human beings from primitive times to the present, like animals, have *ordered* themselves in groups according to their mode of behaviour. These orders are characterized by autodynamics where people depend on their own strength for survival, heterodynamics where people depend on the help of others for survival, and metamorphosis where people transform themselves for survival. In addition, Nitschke draws upon anthropological studies to show that the behaviour in these social orders has a dialectical relationship to the manner in which the people perceive phenomena in regard to time. In other words, people have established different sorts of relationships with their environment depending on whether they have tended to see time as continuity (in which case social forms and figures tend to seem unchangeable), or as having distinct sequences (in which case there is more receptivity to social change), or finally as being characterized by distinct sequences which are significantly parallel in some way (in which case perception of similarities dominates their attitude toward social change). Socialized perception and behaviour are crucial in determining transitions in social orders. The special connection between the behaviour of human beings and their socialized mode of perception in relation to time is described as follows:

> In every order the relation of the temporal parts to one another and the relation of physical bodies to one another is of a special kind. Every order in which human beings of a society are joined together with the forms (*Gestalten*) of their environment is correspondingly characterized by a temporal—corporeal arrangement. Since this order originates in the arrangement of all figures in an environment, it has also been called a configuration. . . . Human beings impart a different significance to individual movements according to the temporal—corporeal arrangement in which they live. They attribute special importance either to the movements which confront unchangeable forms or movements which are commensurate with change in a temporal—corporeal arrangement.[11]

In sum, Nitschke holds that every society in history can

be characterized by the way human beings arrange themselves (autodynamics, heterodynamics, metamorphosis) and perceive time, and this gives rise to a dominant activity (also called a line of motion). The perspectives and positions assumed by the members of society toward the dominant activity amount to a configuration. The configuration designates the character of a social order since the temporal—corporeal arrangement is designed around a dominant activity that shapes the attitudes of the people toward work, education, social development and death. Hence, the configuration of society is the pattern of arrangement and rearrangement of social behaviour related to a socialized mode of perception. It has its analogue in paintings and folk tales because they are dependent on the same socialized mode of perception. In the folk tale the temporal—corporeal arrangement reflects whether there are perceived to be new possibilities for participation in the social order or whether there must be a confrontation when possibilities for change do not 'exist. Thus, the most important factors deciding whether there could be participation or confrontation in primitive societies were not necessarily the modes of labour but social attitudes and behaviour which depended on how the people perceived things. For example, in the early Ice Age, animals were considered sacred as they were the prime source of the maintenance and reproduction of society. The activity of the members of society was governed chiefly by their perception of animals and their attitude toward them. Consequently, their behaviour assumed a line of motion (action) which illustrated the high priority given to the animals. The temporal—corporeal arrangement of this period was stamped by the positions all human beings and things assumed with respect to the hunting, caring for, killing and worshipping of animals. The social configuration was reflected in paintings and folk tales where the lines of motion were predicated on attitudes toward animals. Nitschke shows in his discussion of wall paintings and Indian folk tales and other tales like *Van den Machandelboom* and *Die Hochzeit zwischen Tier und Mensch* that animals had an elevated position in the Ice Age. The tales show that people felt vitalized, strengthened, and more powerful by being close to animals. The large animals endowed human beings with a feeling of strength and vitality, and the actions of animals were imitated in cults showing how human beings sought contact with animals and depended on them for the continuation of the society. As primitive peoples in the Ice and Megalithic Ages began to perceive the relations between themselves and things and time in a different light and to desire change, they transformed their behaviour, thereby causing a temporal—corporeal rearrangement which imparted new meaning to the social order. This often occurred without any change in the mode of production. Thus, positions assumed by human beings acting upon their new awareness led to their placing priorities on another dominant activity which allowed for fulfilling new needs and desires. Power was endowed in a class or group of people who might best facilitate the achievement of the desired goals of the society, or who, at least, made it appear that they could help everyone achieve those goals.

> The modes of behaviour cause human beings to develop the structure of a society in which they can match the desired behaviour. This leads them to accord women a dominant influence in society'at a certain time. In the case of the early Indo-Germans, the ruling class was accorded the decisive role whereas the later Indo-Germans accorded the warriors the decisive role. This decision influences then the social hierarchy. Of course, there are also other factors which have an impact on social structures such as the economy, climate and geographical location. However, what is more significant — and often underestimated — is the desire of a society to be able to realize a behaviour which allows for new similarities and, along with that, for new connections between things being perceived and to the same degree offers the possibilities for confrontation crucial for life or for participation in changes crucial for life (I, p. 193).

By studying and comparing the socially determined configurations in the folk tales of the Ice Age, Megalithic Age, and the Indo-Germanic epoch, Nitschke demonstrates that changes in behavioural attitudes (toward the social function of animals and women) were more important for historical transitions in the social order than work, climate or geography. For instance, he takes such tales as *The Twelve Brothers, The Seven Ravens* and *The Six Swans* and demonstrates how they reflect a situation in the late Ice Age when the attitude toward women was assuming a more significant role than the attitude toward animals in the hunting and grazing society and women were considered the key in providing participation and integration in society. In contrast to the previous period (when hunting and grazing were also the dominant modes of production and animals were considered central to the preservation of society) women were now worshipped as the guardians of culture who provided for the maintenance and continuation of life. The change in attitudes and behaviour toward women led to matrilineal societies in which the *intercession* of the women allowed for participation and development in society. All of this is substantiated by comparing the similarities and differences in the art objects, folk tales, and social activities of peoples from one historical epoch to the next.

Nitschke's findings are significant in that he convincingly overturns mechanistic Marxist theories which have continuously insisted that it is a change in the relations of production or market conditions which determines and accounts for a change in the social order. Though he does not discuss important factors such as class struggle and ideological determination, thereby minimizing Marxist theories of historical development, he still does attribute a crucial role to production and the market in defining a social order, but they are not always primary. This is essential for understanding the change from the folk tale to the fairy tale, which reflects a change in the social order of Germany in the eighteenth century while the same type of agrarian production remained dominant. The move from absolutism to enlightened monarchy or constitutional monarchy in eighteenth-century Germany did not arise because there was a change in the mode of production or market conditions but because the behaviour and attitudes of the Germans based on theories and the perception of time, free will, rationalism, the natural man and revolution led to a conflict with the dominant activity of the older social order which had to be opened up for more participation on the part of the bourgeoisie.[12] As Nitschke has demonstrated, the change in social attitudes and modes of behaviour can forge a new temporal-corporeal arrangement or configuration which imbues the historical epoch with new meaning. At the end of the eighteenth century a new configuration emerged which established favourable *preconditions* for the rise of the industrial society.

Hence, the period was endowed with a new meaning in this configuration. Like all living phenomena, human beings could experience a change in the future. Thus, hope was born that social conditions could become better in the future. Owing to this basic attitude, Europeans began preparing themselves ever since the end of the 18th century to make sacrifices in the present for the sake of the future they hoped to realize.

With the help of this 'inner worldly asceticism,' industrialization could be accomplished in an ideal way. To put it simply, human beings refused to make use of capital gains to set up a pleasant or comfortable life. Instead they used them to build up branches of industrial production for the purpose of attaining more favourable living conditions in later times. . . . Human beings switched to the new industrial production technology only when they took for granted that a sacrifice in the present would bring a better future. In turn this presupposed that they were in the new configuration and thus generally believed that the conditions on earth could change. Whoever did not share in this view of the world was not ready to work in an industry which produced for a future. The fact that this form of society was able to institute itself so quickly is attributable to the Europeans' autodynamic mode of behaviour on their own continent and in America (II, pp. 157-8).

Here the autodynamic mode of behaviour needs more explanation. In his examination of the folk tales in various historical epochs, Nitschke was able to observe three distinct dynamic forms of action developed by the protagonists. As we have seen, these forms of action are significant in that they are related to the modes of behaviour which social groups evolved to defend themselves, prevail over others, or to assert themselves. In this respect one can talk about *autodynamics* in a folk tale where the fate of a hero depends on himself, *heterodynamics* where the hero is dependent on another figure for survival, and *metamorphosis* where the hero undergoes a change to have an impact beyond his life. On the basis of the social and artistic configurations in given epochs, Nitschke studies and compares samples of tales from different countries to determine the major characteristics of a particular culture. For example, most protagonists in the German folk tale are autodynamic, and they generally rise in social class at the end. For the most part, the rise or self-assertion is made possible not so much because of a struggle (*Kampf*) but because of industriousness (*Tüchtigkeit*). The industrious action in and by itself is not the means by which the protagonist rises; rather the efforts made by the protagonist to show his or her industrious nature and reliability bring recognition and reward. In other words, 'the German variants of the tales demand from their listeners — for a long time peasants and craftsmen — that they pursue their lightly regarded activities in an industrious and orderly way even in difficult situations. They promise a marriage that will bring happiness, wealth, and social prestige' (II, p. 31). These acute observations about the distinct nature of the German folk tales are most significant when we consider that the Germans have been susceptible to authoritarian governments and have a long history of accommodating themselves to the demands of the upper classes, i.e., a long history of servility and of reliance on state authoritarianism.

If we carry Nitschke's conclusions about the characteristics of the German folk tale one step further, it becomes clearer why (almost out of historical necessity) the fairy tale was bound to develop. The new social order which received its contours from the Age of Enlightenment could not be depicted in folk tales which had evolved from primitive times and had become centred in form and content on the concerns of feudalism.[13] Although it is true, as Nitschke has shown, that the German folk-tale type stressing the virtue of industriousness as a means of rising in social station continued to exist up to the twentieth century, this oral folk-tale tradition remained tied to the agrarian pursuits of the peasantry and feudal notions and faded in social significance as the need for change in social behaviour was perceived and acted upon by the dominant groups in German society. Along with the institutionalization of the ideas of the Enlightenment, the way was prepared for the development of free-market enterprise and capitalist production. The new configuration in Germany of the eighteenth century encompassed the economic changes made in England and France and brought forth cultural forms of art and music more commensurate with the needs and behaviour of the age, among them the *Kunstmärchen* or fairy tale. Created largely by bourgeois writers of the eighteenth century, the fairy tale transcended the folk tale in Germany by showing how autodynamics could give rise to a new world that breaks radically with the norms of an older, more confining social order. In this respect the fairy tale corresponded to the growing needs of an audience which was becoming more literate, enlightened, emancipated and assertive. In its early phase the fairy tale reflected *conflict*, in other words, the lack of room in society or the lack of real possibilities for social participation desired by talented members of the bourgeois intelligentsia who wanted to create something new and questioned all existing institutions. Out of this conflict or chaos, the romantics sought to open up society, to develop ideas and lines of motion based on a progressive utopian notion and the longing for non-alienating conditions of existence. Thus, the aesthetic design had its point of departure in the gradual formation of a new social configuration stamped by the Enlightenment, particularly by the awareness and attitude that human beings had the free will to determine their destinies rationally. Consequently, the aesthetics of the fairy tale, derived in large part from the folk tale, were imbued with a revolutionary sense that originated in the behavioural and material changes of the social order.

Here it is important to discuss two recent studies on the aesthetics of the folk tale by Volker Klotz and Max Lüthi[14] to illustrate how Nitschke's findings enable us to surmount formalist approaches and provide us with a key to the transition from the folk tale to the fairy tale. Klotz has concentrated on the aesthetic composition of folk tales and has argued that the structure of the tales is based on principles of harmony rather than justice. Thus, he tends to overemphasize the diachronic features of the folk tale in an attempt to elaborate an aesthetic theory founded vaguely on principles of genetic structuralism. His major premise revolves around the following point: 'The harmonious order demands that things apparently disparate be in agreement, that things arbitrarily separated be reunited, that the things transformed by force be returned to their true forms, that the unfinished be rounded out. There is no doubt but that such a world order is a counter model to the historical. . . . The folk tale refuses to elucidate the past, the roots, the motor of disorder. It strives only for the future of the restored order. Disorder is only introduced in order to gain order from it.'[15] Such reduction of the contents of the folk tale to aesthetic principles is highly questionable since it involves a method that dispenses with historical and social change. And, as we have seen in Nitschke's work, it is precisely behavioural and attitudinal change which provides the impetus for the different forms and types of folk tales. Also, thematically it is the quest for power not harmony which sets the design of the folk tale, be the power used for participation or confrontation.

Lüthi is much more discriminating than Klotz, and his numerous works on the aesthetics of the folk tale have made him much more aware of the problems involved in making ahistorical generalizations about folk tales. His most recent book *Das Volksmärchen als Dichtung* is a synthesis of all his attempts to understand why the folk tales have pleased and are still pleasing listeners and readers. In other words, he limits his study to those elements of the folk tale which have made the folk tale anthropologically and aesthetically appealing in all periods of time. His major thesis centres on the beautiful as *movens* and as *absolutum*.

> What is made known to be beautiful in the folk tale partly by explicit designation and partly by the stigmatization of the opposite is therefore not or at any rate not emphatically made known as harmony, evenness, or order but rather as splendour, gold, light — these are, however, not only attributes of wealth and power but also of the divine as they appear in the legends of different peoples and in the visions of numerous mystics.
>
> Where the 'beautiful' is not specifically determined, the listeners of all epochs and regions are allowed the freedom to bring their own concept of the beautiful into play. Insofar as this is the case, the beautiful of the folk tale is timeless and ahistorical — this points to the question which is often posed about the timelessness of folk tales and art works in general.[16]

Indeed, this makes Lüthi cautious in discussing the components of the folk tale as ahistorical and timeless, and he concedes that 'not only are the material basic needs and capacities of human beings in all periods different but so are their intellectual and spiritual needs. The folk tale itself is not ahistorical. It is subject to the change of style in different epochs even though it might be less influenced than the respective literary works written by individuals. Still, aside from traits which are determined by time, different regions and specific classes, it also reveals important and characteristic timeless, supra-regional, and classless elements.'[17] Out of necessity, Lüthi is forced to take a more relative and abstract position than either Nitschke or Klotz. Thus, the hero of the folk tale is anthropologically diagnosed as a *Mängelwesen* (a creature of deficiency) who depends on other creatures and objects to achieve certain goals. But it is only this 'heroic' human being who can combine the help and gifts received to move forward to something new. The protagonist of the folk tale is the carrier of the action who makes detours, experiments, undergoes change. His or her knowing something depends on doing (action). And it is the fascination of the beautiful that shocks and prompts the protagonist to act and become at one with it.

Though there is much to be learned from Lüthi's insightful

study, its aesthetic categories abstracted from all types of *Zaubermärchen* give us a composite view of folk tales which breaks down when applied to folk tales of specific cultures and of particular periods of time. Neither Lüthi nor Klotz considers such problems as the perspective of the teller or collector of folk tales, the aesthetics of reception whereby the role of the audience must be taken into account, the adaptation of the original themes and motifs to changing social conditions, and the ideological content of the aesthetic configurations. Their disregard of sociology and history in developing their aesthetics of the folk tale makes their efforts at explaining the meaning of patterns, style and configurations questionable in the light of Nitschke's more thorough historical materialist approach. This is not to say that Nitschke has solved most of the problems mentioned above. In fact, he, too, neglects the ideological function, use and reception of the folk tales. But, he does — and this is where he provides a better starting point than Lüthi and Klotz — seek to understand the relationship between the social configurations and folk-tale configurations and why they change in different historical epochs. And it is here that his findings can help us elaborate a theory of the romantic fairy tale in Germany.

In sum, Nitschke's study illustrates the historical dynamics between social processes and artistic creation. His focus on the configurations within society and their reflection in the tales during different historical epochs makes it clear that the allegedly indecipherable magic and symbols of folk tales are decipherable and that the key to their interpretation lies in grasping social attitudes and behaviour. Important to note is that the tales were never meant to mystify or enchant listeners for the purpose of leaving them in an enthralled state of reverence for the supernatural. Folk tales consciously *made* and *make* sense. They served to clarify the socialization process and problems of social conflict and participation. Though Nitschke never discusses the relationship of the folk tale to the fairy tale, it was apparent that by the end of the eighteenth century — and here he does talk about the new configuration — the changes wrought by ideas and attitudes of the Enlightenment rendered the oral folk tale as such inadequate to reflect and explain the new style and content of that period. The gradual rearrangement of temporal and corporeal elements under enlightened rulers which prepared the way for industrialization altered artistic production and themes, and the new social configuration burst the seams of

the more traditional folk tale. The consolidation of middle-class attitudes and the incipient development of capitalist technology provided the impetus and subject matter for writers to create something new out of an antiquated form. In addition, we must consider the increased rate of literacy, the vast development of publishing, and the growth of a bourgeois public sphere to understand why the romantics seized upon the fairy tale as a form to convey their visions of a new social order. The romantic fairy tale, particularly in Germany, was the outcome of attempts by educated writers beginning with the Italians Straparola and Basile in the sixteenth century and Perrault and writers of the *cabinet des fées* in the seventeenth and eighteenth centuries to appropriate a popular or folk form of art for a new middle-class reading public. These appropriations assumed different aesthetic shapes and had different ideological tendencies and implications, but the process depended on one common factor: the temporal—corporeal social order was being rearranged in the transition from absolutism to enlightened absolutism and early forms of bourgeois hegemony and capitalism. In Germany, the impact of the rearrangement was greatest about the time of the French Revolution and in the period following this. It was during this epoch that the romantic fairy tale as *Kunstmärchen* developed as a fully autonomous genre, i.e., an artistic form which took as its innate substance the material conditions of the time. Given the rearrangement of the temporal—corporeal social order and discernible trends toward industrialization, the material conditions influenced the particular perspective and form of the romantic fairy tale, setting it apart from the folk tale. Once it is recognized that the fairy tale is not only a diachronic product of a literary tradition which began orally in the Ice Age but also the result of a socio-historical process that gives artistic expression to the revolutionary conditions in Europe of the eighteenth and nineteenth centuries, we can begin to develop an appropriate theory and method to grasp the reasons for the rise of this new genre.

II

Any theory about the rise of the romantic fairy tale in Germany must concern itself with the question why the *Kunstmärchen* seized the imagination of romantic writers and why it became a prevailing form to express the concerns of the romantics at that particular point in history. Novalis elevated the fairy tale to the 'Canon of poetry as it were — everything must be like a fairy tale.'[18] Almost all romantic writers were drawn to the fairy tale and experimented with this form in highly original ways. In fact, it became so ingrained in the German literary tradition that there is hardly a major German writer since the beginning of the nineteenth century who has not in some manner used or created a fairy tale up to the present. All the more reason to ground our theory historically in the material conditions of the late eighteenth century.

Before examining the relevance of Fehér's essay 'Is the Novel Problematic?' for such a theory, I want to remark on two recent studies which touch upon the original project and impetus of the German romantics in conceiving fairy tales. By *project* I mean the manner in which the romantics desired to project a vision of reality upon the world, utilizing a particular art form to elucidate the ambivalent reality of their ontological situation and the social forces acting upon them. Jens Tismar sums up this project succinctly:

> The poetical function of the romantic fairy tales should be understood as a social one. . . . The apparent or symbolically encoded reference to the contemporary social reality is linked to a reflection about the disparity with original conditions. On the basis of reality the fairy tale and folk song appear easy to comprehend in the light of the conditions of the time. The major focus of many romantic fairy tales centres on the attempt to imagine non-alienating world conditions — fairy tale is the 'code' for this — with an innocence which is achieved again through reflection and by the effort to conceive the split in the world as (at least partially) reconcilable without forgetting that this conception is literature.[19]

Claus Träger has gone beyond Tismar in providing us with a broader framework in which to situate the romantic fairy tale. He sees the origins and direction of romanticism in general emanating from 'the futile struggle over the problem to provide non-alienating work and to secure the development of human individuality. One must keep in mind this positive critical premise which was common to all progressive humanitarian thinking of the time in order to gain a sense at the same time of the anti-bourgeois, bourgeois-humanitarian essence of romanticism. Before and along with the early

German romantics, the best thinkers of the continent were challenged by the same phenomenon: the development of capitalist division of labour and its consequences for the integrity of human beings. The essence of the romantic world-view is tied to this unresolved problem. More than anything else, this reveals the genuine utopian character of the romantic models for a life worth living in a most profound manner.'[20] Although Träger resorts to political doctrine borrowed from Lenin to prove how the German romantics' subjective class position ultimately led them to conceive of reactionary utopias which did not serve the progressive visionary needs of the working class, his essay is most useful for defining the dilemma of the German romantics.

No matter what became of German romanticism, it began as a progressive avant-garde *literary* movement. Its thrust not only depended on a negation of the philistine substance and life-style of the emerging bourgeoisie and a protest against the utilitarian ordering of life to further industry, but it was also a *reaction against* the backward feudal ideology and conditions of authoritarianism. This is most explicit in the manner in which the romantics supported the principles of the French Revolution,[21] a point which Träger forgets when he tries to define the romantics as regressive, i.e., turning away from reality to construct impossible dreams of self-realization which harked back to the Middle Ages. On the contrary, the romantics — and here distinctions must be made — could not avoid the *ambivalence* of their situation: caught between the critique of the philistine quality of their own middle class and a critique of the decadence of the nobility and faced with a transitional period when neither peasants nor workers constituted a united revolutionary force in Germany, the romantics conceived artistic forms to clarify the social limitations of personal freedom and to imagine possible situations in which subjective fulfilment might be reinforced by objective conditions that lead to creativity, love and equality. The topos of the golden age had a socio-psychological significance for them which was intended both to affirm their radical visions and critiques and to compensate for the voids in their everyday lives.[22] There is a fine line dividing escapism and progressive utopianism in the other-worldly constructs of the romantics. But I think one misses the point if one assumes that the romantics actually believed they could escape their real situations in fairy tales or project feasible models for future worlds. The struggle to conceive a 'golden age', another world, was the struggle to detach themselves from an *ambivalent* situation in order to gain perspective for change. The locus of this ambivalent situation was the period in which they were most creative: 1796-1816 — from revolution to restoration. Their work was marked and marred by a transitional change in German society from feudalism to early capitalism: the changing contours of the French Revolution from emancipatory movement to nationalist militancy and dictatorship; the constant wars on German soil; the introduction and enforcement of the Code Napoleón in the Rhineland; the reduction of over 300 principalities to 80; the continual censorship of the arts, journals, newspapers, etc.; the changing loyalties of the German states; the growth of the German military and bureaucracy; the improvement and spread of early capitalist technology; the philosophical pursuit of principles of the Enlightenment as well as their betrayal and perversion — all these factors influenced to some degree the substance and form of the romantic project. Certainly — and this is the most significant factor — the emancipation of the individual, eagerly sought by the Enlightenment writers of the eighteenth century, became fraught with difficulties by the end of the eighteenth century since it was no longer possible to assume that the individual could posit himself or herself in the world and become at one with it. This again points to the quandary of the romantic writer: the victory over conditions hostile to self-development and social emancipation could not be accomplished while the socio-political changes fostered conditions which led to the reification of the individual, i.e., the production and use of human beings as (though they were) tools and commodities. Ironically, the romantics had to attack the Enlightenment to try to enrich and fulfil its legacy of humanitarianism.

This dilemma has been examined in detail by Henri Brunschwig, who has remarked on how difficult it was for the romantics as children of the Enlightenment to pursue their goals when the conservative forces in power primarily made use of the Enlightenment to maintain their own power.[23] Thus, the romantic attack on the Enlightenment was in actuality an attack on the *betrayal of the Enlightenment:*

> The interest of the first romantic generation lies in the fact that it brings together the typical representatives of a transitional

57

generation hesitating between two different modes of thought (i.e., the Enlightenment and romanticism). This hesitation originates in the social crisis, which casts doubt on the validity of the promises of the *Aufklärung*. The young dissidents, assembled by chance in the most tolerant and most liberal capital in Europe, believe that the time has come to transform a society which has proved incapable of absorbing them. They proclaim a new era; they are to be its founders, and, worthy ideologues and disciples of the *Aufklärung* that they are, they harness themselves to a gigantic task which they try to perform simultaneously in thought and action. . . . In Prussia the young are consciously revolutionaries, however, and not from the political standpoint alone, on ground where opposition to the existing regime is common, but even more so in the realm of morals; their aim is to destroy the old world in order to create a new. They form a party of the revolution, which they envisage in the broadest sense. All the institutions of the society into which they were born — religion, morals, politics, and art — must disappear.[24]

The ambivalent situation of the romantics who sought a progressive transformation of modes of living, thinking and political systems is reflected in the art forms they developed, and this ambivalence has been most thoroughly studied by Ferenc Fehér in 'Is the Novel Problematic?' His main points which have a bearing on the theory of the romantic fairy tale will be examined here. Fehér's essay has a twofold purpose: to criticize Georg Lukács' *Theory of the Novel* and at the same time to develop his own theory from the critique. In contrast to Lukács, who saw the rise of the novel as problematic because it could not (like the epic) provide resolution, Fehér is more positive and incisive about the origins and future of the novel because he does not hold to a formal idealization of the more classical epic, nor does he claim that the depiction of totality within a harmonious structure contains superior moral and aesthetic values *per se*.

The novel's 'formlessness' and 'prosaic character' corresponds structurally to the formless and chaotic progress through which bourgeois society annihilated the first islands of realized human substance, while also generating a major development of the powers of the species. Thus, the novel expresses a stage in human emancipation not only in its content, i.e., in the notions of collectivity structured by its categories, but also in its form. The form of the novel could not have come into being without the appearance of the categories of 'purely social' society, and the birth of this society is an enrichment, even if we take into account the unequal evolution it produces.[25]

Fehér does not call the form of the novel problematic but rather focuses on the objective problems caused by a change in the socio-economic system which provided a great measure of human emancipation on the one hand and led to capitalist forms of reification and fetishism on the other. Thus, it is the *ambivalence* of early capitalism which constitutes the nature of the novel:

> Methodologically, all of this forces the general analysis of the novel as a new epic genre equal to the classical epic to develop 'on two fronts'. First, in a detailed confrontation with the classical epic, it must prove that the novel entails an *increase in emancipation*, in spite of the loss of the specificity and the formal symmetry of the epic. Secondly, it must show the ambivalence and the striving for autonomy of those elements that within the framework of the bourgeois social phenomenon can no longer achieve high artistic fulfilment. . . . The novel is born in a society without community; the structure of its world is not communal. The world of the novel is not substantial (to use the term of *The Theory of the Novel*). It is dominated by the *duality of the Self and the external world*. This duality means that the individual is neither the direct personification of the prevalent forces in the described sphere of existence, nor are the self-objectifications of the hero immediately given, in forms that can be appropriated and used. This is the source of dilemmas, but it is not in principle 'problematic' (pp. 50-51).

After putting forward this argument, Fehér examines those aspects of the novel which reflect its ambivalent nature: the drive of the protagonist to build his or her own world, the duality of the self and its environment, the exclusion of the public sphere, the role of coincidence, and the fortuitous individual. Essentially he sees all bourgeois novels which can be considered significant (i.e., which make a cultural contribution) as asking one basic, crucial question: 'What can man make of himself?' The very fact that the novel *can* envision (in contrast to the epic) the possibility of a human being's controlling his or her own destiny 'represents a humanizing element that goes beyond the function fulfilled by the epic' (p. 67). Moreover, in direct relation to the Age of Enlightenment and the growth of free-market enterprise, the novel problematizes the pursuit of freedom by the individual whose choices and alternatives are governed by accidents of competition and struggle and by the quality of his or her *activity*. Hence, Fehér used the term 'fortuitous' to describe the modern protagonist whose actions are governed by chance. One could pose the central problem of the novel in this way: the fortuitous individual is fated to be free in a realm where freedom is illusory. The education of the hero in regard to the conditions of socialization in a fetishized world also allows for making the consciousness of the *reader* more aware of the processes determining the alternatives for *the making of oneself in the actual world*. The structure of the novel is governed then by the dialectic of what is predestined and what can be changed within the limits of a predestined framework of activity. Resolution of the contradiction between emancipation and reification in the novel is pre-dicated on socio-economic forces which are constantly changing and moving to constitute a new form of the epic. For the present, the achievement of the novel lies in its refusal to give harmonious form to incongruities and disparities which beset the individual's drive to realize a world with non-alienating conditions.

The rise of the bourgeois novel roughly parallels the rise of the literary fairy tale in Europe. Certainly in Germany the romantic fairy tale assumes a function in relation to the folk tale and the needs of the emerging bourgeois class similar to that of the novel in relation to the epic and the interests of the bourgeoisie. Therefore, much of what Fehér has written about the novel is applicable to the fairy tale. Naturally, there are generic distinctions to be made, but it will be help-ful to indicate where his ideas are applicable and where they might inform a theory of the romantic fairy tale.

First of all, the romantic fairy tale is a thorough confronta-tion with the 'classical' folk tale and demonstrates that there is an increase of human emancipation in the fairy tale despite the loss of formal symmetry and social harmony contained in the folk tale. The formlessness of the tale itself and the activity of the major protagonist, a fortuitous individual, indicate this. Whereas one marvels at the tightly-knit aesthetic composition and clear purpose of folk tales which allow for 'happy' and 'beautiful' resolutions, one is taken aback by the formlessness, apparent lack of design, and open-endedness of the romantic fairy tale. Perhaps one should say 'challenged'. Indeed, the romantic fairy tale is a *challenge* to the folk tale and to the reader as well. From a purely aesthetic point of view, the romantic fairy tale is revolutionary. It explodes the tightly-knit composition of the more feudal-oriented folk tale to articulate the needs and tastes of a bourgeois avant-garde critical both of the archaic nature of feudal societies and of the utilitarian rationalism of the emerging bourgeoisie. The boundlessness of its form and the open problematic endings suggest possibilities for human emancipation which could be *realized* in worlds (utopias) where creativity and Eros are honoured. What is striking about the romantic fairy tale in its inception is that the romantics *play off* the folk-tale symbols, motifs and themes to transcend the conservative notions of both the nobility and bourgeoisie. This is why the early romantics became so critical of Goethe and Schiller, who abandoned their earlier, more radical *Sturm und Drang* positions and sought to integrate their progressive notions within the institutions of the enlightened aristocracy. Novalis' *Klingsohrs Märchen* was in part a radical response to Goethe's *Märchen* and a utopian effort to transcend the confining institutions of aristocratic and bourgeois conservatism. The same can be said about the early endeavours of Wackenroder and Tieck and the later fairy tales of Brentano, Eichendorff, and Hoffmann with some qualifications. Certainly it is possible to argue from Fehér's point of view that the romantic fairy tale was bound to develop on two fronts: (1) in confrontation with the traditional folk tale; (2) in conflict with the exploitative tendencies and interests of the German bourgeoisie in collusion with the aristocracy.[26]

Here it is important that we become more specific than Fehér and point out the peculiar *German* nature of the romantic dilemma. In describing the national character of the Germans, particularly the German bourgeoisie, Marxists have often used the term *Misère* to refer to the wretched way the German third estate became crippled during the sixteenth and seventeenth centuries and divided against itself. The result was that, unlike the French and British, the German middle classes sought ways of compromise with the nobility which would enable them to share in the government and safeguard their vested interests. Ultimately, these compromises led to the bourgeoisie's dependence on the state, no matter what form it took, and to the perversion of the bourgeois public sphere.[27] Characteristic of the German bourgeoisie was its effort through industriousness (*Tüchtigkeit*), duty and morality to establish a public sphere consisting of institutionalized structures which facilitated rational discourse in a formal democratic manner, i.e., public assemblies, schools, theatres, journals, meeting-places, etc. The formation of the bourgeois public sphere at the end of the eighteenth century was a positive result of the bourgeois movement for Enlightenment, but, at the same time, the manner in which it was established also indicated how the ideas of the Enlightenment would be betrayed. Not revolution but compromise and accommodation were the decisive keystones of the German bourgeois public sphere. The middle-class patricians, guildsmen, entrepreneurs and intelligentsia generally sided with the nobility to maintain the interests of monarchical rule and to repress the uprisings of peasants, apprentices and journeymen. Undoubtedly, the conservative movement of the bourgeoisie and nobility was enhanced when the Revolution was turned into a dictatorship in France. The Napoleonic Wars enabled the ruling classes to make it seem that the French were at the root of the German people's oppression, and they made false promises of democratic rule and participation to the people if they would fight against their French 'oppressors'. In any case, the role played by the German bourgeoisie during the romantic period was one which led to the *stabilization* of the society in transition from late feudalism to early capitalism and a reinforcement of aristocratic rule.

As Helmut Böhme has noted:

> Germany experienced the Enlightenment only as absolutism, and that had its consequences. Above all, it was due to 'enlightened absolutism' that the spark of 1789 did not set off an explosion in Germany. As convinced supporters of governmental reforms, members of the third estate did not desire a radical altercation with the nobility and church. They wanted — mindful of the efforts by the princes to eliminate the worst conditions of the *ancien régime* by themselves — a constitutional monarchy in which the government provided for possibilities to develop industry, kept the priests in check, irrigated swamplands, built state schools, took care of the poor, protected the poor against the rich, the peasants against the aristocrats, and the industrious against those people who inherited wealth. In other words, they wanted a bureaucratic state (*Beamtenstaat*) which was not to be run in a corrupt way but according to 'rational' principles.[28]

Böhme makes it clear that, although the industrial revolution was not as fully advanced in Germany as it was in England and France, the socio-economic conditions in Germany were not 'under-developed'. They were different, and the difference depended on how the middle classes absorbed and elaborated the principles of the Enlightenment and developed them within a system of absolutism. Thus, while the principal mode of production remained agrarian in the eighteenth century, social attitudes and behaviour in the urban centres of the German principalities changed and caused a shift in the social order to enlightened monarchy and a gradual change in industrial technology. This transition from feudalism to capitalism was not marked in Germany by a violent *coup d'état* as in England and France. Nevertheless, the German states could not have functioned socially and economically at the end of the eighteenth century without giving the bourgeoisie more privileges, and, as the third estate assumed more control and authority in the authoritarian states of the princes, the economic conditions for a 'better future' under industrial capitalism were being sown. The profit motive and accumulation of capital by the bourgeois class were justified by a utilitarian rationalism (as opposed to the real egalitarian principles of the Enlightenment) and by a hypocritical moralism buffered by the Protestant work ethos which received full articulation in the family novels of this period, the plays by Iffland and Kotzebue, and the didactic stories which were being widely distributed. The energies and capacities of the divided and disunited German people were harnessed by 'bureaucratic states' in the name of nationalism and freedom to oppose the tyranny of the French or some other outside invader, but in actuality the emancipation bestowed upon the people by the 'enlightened aristocrats' from above, with the help of the bourgeoisie, led to new forms of enslavement.

The German romantics were bent on exposing both the new and old forms of enslavement. This is not to say that they had the concerns of the common people at heart. But there is a tendency to forget (especially among critics who like to debunk them) that the romantics were in their early phase *socially concerned* artists,[29] who generally supported the principles of the French Revolution, often wrote essays, articles or statements about the state, received legal training, and assumed positions which made it imperative that they concern themselves with debates about government. Aside from vocational training and pursuits, the French Revolution, the Napoleonic Wars, and changing governments, all contributed to the conception of utopias in their works which must be considered as critical reflections of existing conditions. Since the folk tale inevitably dealt with power and how to order one's life within a realm that greatly resembled a medieval hierarchy, it was natural for the romantics to re-utilize this genre for their own purposes, particularly because they wanted to clarify for themselves the ambivalent situation which caused them so much distress. It is foolish to think of the romantics as escapists. Their distress was tied to the common wretchedness of the German people, and they sought to strike a common chord to which the German people might respond. In the tradition of the *Sturm und Drang* writers, the romantics' *literary protest* was not made solely on their own behalf but also expressed the needs of the oppressed. Their efforts were made in the name of the German national bourgeois movement which failed to realize its revolutionary potential had been discharged by the Enlightenment.

Nevertheless, the folk tale itself was revolutionized to enable the romantics to depict the ambivalent nature of the rise of enlightened ideas, rationalism and free enterprise. This undertaking was both conscious and unconscious and represented one of the major accomplishments of the romantics. From an aesthetic point of view, the romantic fairy tale was conceived for a small bourgeois reading public, and it was intended to *question* and *problematize* the state of the reader, i.e., the reader's objective and subjective situation. The length and form of a tale were arbitrary as long as the tale took as its point of departure a folk tale or another type of *Kunstmärchen*. The composition of each fairy tale had its roots in the social configuration of that period. Obviously, then, each tale demands its own specific analysis because its contours are historically marked. Given the subtle literary dimension and the degree of historical specificity, the fairy tale cannot be changed and remoulded in the same way as the oral folk tale has been. In other words, it may have timeless or universal qualities like the folk tale, but its historical origins inform and even limit in a positive way its universal appeal. The romantic fairy tale marks a historical *rupture* in form and content in literary tradition. The subjective stance of the author *vis-à-vis* the changes of this period sets the mood and disposition of the tale. What is remarkable about the rise of the fairy tale is that valid generalizations can still be made despite the singular qualities of individual tales. These generalizations reveal the extent to which the romantic authors participated in and contributed to an avant-garde experiment.

Beginning with the pattern of the romantic tale, we can

note the following characteristics which distinguish it from the folk tale. (1) Though there is no prescribed form or style for a fairy tale, most use a folk tale or another fairy tale as a point of departure to give expression to the social configuration of the time. Most styles are informed by the social configuration and audience expectations, and the tales are open-ended if not enigmatic. (2) The narrative is often multi-dimensional in contrast to the one-dimensional concrete perspective of the folk tale. The impossibility of bridging the gap between self and existence is stressed. This heightens the antagonistic dualities which reflect the major themes of loneliness, alienation and fetishism. (3) To announce the emancipation of the self, the fulfilment of the Enlightenment's struggle, the fairy tale puts the unusual potential of the imagination on display. In contrast to the sparse description of the folk tale, there is a more elaborate portrayal of inner and outer worlds, unusual use of colour schemes, and the reversal of the traditional stock requisites of the folk tale. The reversal and reutilization of traditional requisites are intended to estrange the reader: to make the familiar appear strange so that the reader will be compelled to take a more critical and creative approach to daily life. (4) The protagonist, generally a male, is displaced, becomes homeless in a world without community. His goal is to transcend the alienating world, i.e., to seek or even create a new world more responsive to his needs. The protagonist is often an artist. At the very least he is associated with creativity. The creative nature of the protagonist, the potential of the individual to develop naturally, is in danger of being *confined*, regulated or manipulated. The quest of the hero, his course of movement, is characterized by an active questioning of what makes man, which suggests its reverse: how can man make society so that man knows and controls the forces acting upon him? The goal of the fairy tale is humanistic but not in a vague sense. It is specific and concrete in its anthropomorphic concern. At a time when the human relations constituting the order of work and play were being administered, rationalized, and instrumentalized in preparation for a new mode of industrial production, the romantics sought to humanize society by revealing the dangers of a growing reification (*Verdinglichung*) and opposing those oppressive forces which blocked self-development and self-government. The bourgeois hero of the romantic fairy tale is by no means a revolutionary, but he does represent the ultimate human refusal to become a cog in the wheel of growing state regulation, industrialization and bureaucratization. (5) Rarely is there a happy end to a romantic fairy tale, and if so, it is not envisioned on this earth but in another world. The other-worldly utopia offers both a critique of and alternative to conditions in the real world of the author and reader. (6) The configuration of conflict and unbridgeable duality suggests, to return to Nitschke, that participation in the socialization process has become difficult and that confrontation is necessary to allow for human development. The configuration reveals the ambivalence of the new temporal—corporeal arrangement. New space is provided for the protagonist to move, and time is uplifted for him to become master of his destiny, but the temporal and corporeal relationships confine the emancipation within state-administered, socio-economic conditions of enlightened monarchical rule. The protagonist is often asked to sell himself in some manner to a repressive, regulated social order, to sell out, to abandon his true worth. Whatever the case may be, he is pitted against demeaning and dehumanizing forces. His resistance remains the key to understanding the revolutionary impulse of the romantic fairy tale.

III

As the literary fairy tale broke away from the folk tale and assumed its own proper form during the sixteenth, seventeenth and eighteenth centuries in Europe, it set certain parameters within which the romantics worked. In other words, despite the great differences among the romantic writers in terms of their style, concerns and ideologies, they commonly took part in developing a new genre which had its roots in the changing social configuration which stamped the character of the social order in its transition from feudalism to early capitalism. Thus, they shared formally the revolutionizing of an older art form and substantively reflected on the new social configuration through the new form of the fairy tale. In particular, as artists or, to be more exact, as professional writers who were confronted by the breakdown of the feudal patronage system they received little financial support from the bourgeois publishing enterprises which replaced feudal patronage. Hence they became acutely aware of the ambivalence of freedom when the socio-economic forces set new standards of production which drove these artists to the margins of society.[30] Not that they led what one might call marginal existences, but they came up against, *were confronted by and confronted*, the solid margins of the new social configuration. Utilitarian rationalism and hypocritical moralism, profit-making and accumulation, state censorship and strict administration of production and commerce, exploitation and alienation — these were the living conditions which set the margins of the romantics' existence and also forged the parameters of the romantic fairy tale.

The situation of the professional writer[31] needs some amplification before we begin examining the romantic fairy tales in detail. As is well known, Lessing was the first prominent *professional* writer in Germany whose experiences as a 'freier Schriftsteller' prefigured generations of bourgeois writers up to the nineteenth century. The fact that publishers in the eighteenth and nineteenth centuries were not capable of paying writers enough to enable them to live off their art, i.e., their production, forced most of them to maintain two professions. Generally speaking, writers took such jobs as teacher, librarian, state official, lawyer or private secretary just to earn money to subsist. At the same time they were active as critics, editors and poets, which brought them little money. In one situation they had to accommodate themselves to the dictates of a system which they despised; in the other, they were free to express themselves and to pursue what they desired to a great extent. No, wonder, then, that art and the artist were described as 'divine'. And this is not an élitist notion. If we understand the concrete material conditions under which romantics laboured — the division of their lives related to the division of labour and the rise of schizophrenia — then it becomes understandable that the artist's vocation represented a *free pursuit*, a total dedication of one's powers to bring about self-realization and unity with objective conditions, and that the realm of art represented a sphere in which the possibilities for overcoming alienation and exploitation might be explored.

As it became more clear to the romantics that it would be impossible to realize non-alienating conditions in the German society, they distanced themselves more and more from the industrious strivings of the citizenry to accommodate themselves to forms of socio-economic rationalization which furthered the domination of the nobility. Again this was not because of the artists' 'élitism' but because of their disappointment in the social changes which were occurring. Nor did they seek flight in their art from daily occupations, nor were they immune to forces of co-optation. As we know, they were all active in mundane positions as lawyer, private secretary, teacher, judge, farmer, etc., and were obliged to make compromises for which they often detested themselves or which they accepted later in resignation. They saw the deficiency in society as linked to their own self-deficiency as some critics have suggested — no one would ever deny the general psychological compensatory value of art. Their art assumed 'divine' proportions and high value because it was an elaboration of their forthright critique of society which was shared by most of the progressive bourgeois writers at the end of the eighteenth century. As J. J. Heiner has pointed out:

> It was precisely the critical reception of Rousseau in Germany which shows that the writers and their readers began to form a progressive anti-feudal and democratic consciousness. After making their careers in the service of the princes and the church, they turned against the state and religion as it became apparent that the political reform efforts of enlightened absolutism would not be sufficient to realize civil rights. Their experience proved to them that, even in its enlightened version, the absolutist monarchy tended to conserve the old estate privileges of the aristocracy, church and guilds. The hopes which writers had for the future were hopes for a free, politically united, and democratic Germany.[32]

Heiner maintains that the progressive tendency of the early romantics became adulterated with religious and monarchical strains of thought and dreams. To a certain extent this is true, but it is irrelevant when we consider that the *anti-authoritarian* impulses of the romantics remained the governing ones even when they made great compromises with the state and church. (Incidentally this can be seen in the case of the late romantic composer Richard Wagner.)

The romantics were *realistically* in touch with the forces splitting them and Germany at the same time, and the value of their work lies in the manner in which they were able to depict their ambivalent situation in Germany. Solutions were impossible. Alternatives for the future were hoped for. The utopian realms, whether designed in their fairy tales as monarchical, republican, or Christian, were *other* than the oppressive, authoritarian regimes of Germany, and they pointed to non-alienating conditions. The dominant forces in these realms were not the people themselves, but Eros and art. Here Eros must be understood in the Freudian sense as 'life instinct'. And as Herbert Marcuse has pointed out, art gives form to and can retain the repressed image of liberation which comes from the erotic element in fantasy. This element 'aims at an "erotic reality" where the life instincts would come to rest in fulfilment without repression. This is the ultimate content of the phantasy-process in its opposition to the reality principle.'[33] Most important for the romantics was the retention of 'the repressed image of liberation'. Here another, longer quotation by Marcuse might help us sum up the project of the romantics, particularly as it assumed aesthetic shape in the fairy tale:

> The development of a hierarchical system of social labor not only rationalizes domination but also 'contains' the rebellion against domination. At the individual level, the primal revolt is contained within the framework of the normal Oedipus conflict. At the societal level, recurrent rebellions and revolutions have been followed by counter-revolutions and restorations. From the slave revolts in the ancient world to the socialist revolution, the struggle of the oppressed has ended in establishing a new, 'better' system of domination; progress has taken place through an improving chain of control. Each revolution has been the conscious effort to replace one ruling group by another; but each revolution has also released forces that have 'overshot the goal', that have striven for the abolition of domination and exploitation. The ease with which they have been defeated demands explanations. Neither the prevailing constellation of power, nor immaturity of the production forces, nor absence of class consciousness provides an adequate answer. In every revolution, there seems to have been a historical moment when the struggle against domination might have been victorious — but the moment passed. An element of *self-defeat* seems to be involved in this dynamic (regardless of the validity of such reasons as the prematurity and inequality of forces). In this sense, every revolution has also been a betrayed revolution.[34]

The anti-authoritarian and erotic symbols in the romantic fairy tales indicate to what extent the romantics were aware of the 'betrayed revolution' in Germany. The French Revolution, the wars on German soil, the promises of the German princes all led to a new social order of domination, but they also 'released forces which overshot their goal', and which, as we shall see, can be found in the romantic fairy tale.

Since it would take a more exhaustive study to cover the

entire development of the romantic fairy tale, I have selected
six tales written between 1796 and 1820 which substantiate
the theoretical premises I have outlined. These tales — W.H.
Wackenroder's *Ein wünderbares morgenländisches Märchen
von einem nackten Heiligen* (1786), Novalis' *Klingsohrs
Märchen* (1801), Ludwig Tieck's *Der Runenberg* (1802),
Clemens Brentano's *Schulmeister Klopstock and seine fünf
Söhne* (1814), Adelbert Chamisso's *Peter Schlemihl's wunder-
same Geschichte* (1814), and E.T.A. Hoffmann's *Klein Zaches
genannt Zinnober* (1818) — represent different historical
stages of the German romantic movement. Most studies of
romanticism have divided the movement into three periods;
early romanticism or the Jena School, 1798-1801 (Tieck, the
Schlegel Brothers, Novalis, Schelling, Fichte, Schleiermacher,
etc.); middle romanticism or the Heidelberg School, 1805-09
(Arnim, Brentano, the Grimm Brothers, Eichendorff, etc); and
late romanticism or the Berlin School, 1814-19 (Hoffmann,
Chamisso, Fouqué, etc.). Though these divisions are helpful,
they fail to take into account other groups and individuals
such as the Swabian romantics, Kleist, Forster, Görres, Hölder-
lin and Jean Paul, who partook in the spirit of this movement.
In general it seems to me to be more accurate to consider
romanticism as comprising three overlapping stages from 1796
to 1820: the theoretical and innovative period which was
characterized by radical experimentation; the folk period,
which led to the exploration of national history and tradition;
and the conventional period, which reduced the originally
complex motifs and themes to formulae for a larger reading
public. In this regard, my selection of tales is an attempt to
understand the specific historical relation of each tale to a
stage in the romantic movement: Wackenroder prefigured in
form and content the great experimentation of the early
romantics; Novalis' and Tieck's tales are examples of this great
experimentation; Brentano imbued the fairy tale with a German *folk* quality; Chamisso and Hoffmann showed to what
extent the already conventionalized forms of the fairy tale
could still be used to present a unique critique of society.

Wackenroder's *Ein wunderbares morgenländisches Märchen
von einem nackten Heiligen* (A Wonderful Oriental Tale
about a Naked Saint) was written during the last years of his
short life when he was under great duress.[35] His father, one
of the leading citizens of Berlin and an upholder of rationalism, opposed his becoming a musician or artist of any kind,
and Wackenroder was obliged to conceal his writing en-

deavours. In the period between 1792 and 1796 he wrote letters to Tieck, his closest friend, which are filled with complaints about the confining, desultory conditions in Germany, and which also expressed hopes for a better life symbolized by art and the French Revolution. 'Only creativity brings us closer to divinity; and the artist, the poet, is creator. Long live art! It alone elevates us above the earth and makes us worthy of heaven.'[36] 'You don't say anything about the French. I certainly hope that you have not become indifferent about them, that you really are interested in them. Oh, if only I were a Frenchman now! Then I would not be sitting here — But unfortunately I was born in a monarchy which fought against freedom, among people who were barbaric enough to despise the French. . . . What is life without freedom? I greet the genius of Greece with joy which I see floating above Gaul. France is in my thoughts day and night now — if France is unhappy, then I despise the entire world and have doubts about its strength. Then the dream is too beautiful for our century. Then we are decadent, strange creatures, not at all related to those who once fell at Thermopylae, then Europe is destined to become a prison.'[37]

Wackenroder praised art in a manner that might seem élitist or escapist to some critics, but there is enough evidence in his works[38] and reports by contemporaries to argue that he actually opposed such art for art's sake tendencies and even maintained that subjective feelings must find a universal, ideal language so that they become intelligible and reach a larger audience. The fairy tale was one way Wackenroder could manifest in such 'ideal' language his love for art which would make his complaint about repression intelligible.

Simply put, the *morgenländisches Märchen* is Wackenroder's critique of utilitarian rationalism. It concerns a naked saint who in some strange way wanders from the heavenly firmament and assumes the shape of a human being on earth. He makes his home in a cave on the fringe of society and suffers from a delusion: he hears the 'wheel of time' droning in his ears continually, and he becomes caught up in it. That is, he spends most of his time turning an imaginary wheel in fear that it might some day stop. He scorns and attacks all those who come near him and question his task, especially those who indulge in petty mundane activities near his cave. Nothing can stop him from turning the wheel, although he wants more than anything else to be set free from it. He especially longs for beautiful things. Then, one night, two lovers take a boatride on a river, and the harmony of their souls touches off such remarkable music that it drowns the noise of the wheel. It is the first time that music had penetrated the saint's hermitage, and it frees him from his earthly form. He ascends into the firmament where he assumes the form of the genius of love and music.

The introductory remarks by the narrator of the tale are significant, for he begins right off by saying that there are strange creatures who are honoured in the Orient as holy beings but who are called insane in his society. This is an explicit attack on the narrow-mindedness of the rationalists of Wackenroder's day and a defence of imaginative non-conformists. The behaviour of the saint sets him apart from other people because he has an *ambivalent* relation to time. On the one hand, he is caught up in the wheel of time which he keeps turning, and, on the other hand, he wants more than anything else to be released from time. Thus, the predicament of the naked saint heralded what was to be a major problem for the romantics in an epoch when time was being rationalized to fit into a rigid pattern. As Henri Brunschwig has noted, the romantics 'are very conscious of the flight of time. They feel that every moment is pregnant with possibilities, and they despair of their inability to choose among them, that is to say, to exclude whatever they would not themselves have elected. But to abstain from choosing means that the passage of time itself makes the choice for them, and this embitters their soul with a melancholy engendered by their impotence to affect the flight of time. This feeling is at the root of their philosophy. What would really suit them would be to live several lives at once. . . . This thirst forever unquenched, this jealously cherished feeling that body and soul must at all times be free to break off any attachment, this abhorrence of the finite — all lead to the perpetual flight toward an ever more distant and ever more exalted ideal uniting contraries in an impossible, a non-human, and miraculous perfection and so removing the necessity for choice.'[39] Wackenroder's tale is almost an artistic paradigm about the romantics' notion of time. The saint can be saved only by love and music which uplift him from the monotony of regulated time. He is set free and moves toward an ideal of infinite time. This ideal serves as a positive contrast to mundane reality which is associated with images of confinement and enforced regulation. It is also indicative of the romantics' quest to become masters of time. This is why

72

music and love are the two most important components of the utopian vision. They offer compensation for the deficit of a regulated reality in that they allow for the free expansion of the saint's spirit. His creative energies, held in check by the wheel of time are discharged and find their genius in another world.

The position assumed by the naked saint with respect to the wheel of time and to the other characters of the tale reveals Wackenroder's critical attitude toward the dominant activity of his times. Industriousness and regulated behaviour which benefited authoritarian rulers set the basis for a mode of life rejected by him, Tieck, and the other early romantics. Particularly in Prussia the principles of the Enlightenment had become extremely vulgarized and were used to rationalize the arbitrary domination by the state. Hence the ambivalent behaviour of the saint toward time is interesting since it reflects Wackenroder's dilemma. As a child of the Enlightenment, he was drawn to notions of reason and regulation; however, upon perceiving how these enlightened notions were applied to enslave man's creative spirit, he sought alternative forms of behaviour. In capsule form, then, Wackenroder's tale lays out the needs of a young generation of intellectuals who sought to overcome the contradictions of their time through their critical spirit and oppositional behaviour. Moreover, his fairy tale departs radically in design from the folk tale. Gone are kings, queens, struggles for power and wealth, marriage, and the rise in social status. Instead we have an outsider who *remains* an outsider, an artist type, who becomes the genius of love and music. Power is not pursued, rather freedom and non-alienating conditions. As it takes shape, the tale is a celebration of the imagination in protest against the banal existence to which people on earth are sentenced. Unlike the folk tale, here the narrator editorializes and evinces a dedicated sympathy for his protagonist. His is a perspective which sees the exemplary in non-conformist behaviour. Hence, again in contrast to the folk tale, the ending is left open. The infinite goal, though reached, cannot be attained on earth. Conditions are not yet ripe for individuals like the saint to be accepted in the society of the wheel of time.

Most of Wackenroder's work in *Herzensergiessungen eines kunstliebenden Klosterbruders* and *Phantasien über die Kunst* can be considered a prelude to the great experimentation of the early romantics. Certainly Novalis was much more experimental, abstract, and erotic, and in this regard he was much more of a revolutionary than Wackenroder. He constantly sought to work out a radical position in his poems, essays, novels and fairy tales, and the fact that he made numerous enigmatic and contradictory remarks about monarchy and religion did not detract from his basic effort to conceive a realm *in opposition* to the position of the decadent aristocracy.[40] His pietistic upbringing, support of the French Revolution, and serious study of idealist philosophy led him consistently to place great faith in the democratic potential of human willpower and creativity. His disappointment in the failure of the Germans to realign society along more egalitarian lines led him to put forward ideas about government and self-government which might provide the basis for realizing more harmonious conditions and for establishing the rights of human beings as humane creatures.

> Absolute equality is the greatest trick possible — the ideal — but not natural. — According to their natural disposition human beings are only relatively equal — which is the old inequality — the stronger also has a stronger right. Likewise, human beings are according to their natural disposition not free but, rather, more or less bound.
>
> There are few human beings who are human beings — this is the reason why there is so much difficulty in establishing the rights of human beings, as really extant.
>
> Be human beings, then the rights of human beings will devolve upon you by themselves.[41]

Most of his creative work which was completed in the last three years (1798-1801) of his life was aimed at *humanizing* human beings, and there is no doubt that the fairy tale assumed the most significant place among his radical writings: 'The genuine writer of fairy tales is a seer of the future. (With time, history must become a fairy tale — it will become once again what it was at its inception.)'[42]

Underlying all of Novalis' three major fairy tales — *Hyazinth und Rosenblüte* from *Die Lehrlinge zu Sais* and the *Atlantis-Märchen* and *Klingsohrs Märchen* from *Heinrich von Ofterdingen* — is the same notion of time as was developed by Wackenroder. Regulated time must be uplifted so that the creative spirit can be set free to reorder the universe more in keeping with the erotic needs of human beings. For history to be man-made, the orderly components of restrictive time must disintegrate, and out of chaos a new creative principle will emerge to give shape to a new world. However, this does not occur easily. As Sophie says at the end of *Klingsohrs Märchen*: 'The new world is born out of pain, and the ashes will become dissolved in tears and made into the drink of the eternal life.'[43] The line of motion in *Klingsohrs Märchen* is indeed characterized by dislocation, disorder and confrontation. The major force of conservatism and petrifaction is the Scribe, who is constantly associated with the vulgar Enlightenment. It is he who controls the spinners of fate, kills Sophie, and endeavours to legislate how life should be conducted according to rational principles. Only in confrontation with the Scribe can a new world come into being, and it is significantly Fable (art) who binds love (Eros), peace (Freya), and wisdom (Sophie) together to conquer the Scribe and unite three different realms. Consequently a new world does come into being, but it is a transcendent world, a world apart which serves as a measure for the reader's real world. The *ideal* propensities of this fairy-tale world, however, are meant to be the possible *historical* dimensions of the real world, for we know that Novalis envisioned history's becoming a fairy tale. Clearly, his fairy tale is forward-looking and has nothing to do with medieval concepts and absolutism. Nor is Novalis unrealistic in his expectations. The world will become as human beings are, and the erotic nature of the new realm is made convincingly manifest. The behaviour exhibited by Fable, Eros, Freya, Arctur, the mother, father, and Sophie reveals a sensual mode of relating which allows for mutual respect and equality. When Eros loses control, it is Fable, i.e. art, which brings the life instincts back to their senses, gives them shape, gives them peace (Freya). Non-alienating conditions must first be established for human beings to become human, for a state to rise which will humanely meet the needs of those same human beings. So *Klingsohrs Märchen* teaches us a lesson about the future: 'Nature will be moral — when it does what art wants out of genuine love for art — when it abandons itself to art — and art will become moral when it lives and works for nature — out of genuine love for nature. Both must do it simultaneously, of their own choice — for their own sake — and of another's choice for something else's sake. They must come together in themselves with the other and with themselves in the other.

'When our intelligence and our world harmonize — then we are like God.'[44]

The aesthetic design of *Klingsohrs Märchen* is intended to bring out the divine nature of art and the creativity of human beings. Novalis was fond of saying that to become a human being is an art, and his stress on the sublime role of the artist in society had nothing to do with élitism. Quite clearly, he recognized that society was an artefact, i.e., a product of human workmanship, and that nature — the environment *and* human nature — had to be moulded in such a way that the elemental drives of nature would be given free rein by the human intelligence which could construe democratic and egalitarian principles for social behaviour. In *Klingsohrs Märchen*, the thread of action woven by Fable makes up the fabric of a new world that unites a 'genuine love for nature' with a 'genuine love for art'. The focus of the tale is on Fable who 'loves and works for nature'; that is, she endeavours to comprehend the essence of all things in order to bring about a sense of justice and balance. Her answers to the Sphinx reveal to what extent she is capable of fulfilling such a task:

' "What is more sudden than lightning?" — "Revenge," said Fable. — "What is most perishable?" — "Unlawful possession." — "Who knows the world?" — "Whoever knows himself." "What is the eternal secret?" — "Love." — "Where can we find love?" "With Sophie." ' [45]

Here we must expand upon Novalis' notion of love if we are to understand how it is related to creativity and underscores the aesthetic pattern of the tale. In her book, *Weiblicher Lebenszusammenhang*, Ulrike Prokop makes the following significant observation:

> Like the early romantics, the young Hegel sees the model for non-alienating institutions in the example of love as a communicative relationship. Thus, he interprets the concept of Christian love as that free flowing of social needs and interests which does not necessitate the regimentation by legal institutions since it emanates from spontaneous agreement. Hegel describes love as a principle which lifts barriers and creates vital relations among human beings and, because of this, also makes the human being really alive for himself or herself. . . . Love is the expression for the bourgeois-revolutionary concept of the universally developed human being and for the relations which he or she undertakes. This is still the theme of the romantic protest: love, as reconciliation in the dialogistic recognition of the other, in which the I recognizes itself again, is not limited to the family. [46]

Novalis' fairy tale gives full expression to this notion of romantic love. Freya is desperate because conditions in the kingdom of Arctur have become petrified. In the bourgeois realm on earth, Eros is still in his infancy and does not know how to control his instinctual impulses. Otherwise, there is, at first, a beautiful image of sensuous, fluent and erotic communication between the father, Ginnistan, Sophie, and the mother. All this is destroyed once Eros departs with Ginnistan for the kingdom of Arctur, and once the Scribe incarcerates and destroys the members of the family. Fable's artistic task is to overcome barriers of rationalism set by the Scribe so that there can be free love. This is not to be understood in the sense of licentiousness. Like most of the early romantics, Novalis objected to love as possession, and he wanted to open channels so that love might consist of genuine communication and respect for the needs of others. In turn, this would allow for recognition of the self and free self-development. For this to occur, the old forms of behaviour had to be destroyed and replaced. Thus, the conflict with the Scribe is in effect romanticism's struggle against the restrictions of the vulgar Enlightenment.

Like Wackenroder, Novalis conceives the movement in the fairy tale as a process of self-realization and creativity. Love and art can flourish only if a new temporal—corporeal order is brought about. Thus, the aesthetic pattern depends upon constant movement between different realms and consists of metaphorical associations with old and new worlds. Novalis consciously played off folk tales and Goethe's *Das Märchen*. The complex network of mythical and allegorical figures defies exact interpretation, but the creative process of Fable does make it clear that the art work of the fairy tale critically reflects the reified *artificiality* of human relations in society at the end of the eighteenth century. Paradoxically the artistically conceived relations in Novalis' fairy tale — sensuous, free-flowing, democratic — are more natural than those in real society. This is the *historical* mission of the fairy tale: the raising of barriers of prescribed time to allow for love and creativity to take their natural course can lead to man's making history in a true sense. Real history can only commence when human beings are not treated as tools and subject to the whim of chance but when they creatively make full use of their human nature and use time for creating non-alienating conditions of work and play.

In the introduction to his collection of fairy tales and plays in the *Phantasus*, Tieck has one of his characters talk about *Naturmärchen* which mix 'the lovely with the horrible, the strange with the childlike and confuse our imagination to the point of poetical insanity in order to dissolve and set it free only in our inner world. . . . There is a way of looking upon ordinary life as upon a fairy tale. This is precisely the way that someone can be made familiar with the wonderful as though it were an everyday occurrence. One could say, everything, the most common thing, only possesses truth like the most wonderful, the easiest and the funniest things, and only takes hold of us because this allegory in the last instance serves as a construct for everything, and this is also why Dante's allegories are so convincing because they have been honed down to a reality that can be grasped most readily. Novalis says: 'only *that* story is a story which can also be a fable.'[47] Like Novalis, Tieck wanted his fairy tales structured allegorically to carry polarities of reality. When he discusses the fairy tales in *Phantasus*, he discusses them in relation to a reality which he wants made strange so that the familiar can become known to us through such estrangement. Novalis thought of this as one of the underlying principles of romantic poetry.[48] The allegorical function of the fairy tale was to provide the form and set a configuration which embraced reality and brought it home to the reader.

To bring something home to the reader for Tieck meant shaking the expectations of the reader. Ever since he began writing tales and editing stories for the publisher Bernhardi in the 1790s, Tieck sought to turn upside down the meaningless homilies of didactic writers who preached moral lessons. The world had become immoral and empty for Tieck, and he often raised the question whether we are insane because we have not gone insane — a question that was on the minds of most of the romantics. After leaving the university and leading a precarious life as a professional writer in the late 1790s, Tieck underwent a severe depression in 1802.[49] This can be attributed to many factors: the death of Novalis, who had replaced Wackenroder as his best friend, the distribution of the early romantic school in Jena, the disappointment in the French Revolution and its consequences for Germany, i.e., the stifling atmosphere of utilitarian rationalism which was becoming more prevalent in Germany. 1802 signalled a crisis in his life, and he stopped writing original narratives for almost a decade. But before he did this, he wrote one of his most significant fairy tales, *Der Runenberg*. The essence of Tieck can be found in this spine-chilling tale.

Christian, the young protagonist, flees his home because he dislikes the orderly gardens and flatlands in the confines of the castle where his father works. He heads for the mountains and the loneliness of nature — the words *einsam* and *Einsamkeit* recur throughout the tale. In the mountains he meets a stranger, an old miner, who directs him to the Runenberg. After a nocturnal encounter with an enchantress (probably Isis), who presents him with a tablet of marvellous crystals, he awakens not sure whether he has dreamt or gone insane. He hurriedly abandons the mountains for the lowlands and seeks refuge in a small orderly town with pious people. After proving his industriousness, he marries Elisabeth, the daughter of the richest farmer in the region, and soon becomes a success himself. However, a man resembling the stranger whom he had met in the mountains comes by and stays with him for a year. This man and later an old woman, who resembles the enchantress, rekindle his longing for life in the mountains and for the crystals, which he thinks he has betrayed. His father and wife endeavour to convince him that he is possessed by the Devil and that the crystals are just ordinary rocks. But their arguments are in vain. Christian departs to seek the treasures in the mines. Soon after this his father dies, and after waiting several years, Elisabeth remarries. She and her new husband encounter one misfortune after another so that she becomes poverty-stricken. At this low point in her life she encounters a wild stranger from the woods carrying a bag of rocks which he believes to be crystals. This man turns out to be Christian, and he frightens both Elisabeth and their daughter. He rests but for a short time, does them no harm and returns to the woods where his mistress, the enchantress of the crystals, awaits him.

The dichotomy is clear and made even more explicit by the imagery used by Tieck. The mountains, crystals, wilderness, and nature all represent freedom, particularly freedom of the imagination, perhaps even art and the profession of the artist. The town, church, gardens, and plants represent the rooted, pious Christian way of life, tradition, the confines of the well-ordered and well-regulated. Christian breaks out of his home to fulfil his calling in the mountains, but he fears the loneliness (the calling of the artist) and returns to the orderly life by marrying Elisabeth. But this life never did and never can satisfy him. He is torn by his yearnings for the crystals and finally abandons home and security to follow his imagination. Christian goes off to live in another world on the fringe of society. Though his wife considers him insane and unfortunate, it is not certain that the narrator shares this view. In fact, Elisabeth is just as spiritually and materially destitute as Christian at the end of the story.

There is no moral to Tieck's story. The ending is left open. Nobody lives happily ever after. All the traditional·expectations of readers and motifs of the folk tale are reversed.[50] Christian is un-Christian, the good life leads nowhere, the strangers do not help but remain enigmatic. There is no hold on reality, but neither does the imagination still Christian's yearning. The story is one of dislocation and confrontation. As in his other famous fairy tale, *Der blonde Eckbert*, the prevailing mood is one of *Waldeinsamkeit* — a chilling loneliness, an alienation which results from a split that cannot be subjectively or objectively resolved. The marginal existence is all that is possible when the daily life is deprived of the erotic impulses of fulfilment.

As a member of the early romantic school, Tieck clearly rejected the provinciality of small-minded rationalists. All his fairy tales attempted to explode the bounds of instrumental thinking and provincialism. In the process the tight, feudal structure of the folk tale was both decomposed and universaized. The imagination was set free to explore seemingly limitless possibilities for expression and self-realization. However, as Tieck recognized only too well, the new art forms and state of emancipation of his time were *ambivalent*. The journey from the home of provincialism to the home of cosmopolitanism was not a linear progression, and the contradictions were made manifest in the razor's edge of a divided existence which his protagonists had to endure in his tales.

Whereas Wackenroder, Novalis and the other early romantics were cosmopolitan, if not international in their outlook, even if they did treat distinct German themes, the middle romantics were influenced by the rampant nationalism of the early nineteenth century. Brentano, Arnim and the Grimm Brothers all studied German folklore, and there was a definite conservative tinge and anti-French bias to their writings. The conservatism was not necessarily reactionary. The middle romantics sought to give the Germans a national identity and unify the people around a Germanic tradition which was based on plebeian values of honesty, courage, fidelity, purity, etc. At any rate, nationalism at that time was associated with the movement for freedom against oppressive rule, and the romantics of this period endeavoured to awaken a national consciousness so that the German people might realize their emancipation themselves. At the same time, these writers were trying to establish *their own* identity as writers. Brentano particularly suffered from self-doubts throughout most of his life.[51] He was a purist of sorts and hoped either through religion or through art to be able to lead a life without pretensions, an open life without inhibitions. This was one of the reasons he was drawn to the folk or nationalist movement. On the one hand, there was something idyllic and pure in the way of life of the German common people. On the other hand, he mocked their simple ways. This love—hate attraction drew him to a serious study of folklore.

In 1798 he moved to Jena where he met the early romantics who encouraged him to pursue a literary career. After the composition of his remarkable, what he called wild, romantic novel, *Godwi*, he travelled in the Rhine region from 1799 to 1803 and collected material for folk songs and tales. About this time he conceived the idea to adapt Basile's tales from the *Pentameron* for German readers — the original impetus coming from the early romantics, especially Tieck, despite the fact that he found Tieck lacking in humour. He began this project in 1805 and completed the short Italian fairy tales in 1807. The longer ones were finished in the period between 1813 and 1817 when he spent most of his time in Bohemia and Berlin.

Brentano's fairy tales mark a definite break with those written by the early romantics. Not that his themes changed radically, nor his critical perspective on society. Brentano's tone and disposition were different. He endeavoured to attain a pure lyrical quality and endow the heavy German language with a lightness and insouciance which signalled his own pursuit of a life without restraint. Often struck with depressions, Brentano used the brisk humour and music of his fairy tales to maintain a balance between his moods of ecstasy and despair. In a letter to Frau von Ahlefeld about the *Gockel-Märchen*, he wrote: 'If the fairy tale pleased you, that's good. I wrote it mainly under great distress and could not for a moment allow my great sufferings to be noticed. So I assumed the attitude of a child in order to fool people and cover my torn heart.'[52]

Schulmeister Klopstock und seine fünf Söhne (The Schoolmaster Klopstock and His Five Sons) was written during the same period as the *Gockel-Märchen*. It is based on Basile's *The Five Sons* and is approximately ten times its length. Both tales are derived from the traditional folk-tale theme of a father who has five good-for-nothing sons. He sends them out into the world to learn a trade. They return after a year, all having learned skills which then enable them to unite to save a princess. Since there are five, the king does not know which son to choose for his daughter's husband. So he chooses their father, and all are happy. Basile basically follows this theme, but Brentano makes considerable alterations which indicate his *German* perspective.

First of all, the father Klopstock is a schoolmaster, and a catastrophe has destroyed his town. Not only has the school been burned down but all the inhabitants and all the school-children have been killed. This devastation is an immediate allusion to the Napoleonic Wars and the upheavals experienced during that time. Secondly, the father does not send his sons out into the world because they are good-for-nothing but because he wants them to become good for something. The five of them, Gripsgraps, Pitschpatsch, Piffpaff, Pinkepank and Trilltrall, are to learn a calling, and, since Brentano constantly delighted in using puns, their names indicate their callings, 'and they comically run off when they hear themselves 'called'. After a year, they return, and here Brentano makes radical changes to the original Basile tale. Not only does he amplify the narrative by having each son tell a humorous anecdote of how he discovered his calling, but the focus of the tale switches to Trilltrall, the poet. At first, since Trilltrall looks wild and ragged and behaves strangely, his father calls him a fool. With his long hair, tanned face, and counter-cultural habits, the young man certainly resembles the first of the hippie poets. But soon the attention focuses on Trilltrall's story of how he met a hermit who taught him the song of the birds and other animals. Trilltrall's adventures are also connected to the princess Pimperlein, who has been abducted by the nightwatchman Knarrasper. Trilltrall persuades his father and brothers to form a rescue party to return her to the kingdom of Glocktonia. They are, of course, successful, but instead of father Klopstock's marrying the princess, it is Trilltrall who is chosen by the princess, and they set up an animal park and breeding place for birds on the small property allotted them.

Though there is little indication of the 'torn heart' of the poet Brentano in this tale, the theme again suggests the impossibility of living freely and according to one's calling in the real world. The father and five sons are literally burned out of their home, dispossessed. Their skills are developed to move to a new world. This world of Glocktonia, obviously

one of music and harmony, is threatened by a nightwatchman, who is associated with the police and forces of darkness.
This intruder is vanquished by the united strength of the sons
whose creative skills are exhibited in the course of the struggle.
In the end they are all equally rewarded and can pursue their
callings in peace. This realm, as the narrator remarks, is not
of this world, but it does exist, for he claims that he had been
there once. Brentano's light humour here masks anguish and
disappointment, for he must contend with a different type
of reality.

As in most romantic tales, the mirth and humour serve to
mark a critical distance so that the author can maintain a
balanced perspective on the changing times without being
overwhelmed and devastated as happened in the beginning
of Brentano's story. Rooting a traditional folk tale in German
conditions meant also an uprooting of the original themes
and motifs. Brentano celebrates a life of the carefree imagination, of the bohemian, in contrast to the folk tale which
reasserts the position of the father as the justifying principle.
Trilltrall is chosen by the princess, not the father by the king.
So it is love and music again which are elevated to the guiding
forces of an ideal realm, and these forces are more democratic than the ones which existed in the folk tale. After all
they have been set free by the united power of the sons who
have become good for something. Barriers are broken by the
artist's being chosen by a princess and by the democratic
sharing out of the reward. As in Novalis' *Klingsohrs Märchen*,
the pattern of the tale is a process of creativity. In Brentano
the words and metaphors resound musically and exude a
German folk quality which rings pure in contrast to the artificial tones of German society. Though Brentano does not
address the problem of decadence and repression directly
in the tale, it is clear that the nightwatchman represents the
intrusion of repressive forces (be they French or Prussians),
and his imaginative play is a spoof about rationalism, his
defiance of the enemies of fantasy.

This move toward humour and irony in order to attain a
critical distance was especially typical of writers in the late
period of romanticism. As the conventions of German life
became more bureaucratized and reified, they elicited even
more ironic replies from the late romantics: they conducted
experiments to 'conventionalize' the fairy tale to show the
necessity for becoming unconventional.

Chamisso's *Peter Schlemihl* is a good case in point. The

story is well known. Written in the first person in the form of a private account by Schlemihl to Chamisso, it relates how Schlemihl encountered a strange man who performed magic tricks in the salon of a rich patrician in Hamburg. This stranger purposely seeks out Schlemihl, whose shadow he had admired, and makes him an offer to exchange his magic sack which will bring the young man wealth and power for the shadow. Schlemihl agrees immediately, and, although he has become rich, he is treated as a social outcast because he has lost his shadow. Wherever he goes, people spurn him. He even loses his fiancée because she will not marry a man without a shadow. Thus, Schlemihl endeavours to buy back his shadow from the stranger only to learn that he is the Devil and that he will only return it if Schlemihl sells him his soul. Schlemihl refuses because the sight of the soul-less patrician John, whom the Devil pulls out of his pocket, horrifies him. In fact, he becomes disgusted with his own greed and discards the magic sack. Left without money *and* shadow, Schlemihl finds a pair of seven-league boots which enable him to move across the earth with ease. Schlemihl now becomes a nature explorer (scientist), and, though still an outcast of society, he teaches and dedicates all his discoveries to mankind. His account closes with the hope that Chamisso will tell his story as a warning to all people after his death.

Chamisso wrote this story which contains many auto-biographical elements in 1813 while under duress.[53] He had recently made a decision to concentrate on his scientific studies at the university instead of poetry. However, the war against the French erupted, and pressure was put on the ex-patriate Frenchman to join the Prussian forces. Torn because of his doubts as to whether the war against the French would actually bring freedom, and troubled because of his French origins, he refused to serve in the Prussian corps and retired to the country for several months where he did botanical research and wrote *Peter Schlemihl*, a story that was originally written to entertain the wife and children of his friend Hitzig. It is obvious that his desperate situation as an ex-patriate determined the theme of the story. But even more, we must consider that Chamisso was a former French aristocrat whose admiration for the ideas of Rousseau prevented him from establishing himself in German society. His close circle of friends were artists, musicians, publishers and scientists, who were members of the progressive intelligentsia.

Chamisso felt uprooted for the most part of his life, and the tale indicates why it was impossible for him to root himself in German soil.

Most critics have focused on the meaning of the shadow in interpreting *Peter Schlemihl*. Obviously, it is significant — the loss of integrity, the loss of soul, the loss of status — but Schlemihl's movement and behaviour in relation to other people is even more significant. Chamisso is dealing with the theme of alienation, and he is trying to comprehend the causes. The loss of the shadow whether it is the loss of integrity or social status designates Schlemihl as *different*. Both when he has money and later when he serves mankind, he is singularly different from the others and remains stigmatized, an outcast, despite the fact that his work is recognized as valuable for the progress of mankind. In short, Chamisso describes a society which has become fetishized. In other words, it is the *sign* of a person, the commodity form, which designates acceptance. Human essence cannot be ascertained because the emphasis on *form* mystifies and hinders people from grasping those conditions which give birth to the form. Schlemihl himself cannot grasp these conditions either and remains a distraught victim of a society which cannot see beyond its own shadow. Chamisso uses numerous folk-tale motifs such as the selling of the soul to the Devil and the seven-league boots in a manner which makes the fantastic seem real. Like Hoffmann and Tieck, to whom he makes reference, he means to link the realities of the interior and exterior worlds, for he sees them as forged by the same material conditions. His ironical stance toward his protagonist allows him to use humour for social criticism. Though Schlemihl remains shadowless and homeless, he has realized what the social causes were which had caused his alienation. His resistance to pressures of the fetishized world enables him to gain some contact with his potential for making a contribution to the welfare of humanity. Ironically, it is only as a wanderer, on the margins of society, that he can gain a sense of true community. Underlying the humour of this situation, then, is a bleak vision of a world without community.

This bleak vision is sharpened by E. T. A. Hoffmann's conventionalizing of the fairy tale to show how the German people were not only in danger of losing community but also humour and imagination. Toward the end of Hoffmann's tale about *Klein Zaches*, the crude and pompous dwarf, who has become a minister, ends his career ignominiously by drowning in a silver pot, and the court doctor tries to explain the cause of death to the Prince Barsanuph:

> If I were content to swim around in superficialities, I could say that the minister's death was caused by his lack of breath which was brought about by the impossibility to get his breath and this impossibility was in turn induced only by a certain factor, by humour, which overthrew the minister. I could say that in this way the minister died a humorous death, but far be it from me to be so shallow, far be it from me to cherish such a desire to use vile, physical principles to explain things which can only find their natural irrefutable substantiation in the field of pure psychology.[54]

But the fact is that the ugly runt Zaches *was* killed by humour, and that Hoffmann's irony was used consistently as compositional and substantive principle for his tales and novels. As the most consummate romantic writer of fairy tales, Hoffmann learned to conventionalize and then play with the fairy tales of other romantics as well as with folk tales. Being among the last and the most explicitly political of the romantics, he learned to disguise his sharp barbs against the Prussian state with humour which allowed him to keep his distance and so survive an existence of travail and pursue a life of creativity. Certainly he would have died a much earlier death figuratively had he not used his humour to gain a hold on himself and 'to kill off' his enemies.

Beginning with his first major tale, *Der goldene Topf* (1814), Hoffmann served notice on the 'society of Enlightenment' that he would be judging it severely. He has his protagonist Anselmus reject a secure career as privy councillor for a life in poetry with the salamander Serpentina. By 1818, Hoffmann as a judge in Berlin had not only seen the dawn of the restoration but had experienced the brutal force of political repression and recrimination against which he fought. Thus, his depiction of society in *Klein Zaches genannt Zinnober* is even more harsh than it was in his earlier tales. In the principality of Kerepes where the tale takes place, we learn that what once had been a paradise for poets, elves, fairies, i.e., the imagination, under the rule of Prince Demetrius, has been transformed into a police state by his successor Prince Paphnutius, who decides to introduce the principles of the Enlightenment into his kingdom. But, as the Prime Minister explains to the prince, 'before we go ahead with the

Enlightenment, that is, before we cut down forests, make the rivers navigable, plant potatoes, improve the village schools, plant acacia and poplar trees, teach the young to sing evening and morning songs in two voices, lay out roads, and introduce vaccinations, we must banish from the state all the people who hold dangerous opinions, do not pay reason its due, and lead the people astray.'[55] In particular, the Prime Minister singles out the fairies as 'enemies of the Enlightenment', who have caused the state to remain in total darkness. 'Their work with the miraculous is pernicious, and they do not hesitate to use the name of poetry to spread a secret poison which makes the people totally incapable of serving the Enlightenment. Furthermore, they have such insufferable habits which go against the police that they therefore should not be tolerated in any cultivated state.'[56] The arguments of this minister are so persuasive that most of the fairies are exiled to Dschinistan, and a police action begins which lays the conditions for Klein Zaches, later under the rule of Prince Barsanuph, to take over the state as minister. This misbegotten, ugly dwarf who screeches when he talks and treats people in mean and nasty ways, ironically becomes the protégé of Rosabelverde, one of the few remaining good fairies in the kingdom, who takes pity on him in the hope that he may further the cause of the imagination. Using her magic indiscreetly, she enables him to make it seem that all his mean actions and ugly features are attributed to other people while everything good is attributed to him. For the most part, however, his actions only bring out the insufferable qualities of the 'enlightened' world. Because of this he is soon promoted to minister and will marry the lovely Candida, daughter of the famous professor of physics Mosch Terpin. This leads the real protagonist of the narrative, the gifted poet and student Balthasar, who is in love with Candida and who sees through Klein Zaches (now named Zinnober), to seek help from the magician Prosper Alpanus, who had managed to survive the police action of the Enlightenment and works to save the poetic forces in the kingdom. Since Alpanus realizes that Balthasar has great poetical talents and that the forces for true enlightenment and imagination are endangered by the barbaric, crude behaviour of Zinnober, he gives Balthasar the secret which will expose the dwarf. Once exposed, Klein Zaches dies a humorous death. He tries to escape the outraged people who now realize how he has deceived them, and he falls into the silver pot and drowns.

Balthasar marries Candida and settles down on an estate bequeathed to him by Alpanus before the magician leaves for the Orient. Alpanus has made such a gesture because Balthasar understands the 'wondrous voices of nature' and possesses 'the pure heart of which yearning and love are fused'.[57] Indeed, Balthasar becomes a good poet, and Candida develops her natural talents in the marvellous realm in which they are privileged to live.

Throughout this long, complex narrative the narrator constantly interjects ironical remarks which belittle the presumptuousness not only of the banal rationalists but of the pretentious poets. Like Novalis — and, in fact, all the early romantics — Hoffmann was just as much against the misuse of the imagination (*Schwärmerei*) as he was against the abuse of the imagination. The imagination and art were serious,[58] and it was not until the talented individual had undergone severe tests that the title of poet could be bestowed upon him. In *Klein Zaches*, there is a clear indictment of the new social order of utilitarian enlightenment which leaves little room for the development of creative individuals. Thus, what does 'develop' is misshapen. What is misshapen is also partly due to a poor use of imagination and reason. This perversion of the imagination and reason is the outcome of material conditions in a *police* state. The skills used by the magician Prosper Alpanus are directed to offset repression and develop creativity so that hypocrisy and treachery will be exposed. Art is not used for its own sake — something which Balthasar must learn. And even when the young man does learn what it takes to become a poet, he must live on the fringes of society. Happiness is impossible *in society*. The movement towards resolution does not mean that participation is possible in the socialization process. On the contrary, this allegedly 'enlightened' process is confronted, turned inside out, and exposed as an actual betrayal of the real humanitarian principles of the Enlightenment. Moreover, the revolutionizing force of movement in the tale speaks in the name of the betrayed principles of the French Revolution.

Yet, Hoffmann's mode of presentation and the motifs which he employs are anything but revolutionary. He is the great conventionalizer of the romantic movement. This is not meant in a pejorative sense. His achievement lies in his ability to conventionalize the early romantic notions of love and art with plots and characters reminiscent of the *commedia dell'arte* so that they typify characters and situations which were easily recognizable to a larger reading public. At the same time he retains the original anti-capitalist impulse and critique which he adroitly weaves with strands of both the folk-tale and fairy-tale motifs to make the borders between reality and the imagination disappear. Thus we have the conventional romantic story of the aspiring young poet who falls in love with the seemingly unattainable beauty from the upper class, a 'princess', and there is a magician who helps him not only to win the princess but to become a fully-fledged poet. This fantastic level of the fairy tale (a transformation of folk-tale motifs) also contains a fairy godmother, a grotesque dwarf, a comic foil and a foolish prince. But there is another level and a more real side to all these events and characters that concerns a story about police repression in Prussia with which Hoffmann's audience was well acquainted. The exaggerated features of his droll characters and the ridiculous melodramatic situations in which they find themselves were purposely elaborated to let the readers uninhibitedly enjoy the critical power of the imagination. Consequently, the intricate pattern of flashbacks, interludes, and narrative irony suggests how difficult the creative process joining art with love had become by 1818. The conventionalization of the early romantic project was an attempt to locate and typify the absurdity of a social reality that had lost its sense of humour and was busy repressing the forces of the imagination.

When we talk about the revolutionizing force of the romantic fairy tale, we must first begin by talking about the way the romantics revolutionized composition to create their worlds. In the short synopses of the tales which I have presented, I have not attempted to explore in depth the remarkable aesthetic experiments undertaken by the romantics. Nor shall I begin such an analysis at this point since each tale would demand a long, detailed explication. However, I should like to conclude by examining certain common features which link the revolutionizing of forms to the revolutionary impulse of the period.

Fehér talks about the 'formlessness' of the novel, and certainly this is the case with the romantic fairy tale. Unlike the compact pattern of the folk tale which, as V. Propp has demonstrated,[59] can be structurally charted, the fairy tale knows no such limits or perimeters. Wackenroder's narrative is about six pages in length, utilizes poetry, and maintains a serious, but ironic perspective. Brentano's carefree tale is about sixty pages, contains poetry, subtle puns, and stories within stories, and evokes a musical mood. Hoffmann's *Klein Zaches* is over a hundred pages and contains flashbacks, stories within stories, and ironical interjections. Each one of the romantic fairy tales is distinctly different in composition, but they are the same in that they explode the bounds of the folk tale. Not only that, they explode the bounds of other *Kunstmärchen*. Novalis transcended Goethe's tale as a model when he wrote *Klingsohrs Märchen*, and Hoffmann endeavoured to surpass the fairy tales of Tieck, Fouqué, and other romantics as well as his own when he wrote *Klein Zaches*. The 'formlessness' of the fairy tale obviously emanates from the writer's exuberance at the discovery of the self and the power of the imagination to proclaim independence from the severe strictures of eighteenth century regimentation. The freedom sought by the imagination was a result of the establishment of a new social configuration. Thus, a form representative of a past or passing social and cultural order could not dictate a new artistic conception. It could only help determine new notions in that it provided a standard, a pattern, against which the writers rebelled and measured their new-found worth. Formlessness then became form which had its own determinants when understood in the light of the transition from one socio-political order to a new one and the ambivalent attitude of the romantics toward the Enlightenment and incipient modes of capitalist rationalization.

Here, too, one must consider the temporal aspect in the fairy tales. Most of them involve an 'uplifting of time'. By this I mean that they dissolve normal sequential patterns and fuse the boundaries between fantasy and the real world. Time becomes timeless so that the protagonist can create his or her own time, so that the temporal—corporeal arrangement can be moulded to the pursuits of creative individuals. The mastery of time by human beings in a period when time was becoming more rationalized according to the needs of bureaucratic administration and early modes of industrial production is a significant theme in the romantic protest against reification. Self-mastery and self-determination are crucial aspects for the romantics' notions of creating new social orders. Their anti-authoritarian and anti-capitalist position takes form in the formlessness and timelessness of their tales.

The Romantic Fairy Tale in Germany

What are the determining elements in the formlessness and timelessness of the romantic fairy tale? All the romantic writers argued for taking the imagination more seriously. They aimed at making the line between the fantastic and the realistic disappear to show the unlimited potential of the human being for self-realization. The aesthetics called for reversing the already reversed principles of Enlightenment which were being utilized to deplete and enslave the humane essence of human beings. The flux of lines in the fairy tale causes an upheaval of categories of specialization which are examined critically from the narrative point of view. This flux gives birth to a configuration which measures the marginal limits of the extant social configuration. For instance, in the folk tale there is a definite hierarchical structure. Participation in this structure is (depending on the historical period) generally desired, and power and wealth are the dominant concerns of the protagonists. Folk-tale heroes want to rule over others or want power to be used justly. In the fairy tales of Wackenroder, Novalis, Brentano, Hoffmann and other romantics the old social order is upset, burned down, destroyed or made to seem ridiculous. Out of the needs of the major protagonist — generally speaking an artist, explorer or creative individual — a new realm arises which levels false distinctions and is based on egalitarian principles. The design of the tale is predicated on dislocation and confrontation in which imaginative energies are used to conceive of a realm apart from the real world which is stifling or has fallen apart. Imagination and self-realization are celebrated as activities in contrast to the celebration of power, i.e., 'might makes right', in the folk tale. The protagonist in the fairy tale does not want to rule over other people but over the dualities in his or her own life. The naked saint wants to be freed from the wheel of time and become the genius of music and love. Fable wants to unite the 'erotic' forces gone astray and create a new world free of restraint. Christian wants to overcome his contradictory drives. Trilltrall wants to follow his creative calling and realize his love for the princess. Schlemihl wants to make a real contribution to humanity. Balthasar wants to become a poet and consummate his love for Candida. The *centre of attention* in the configuration of these tales was a *side issue* in the social configuration in Germany; i.e., the social concerns of the romantics were shunted aside by ruling classes. Thus, the movement of the tales ultimately revolves around conflict

91

and the projection of alternatives to the socialization process which was becoming institutionalized in the German principalities. The conflict was not a simple black—white issue. The romantics were not fools. They recognized the great accomplishments of the Enlightenment and saw the powerful potential of early capitalist technology. But they also saw how these advances in thought and industry were being used to affect and enslave their own consciousness and behaviour as well as those of the people in general. And their tales sought to recover the revolutionary potential of the new inventions and thought for the information and formation of a new social order which was still in transition. Their awareness of the ambivalence of what was called progress and enlightenment caused them to point to the deficiencies they noted in their own lives and in the living conditions in Germany. The stress on free play, love, harmony as activities, and the formlessness and timelessness of the tales point to the revolutionary impulse behind their designs. The fact that these activities were not realized in new, life-giving, non-alienating forms cannot be attributed to the passivity or resignation of the romantics, a small group of artists who were divided against themselves and their audience. As the tales amply demonstrate, creative individuals were made into fortuitous creatures whose qualities were determined by material conditions and their choices of action. Generally speaking, the actions of the protagonists led to an opposition with society which divided them, set them apart. Their value as revolutionary figures does not lie in the fact that they show us how to build the new 'socialist society', but in the fact that their failures *realistically* show the deficiency of the times. It is in their 'great refusal' to be formed by the powers of domination that the failures and formlessness of the fairy tales are revolutionary.

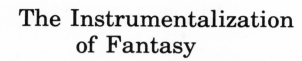

4 The Instrumentalization of Fantasy

Fairy Tales, the Culture Industry and Mass Media

> Every ruling class produces sensual present-day products of
> a better life. It produces needs in the masses which it can-
> not satisfy. To be sure, the palaces are not built for the
> masses. However, the needs of the masses are measured by
> them. This is most fully and freely articulated by fairy tales.
>
> Oskar Negt and Alexander Kluge,
> Öffentlichkeit und Erfahrung

Ever since the eighteenth century German bourgeois writers
have shown a marked propensity to write and study folk and
fairy tales. One might snidely assert that this is perhaps what
has been wrong with German bourgeois thinking. However,
such a snide remark would miss the real significance of this
phenomenon. The discovery and serious study of folklore
during the latter half of the eighteenth century tapped a rich
vein of culture which is still being explored today and is
vital for a concrete realization of humanistic utopian projects.

It was Herder who first kindled the interest in German
folklore, and his ideas set fire to the imagination of other
talented writers of this period such as Goethe, the poets
and dramatists of the *Sturm und Drang* movement, and
those progressive thinkers interested in waking the national
consciousness of the German people. Once the romantics
turned their attention to the folk and fairy tales by the end
of the eighteenth century, Novalis was able to proclaim:
'The genuine fairy tale must be at the same time a prophetic
portrayal — ideal portrayal — absolutely necessary portrayal.
The genuine fairy-tale writer is a seer of the future. (With
time history must become a fairy tale — it becomes once
again what it was at the beginning.)'[1]

History as a fairy tale. It is easy to laugh about this as
typical romantic escapism, but the utopian landscape etched
by Novalis in his fairy tales was created in rebellion against

the manner in which reason had already become instrumentalized to serve the arbitrary interests of authoritarian powers. The Enlightenment had become utilitarian and rationalized human production for economic exploitation and profit, thereby warping the people's sense of their own history. For Novalis, history was a reappropriation of nature and human resources through love and the imagination by individuals jointly striving and helping one another to reach their full potential in harmony. The fairy tale showed the way toward self-realization, or, in other words, the alternative path history could take if human beings actually took charge of their destiny.

Novalis was already fighting a losing battle with his fairy tales and radical theories. But, as I mentioned before, that did not stop the great German bourgeois minds from writing and using folk and fairy tales to criticize the dehumanizing forces of rationalism and capitalism up to the present. Undoubtedly the love of the fantastic in their symbolic works can be interpreted as retreat and privatism, but this love also signifies an active utilization of the imagination to oppose social manipulation and arbitrary domination. The telling of a folk or fairy tale is accomplished by an autonomous exercise of the imagination which endows the creator with a sense of his or her own power and challenges the self-destructive dictates of reason. Equally important is the creator's direct connection with an audience, social experience and nature. As Walter Benjamin has emphasized, 'a great storyteller will always be rooted in the people'[2] since he or she has the practical task of communicating wisdom as a use value to the people, and such mediation can effectively bring audiences closer to nature and endow them with a sense of possibilities for self-realization. Benjamin particularly praised the folk tale as the highest form of narrative:

> The folk tale, which to this day is the first tutor of children because it was once the first tutor of mankind, secretly lives on in the story. The first true storyteller is, and will continue to be, the teller of folk tales. Wherever good counsel was at a premium, the folk tale had it, and where the need was the greatest, its aid was nearest. This need was the need created by the myth. The folk tale tells us of the earliest arrangements that mankind made to shake off the nightmare which the myth placed upon its chest. . . . The wisest thing — so the folk tale taught mankind in older times, and teaches children to this day — is to meet the forces of the mythical world with cunning and high spirits. (This is how the folk tale polarizes *Mut*, courage, dividing it dialectically into

The Instrumentalization of Fantasy

Untermut, that is, cunning, and *Übermut*, high spirits.) The liberating magic which the folk tale has at its disposal does not bring nature into play in a mythical way, but points to its complicity with liberated man.[3]

Like Novalis, who sought to retain the original purpose and aura of the folk tale in his fairy tales, Benjamin sees the folk tale as a quasi-magical mode of connecting the people with their own nature and history. Myth as the social construct of instrumental reason must be pierced and exploded by the powers of the imagination which maintains a use value by providing counsel to the people and by restoring the immediacy of nature to them. The folk tale then was a model of narrative art which, despite its gradual demise in the age of mechanical reproduction, could still serve to point the way toward the making of real history. In the twentieth century this would mean that a tale would have to provide counsel against authoritarianism and commodity fetishism and subvert instrumental rationality with the imagination. Take this fairy tale as an example.

> *Once upon a time there was a rich young man. He was so charming and endearing that everyone liked him. And he was endearing not only to people of his own kind but especially to people who were beneath him. When he entered his father's store, he talked charmingly with the employees, and, with each purchase he made in the city, his clever conversation put each salesman or saleslady in a friendly mood for the rest of the day. His refined character showed itself in everything he did. He became engaged to a poor young woman and sympathized with poor artists and intellectuals.*
>
> *Then, one day, his father's business went bankrupt. The excellent qualities of our prince did not change in the least. Just as before he chattered charmingly when he went shopping, maintained his connections with the artists, and did all he could for his fiancée. However, behold what happened. The salespeople became irritated by him because he kept them from their business. The artists discovered that he was totally unproductive. And even his poor girl friend found him untalented and insipid and finally left him in the lurch.*
>
> *This is an old story. It would not be worth while telling again if people did not generally misunderstand it. It was not the prince in particular who remained the same, and the others who changed — that would be the usual and superficial interpretation — rather the other people remained the same while the collapse of the father's business had the effect of endowing the character of our*

*prince with an entirely different meaning. An endearing charac-
teristic of a person can become imbecilic without having anything
change about the person except his bank account.*

*What would have been more conspicuous and more uncanny
than in our story would have been a different set of circumstances showing that the people knew about the collapse of the
father's business for some time while the young man himself
knew nothing about it. Then the talented prince would have
turned into a cretin without having the slightest thing changed in
his consciousness. So little are we dependent on ourselves.*[4]

This fairy tale was not written by a romantic but by a
man named Heinrich Regius in 1934. Actually, Heinrich
Regius was a pseudonym for none other than Max Horkheimer, one of the founders of the Institute for Social Research in Frankfurt am Main. It is interesting to see how
Horkheimer uses the fairy tale to demystify the operations
of commodity fetishism in capitalist society. This is not the
place to begin a detailed interpretation of Horkheimer's
fairy tale, but it is the place to question the potential of the
fairy tale, whether it be communicated in Horkheimer's
narrative style or through the mass media, to lay bare the
degrading tendencies and exploitative machinations of the
culture industry so that audiences, unlike Horkheimer's
prince, can become *dependent on themselves.*

It is somewhat ironic that Horkheimer and the Frankfurt
School of critical theory which expended most of their
energies to recuperate the emancipatory potential of reason
should actually set the parameters for a critical analysis of
the fairy tale and imagination. However, there is no contradiction here, for they themselves relied upon and defended
the imagination to break the stronghold of reason used by
privileged classes for domination in a society oriented toward
the reification and standardization of human beings as commodities by authoritarian interest groups. Thus, we can best
grasp the contemporary potential of the fairy tale as a liberating cultural force by placing it in the context of what Horkheimer and Theodor Adorno called the culture industry.
This term denotes the mode by which cultural forms are produced, organized and exchanged as commodities within a
capitalist socio-economic system so that they no longer relate
to the needs and experiences of the people who create them.
Such a process prevents us from realizing who the actual producers of wealth and culture are with the result that humanity
is reduced to the level of a thing. Cultural objects appear to

possess a life of their own beyond the control of the actual creators who also lose control over their own destiny.

In the following study I want to elaborate on some of the basic notions of the culture industry theory in order to comprehend the impact of technology on the historical development of the folk tale as a fairy tale, i.e., as a mass-mediated cultural form. Since this is such a vast topic, I shall focus primarily on the ways that the fairy tale is mediated by the film in such cases as *Snow White*, *Wizards*, *Star Wars*, and *Rocky*, and I shall relate these fairy-tale films to Ernst Bloch's utopian concept of the fairy tale in order to offset the pessimism and uncover the weaknesses of the culture industry theory. Ultimately this will lead us back to Novalis' insistence that history must become a fairy tale with time and Horkheimer's implicit assertion in his fairy tale that we must become dependent on ourselves to make history.

As early as 1944 Horkheimer and Adorno demonstrated in *Dialectic of Enlightenment* the ways and means by which the culture industry employs technology and instrumentalizes reason to extend the domination of capitalism and make human beings and their cultural expressions into commodities. Concerned about how the Enlightenment itself betrayed the very principles of critical and rational consciousness for liberating the human spirit which it had first championed, Horkheimer and Adorno argued that the organization of the socio-economic system based on private property, competition and profit was arbitrarily developed through rationalism to prevent human beings from realizing their full potential as imaginative and thinking human beings. Human beings have become little more than tools, for as they were required to place their skills and thought at the service of a system which uses industry and technology to increase the profit and power of élite groups, they were prevented from pursuing their own interests and internalized the norms and values of capitalist commodity production. Progress as the advancement of machines and technology for production has become identified with the power of the capitalist system to dominate and manipulate humanity and nature. Both reason and imagination have atrophied. According to Horkheimer and Adorno, the role played by culture since the eighteenth century to reinforce the dehumanization process of capitalism has become the key to comprehending how and why this system continues to endure. They are particularly sensitive to totalitarian tendencies in culture, and here they stress that the process by which people and cultural forms are made into commodities through the mass media in the twentieth century has all but crippled the ability of human beings to distinguish the real from the unreal, the rational from the irrational. Cultural production then results in making people into consumers who out of a sense of confusion and impotence gratefully relinquish their own autonomy to allow the bureaucracy or industry to make decisions for them. 'The stunting of the mass-media's consumer's powers of imagination and spontaneity does not have to be traced back to any psychological mechanisms, he [the consumer] must ascribe the loss of those attributes to the objective nature of the products themselves, especially to the most characteristic of them, the sound film. They are so designed that quickness, powers of observation, and experience are undeniably needed to apprehend them at all; yet sustained thought is out of the question if the spectator is not to miss the relentless rush of facts. Even though the effort required for his imagination is semi-automatic, no scope is left for the imagination.'[5]

Since the imagination and reason became the key targets of the culture industry, Adorno and Horkheimer focused on the illusions used by the media to deceive the masses. The structure of mass amusement now resembles that of the production line and is intended to lull and distract the masses into believing that the goods they consume and produce actually nourish their potential to develop. Yet, the purpose of production is to make the people into bigger and better consumers with no regard to the quality of the things they produce and consume. Cultural expressions are mediated for the people by an industry which seeks to make the masses into automatons not autonomous beings.

Amusement under late capitalism is the prolongation of work. It is sought after as an escape from the mechanized work process, and to recruit strength in order to be able to cope with it again. But at the same time mechanization has such power over a man's leisure and happiness, and so profoundly determines the manufacture of amusement goods, that his experiences are inevitably after images of the work process itself. The ostensible content is merely a faded foreground; what sinks in is the automatic succession of standardized operations. What happens at work, in the factory, or in the office can only be escaped from by approximation to it in one's leisure time. All amusement suffers from this incurable malady. Pleasure hardens into boredom because, if it is to remain pleasure, it must not demand any effort and therefore moves rigorously in the worn grooves of association. No independent thinking must be expected from the audience: the product prescribes every reaction: not by its natural structure (which collapses under reflection), but by signals.[6]

Happiness or gratification of pleasure promised by the culture industry turns out to be a dulling of the senses. The utopia of the mass media resembles those technological wonders like commercial health clubs and fancy convalescent spas frequented by people who are conned into believing that a new life can be automatically induced. Since the conditioning images and products of mass media are aimed at making all producers into passive consumers and all art works into commodities, the autonomy of both producer and product are circumscribed by the conditions of the market. Production for consumption and profit become values in and for themselves. Human beings trade themselves and their products as wares for money and success. They lose touch with their innate abilities and talents and lose sight of the manner in which they project themselves on to the world. The subjectivity of the individual has been so invaded at work and in the home by standardization demands of the production line through the mass media and technological inventions that it is difficult to talk any longer about the autonomy of the mind.

In effect, Adorno's and Horkheimer's study of the culture industry for which the ground had already been prepared by previous works of the Frankfurt School in the 1930s[7] posed the major question of our time, a question which had been particularly intensified by the rise of fascism since the 1920s. Given the extent to which the state and private industry have collaborated to increase their power to administer and bureaucratize our public *and* private lives through technology, can one actually speak about subjective self-realization and self-determination? Or, to put it another way, has reason become so instrumentalized for the purpose of capitalist realization that human beings have become depleted of their inherent creative and critical potential to shape the destiny of humankind? The question pursued by Adorno and Horkheimer has also been posed by other members and disciples of the Frankfurt School. In particular, Herbert Marcuse has written extensively on this question in *Eros and Civilization*,

One-Dimensional Man, and *Counter-Revolution and Revolt*. Marcuse's great achievement has been to make clear how the capitalist ideology of political domination not only pervaded the social organization of human beings but was constitutive to the form and content of technology itself. Thus, 'the technological *a priori* is a political *a priori* inasmuch as the "man-made creations" issue from and reenter a societal ensemble. One may still insist that the machinery of the technological universe is "as such" indifferent towards political ends — it can revolutionize or retard a society. An electronic computer can serve equally in capitalist or socialist administrations; a cyclotron can be an equally efficient tool for a war party or a peace party. . . . However, when technics becomes the universal form of material production, it circumscribes an entire culture; it projects a historical totality — a "world".'[8] The consequences of Marcuse's theory are just as frightening as those of Adorno and Horkheimer: the total immersion of culture by a technology politically and socially geared to curtail critical thinking and autonomous decision-making leads to a rationally totalitarian society. In this regard, the mass media function to curb the emancipatory potential of creative art and can serve to instrumentalize fantasy.

The pessimistic outlook of the major members of the Frankfurt School has been balanced somewhat by Jürgen Habermas who makes a distinction between instrumental action governed by technical rules based on empirical knowledge and 'communicative action or symbolic interaction, governed by binding consensual norms which define reciprocal expectations about behavior and which must be understood and recognized by at least two acting subjects.'[9] In contrast to Marcuse, Habermas shifted the focus from technology as the framework within which capitalist ideology was made manifest and controlled the lives of individuals to the institutional framework of the bourgeois public sphere which determines and embraces the socialization process *and* technology composed of systems of instrumental and strategic action. As a historical sociological category the public sphere designates those forms of communicative action developed and institutionalized by the bourgeoisie in the eighteenth century between the private sphere and the state to foster rational discourse and a democratic decision-making process. The causes of the loss of individual autonomy and democracy and the increased technological control of our lives by capitalist interests can only be comprehended, according to Habermas, if one studies how private interests have manipulated and dominated public opinion in the public sphere and how the state has intervened on behalf of these private interests which have developed monopoly power. The result has been a perversion of the public sphere or what Habermas calls a 'refeudalization of the public sphere'[10] where the state openly and arbitrarily exercises its control to further the interests of large monopoly and conglomerate concerns. 'The substitute program prevailing today . . . is aimed exclusively at the functioning of a manipulated system. It eliminates practical questions and therewith precludes discussion about the adoption of standards; the latter could emerge only from a democratic decision-making process. The solution of technical problems is not dependent on public discussion. Rather, public discussions could render problematic the framework within which the tasks of government action present themselves as technical ones. Therefore, the new politics of state interventionism requires a depoliticization of the mass of the population. To the extent that practical questions are eliminated, the public sphere also loses its political function.'[11] Central, then, for Habermas is a theory of communication not technology, and thus he seeks to overcome the gloom of the Frankfurt School by positing an emancipatory notion of rationalization which is based on 'public, unrestricted discussion, free from domination, of the suitability and desirability of action-orienting principles and norms in light of the sociocultural repercussions of developing subsystems of purposive-rational action.'[12] The possibility for repoliticizing the public sphere to allow for democratic decision-making and individuation has become the subject of numerous studies in West Germany. The debate among those critics concerned with the culture industry has centred on ways to expose and oppose the commodity fetishism based on the economic exploitation of the subjective needs of the masses[13] or on ways to create a counter public sphere.[14] In particular the notion of a proletarian or plebeian public sphere as developed by Oskar Negt and Alexander Kluge provides a solid theoretical starting point for moving beyond the pessimistic position of the Frankfurt School, and this will be discussed later in more detail. Whether the point of view is pessimistic or optimistic, all the studies of the mass media recognize their power and tendency to increase the effectiveness and manipulation of the culture industry. Consequently, they continually pose the question which Habermas places at the end of one of his more recent books: 'The end of the individual?'[15]

Among Anglo-American radical commentators on mass communications, the Frankfurt School's critique of the culture industry has not had a profound effect, although an influence can be traced through the mediations of Marcuse, Hans Magnus Enzensberger,[16] Raymond Williams,[17] Stanley Aronowitz[18] and Stuart Ewen[19], whose works have had comparatively wide circulation in the United States and England. However, the dominant tendency in the US and England in the field of mass communications has been toward empirical and quantitative studies which concretely demonstrate the growing power of monopoly interests. In other words, many empirical studies, without studying or taking into account the works of the Frankfurt School, have actually substantiated critical theory's general thesis about the growing totalitarian domination of mass media. As a result of the Vietnam War and the Watergate scandal, more and more studies have concerned themselves with the manipulation and machinations of the culture industry. Two works by Herbert I. Schiller and Michael R. Real are good examples of the exhaustive research and critical analysis of the mass media which address themselves to the question of the cultural industry's control over human behaviour.[20] Schiller's *The Mind Managers* covers the areas of governmental co-operation with private concerns, the military corporate industry, the entertainment sphere, the polling industry, international conglomerates, and the legal system of repression. In each case he proves conclusively that the circulation of images and information are not neutral but contain ideological messages which intentionally create a false sense of reality and produce a consciousness that is at the mercy of a commodity industry seeking profit and creating divisiveness and alienation among the people. Real's book is more specific than Schiller's in that he focuses on culture. Still the thrust is the same:

> Mass-mediated culture primarily serves the interests of the relatively small political economic power élite that sits atop the social pyramid. It does so by programming mass consciousness through an infrastructural authoritarianism that belies its apparent superstructural egalitariansim. For example, while allegedly 'giving people what they want,' commercial television maximizes private corporate profit, restricts choices, fragments consciousness, and masks alienation.[21]

The Instrumentalization of Fantasy

Real's study is significant in that he elaborates a category of 'mass-mediated culture' which can be effectively used in clarifying how the culture industry maintains its pervasive influence on mass behaviour. After making distinctions between élite, folk, popular, and mass art as well as discussing other concepts of high and low culture, Real argues that technological developments particularly in the age of mass reproduction have given a new orientation to culture which he defines as the systematic way of construing reality that a people acquires as a consequence of living in a group. Technological developments have brought about a radical shift in the cultivation of culture.

> The increasing dissemination of culture through mass instruments of communication blurs the traditional distinctions between élite, folk, and popular art. A person preoccupied with élite art may pursue it by reading poems and plays that are *mass* printed and distributed, and by listening to classical music on recordings that are *mass* pressed and marketed. On the other end of the spectrum, a West Virginia mountaineer may satisfy his liking for folk music through the local outlet of the *mass* medium radio. In both cases the traditional concepts of personalism, immediacy, spontaneity, creator-orientation, and similar qualities, which are said to distinguish élite and folk art from mass culture, disappear in the process of reproduction and distribution.[22]

Thus, Real uses the concept of *mass-mediated culture* 'to refer to expressions of culture as they are received from contemporary mass media, whether they arise from élite, folk, popular, or mass origins. This redefinition of focus assumes that all culture when transmitted by mass media becomes in effect popular culture. Popular culture *not* transmitted by mass media exists but has decreased in importance both aesthetically and socially.'[23] As in most studies of the culture industry, Real documents the dangers inherent in a social system which now has the technological capacity to administer and control the thinking and behaviour of all its members. The totalitarian 1984, as Orwell portrayed it, appears to be right around the corner. Yet, Real, Habermas, Marcuse, Negt, Kluge, and other radical critics are not totally pessimistic about the chances of avoiding 1984. Culture can still be reappropriated by the masses to serve the emancipatory interests of humanity. As Fred Inglis has pointed ed out, it would be a gross mistake to consider mass communications in the culture industry as locked in a fixed and monumental edifice.

Public communications are too porous to occupy the edifice. It is therefore possible to make some suggestions to that small minority — and it will always be a small minority – who are ready to see the understanding of the mass media as part of education. . . . The main instrument for the innovation of knowledge is no doubt mass communications: the consciousness they register is what controls the march of history far more than new technologies. Now there are significant connections between public communication and mass education and it seems a reasonable guess (though only a guess) that the two institutions contain enough men and women interested in reversing the dominant flows of information to have some effect. Inasmuch as all change must have its expressive social institution, then education — in however novel, communal, and deschooled a form — must remain institutionalised if rational social criticism is not to die of attrition.[24]

Inglis focuses largely on how educators can help offset the negative trends of the mass-mediated culture, and his suggestions are not only worth the effort but are actually being implemented by progressive educators at many schools and universities in the West. However, he approaches the problem of mass manipulation too much from the point of view of the intelligentsia and does not see how the culture industry itself produces new needs and interests in mass consumers which impel them to use their imagination against the instrumental purpose of the culture industry. In other words, the technology and ideology of the culture industry are responsible for developing needs, wishes and a consciousness which often stand in contradiction to the industry's rationale. Essentially it is impossible to instrumentalize fantasy completely, and the basic question of genuine social emancipation concerns whether the images of fantasy production can be organized by the producers themselves in their everyday reality to put an effective end to exploitation, alienation and injustice. But, before we discuss the different possibilities for radical alternatives to the culture industry, let us examine how the critical premises developed in the critique of the culture industry can help us grasp how mass-mediated folk and fairy tales function in our present society. Only by firmly grappling with the way our reason and imagination are being used against us can we learn to use them for our well-being. To quote Inglis again:

104

The Instrumentalization of Fantasy

At the moment, we live out a constant and hateful reversal of
poles, where public power lies in a mystery beyond the tabernacle,
and the sanctities of our intimate relationships are defiled and
paraded in public. One way at least of starting to clear up the
confusion is to identify who is trying to control us, and how. It
is only by being able to meet another person straightly that you
can decide what you are worth to yourself.[25]

In what ways has the fairy tale as a mass-mediated cultural
form been used to further the interests of the culture industry? Have the utopian impulse and the alternative social
orders of serious fairy tales been totally defused by the
machinations of the culture industry? Is there no room left
for the imagination in mass-mediated culture to suggest
alternatives for autonomy and self-determination by the
people? Has the bourgeois public sphere become so corrupt
and is its manipulation of public opinion so total that the
creation of an alternative public sphere is no longer possible?
A discussion of the fairy tale and its function in the mass
media can help us assess the limitations placed on the imagination and counter-cultural forms and also point the way
toward possible solutions. However, the topic is vast as are
the problems. Let us briefly address ourselves to the magni-
tude of the problem.

The reception of folk and fairy tales in the Western world
(and to a great extent throughout the world) has been heavily
influenced by the Walt Disney industry and other similar
corporations so that most people have preconceived notions
of what a fairy tale is and should be. The media rely on our
preformed imaginations to suggest in every manner and form
that Disney-like utopias are ones which we should all strive
to construct in reality, and, if that were not enough, we even
have concrete Disneylands as blueprints for our imagination
to show that they can be constructed. To counter this
corporate inundation of our imagination, the familiar fairy
tales must be made strange to us again if we are to respond
to the unique images of our own imagination and the possible
utopian elements they may contain. Otherwise the pro-
grammed fairy-tale images will continue to warp our sensibili-
ties in TV advertisements such as the ones which have women
transformed into Cinderellas by magically buying new dresses,
paying money for beauty treatments in a health spa, using
the proper beautifying cosmetics. Then there is the beast
turned into a magnificent hunk of a prince by shaving with

105

the right brand of shaving cream, using the proper deodorant, and grooming himself with the best hair tonic. One comes across fairy-tale motifs everywhere. For instance, the following advertisement which appeared in a local newspaper for a commercialized fairy-tale film is typical of advertising's commodification of fairy tales: 'Dorothy's off to see The Wizard! The Scarecrow is a surfer . . . The Tin Man is a greaser . . . The Lion is a biker . . . The Wicked Witch drives a semi . . . The Good Fairy is gay . . . The Wizard is a rock superstar in . . . 20th Century Oz. Just follow the yellow rock road.'[26] Obviously the yellow rock road will lead us to buy a ticket to the wonderful land of Oz which will allow us to suspend our sense of reality for two hours.

The vast use of fairy-tale and folklore material in the mass media has only recently been studied by critics. Some references to the incorporation of fairy tales in the mass media are made in Raphael Patai's book *Myth and Modern Man*.[27] However, he is too eclectic in his examples — often confusing myth and folklore — to enable us to comprehend the ramifications of mass media's use of the fairy tale. More systematic are two studies on folklore in the mass media by Tom Burns and Priscilla Denby.[28] Burns spent one entire day watching television in 1969 and recorded 101 traditional folklore items or themes. He discovered that the use of folklore was rampant in all sorts of programmes and also employed extensively in advertising. For instance, 'four out of the five advertisements using Märchen material draw upon familiar characters and plots and fit them to a product. The Proctor and Gamble use of Cinderella to push the cleaning agent, "Mr Clean", is typical:

One older sister: Cinderella, wash the floor.
Other older sister: Yeah, wash it, and then re-wax it.
[Sisters leave for the ball.]
Cinderella: Wash, wax, pfui.
[Fairy Godmother appears.]
Fairy Godmother: Phew, ammonia. That strips wax. But use Mr Clean with no ammonia. Mr Clean gets the dirt but leaves the wax shining and you get a shine.
Cinderella: Wow.
Fairy Godmother: And now off to the ball?
Cinderella: Ball-schmall. Tonight's my bowling league. 'Bye.[29]

Denby's study went beyond that of Burns in that she collected folklore material from magazines, newspapers, plays, television, radio, cartoons, records, films, advertisements, local festivals, restaurants, etc. She also expanded her categories to include folklore *qua* folklore (articles about folklore; folklore as foundation, mimetic folklore), folklore as folklure (for selling and decorative purposes), and folklore as an aside. She reached the conclusion that folklore as employed in the mass media had nothing more to do with the original purpose of fostering and reinforcing a traditional image, unifying people, and passing on tradition. It has become more international and universal.

> In a sense, the folklore as found in the media is meant to be a psychological magic wand; it can systematically inform and directly instruct one to revert to a simplistic life style, or it can subtly suggest that the world is somehow based on unreal forces over which one has no control anyway. It can thus serve as an escape, conscious or otherwise. Then again, it may also serve to demonstrate that society has become too technological to ever become 'folk' in nature again, and, ironically, that the current emphasis on folklore and superstition which are sought as aids, only serve to further complicate and obscure the issues (a point of view prevalent in the more sophisticated or intellectual magazines). Thus, media folklore can be seen as a panacea or an obfuscation.[30]

Whether as panacea or as obfuscation, Denby has placed her finger on how mediated folklore is instrumentalized to mislead audiences and mystify the cultural system which produces images to distract and manipulate the imagination. The system of mass communication and its links to capitalist commodity production are ultimately affirmed by folkloristic plots and images which leave the audience happily passive or disturbed and impotent. Both Burns and Denby conducted their studies under the correct assumption that traditional folklore loses its strong cultural meaning when lifted out of its usual context of performance, setting and audience. But, unfortunately, they do not discuss in depth how the new commercial context of mass media determines the function and meaning of folklore. Once folklore is mediated it loses the folk aspect. In the case of the folk tale, its mediated form is the fairy tale and its context is the culture industry.

The effects of the culture industry on folk and fairy tales were touched upon in part at the 15th Congress of the International Board on Books for Young People

(IBBY) held at the Pandios School of Political and Economical Studies in Athens from September 28 to October 2, 1976. The two most important papers concerned with the subject of fairy tales and the mass media were 'Le Merveilleux dans la Littérature pour la Jeunesse à L'Ere Technologique' by André Kédros and 'Fairy Tales and Technocracy' by Kypros Chrysanthis.[31] Though neither Kédros nor Chrysanthis deal explicitly with the mass-mediated fairy tale, their papers are worth summarizing since they shed light on the extensive nature of the problem posed by technology and the mass media for fairy tales and fantasy literature.

After painting a depressing picture of how the technological society of consumption places children under enormous stress and fragments their lives to further the interests of bureaucracies and big business, Kédros argues that the marvellous must assume a new and special function in children's literature in keeping with the changing times. The traditional folk and fairy tales and old-fashioned stories cannot help children grapple with contemporary social problems.

> Children (and not only children) need a kind of modern marvellous element *(le merveilleux)* capable of exorcising the menacing technological environment and showing ways which lead to the mastery not only of nature but of technology itself. Our children need a marvellous element which, through the fantastic, the unusual, the bizarre and also (why not?) through comedy and modern myths, deranges and masters the machines, the apparatus, the great enterprises and large firms, the rigid bureaucratic conditions and blind laws of the market. They need a miraculous element which introduces the sun and festivity into the terrifying rationality of our technological societies by making them see how technology, thanks to new human relations, can contribute to everyone's development. From this perspective the marvellous becomes a vital need: it gives children stability and moral support to a great extent and makes them aware of their future responsibilities.[32]

Kédros borrows notions from the French School of psychology (Derrida, Lyotard) in defending the power of the miraculous in literature: 'While mastering technology, the marvellous could thus serve at the same time to foster critical and open attitudes in the child's thinking. In this "constructive derangement" *(déréglement constructif)* humour could play a considerable role.'[33] In other words, the miraculous and the comical have an alienating effect and can provide children with the necessary distance to deal with socio-psychological pressure and to gain a sense of themselves.

Whereas Kédros sees modern technology and commodity production as setting conditions for a new type of fantastic literature, Chrysanthis assumes a slightly different viewpoint:

> When one tries to define the position of the fairy story in this technocratic age of ours one must bear two important points in mind. Firstly, that in most parts of the world, and not only in the developing countries, the rural population is far greater than the urban, and it is this rural tradition that consciously lives its folk traditions, since even the educated in these areas have not ceased to be influenced by the folk tradition, at any rate subconsciously. And secondly, that technology has achieved unhoped for wonders but yet has not been able to change the spirit of man, since man has not been given that long period of time required for him to adjust gradually to new technological concepts. . . . On the basis of what I have said I think that the fairy tale's place in children's literature must be preserved, with, of course, careful adaptations to the new circumstances created by technocracy.[34]

Chrysanthis believes that folk and fairy tales provide children with a sense of tradition and self-knowledge. The mass media of technology have not altered the folk tradition because they have not created a new conception of the world, at least among the great mass of people. Consequently, they can be used as services to implement the folk tradition and to create new fairy tales which enhance the entrenched humanistic values and customs of individual communities.

In general, Chrysanthis is surprisingly naïve in his assessment of technology and the mass media which he never adequately describes. It is as though the media could easily be placed at the disposal of educators and professional artists interested in children's welfare and a humanitarian folk tradition. Nor does he bother to examine the ideological content of the folk and fairy tales he discusses. Furthermore, he underestimates the spread of technological control through the mass media in rural areas and is not aware of how the folk tradition has already been disrupted by science and industry. Indeed, he appears to contradict himself when he concludes that the fairy tale must adapt to 'circumstances created by technocracy', which are never explained. In contrast, Kédros is more thorough and aware of the complexities involved in creating a 'new kind of miraculous element' in children's literature which must oppose the dominant images of the culture industry.

> But in order for the marvellous to operate both as antidote and catalyst of constructive forces, it becomes necessary for the creators of works addressed to the young to supplement their talent with a more profound knowledge of the problems of our times and of the educational, social, and especially political means to resolve these problems. In introducing all the richness and contradictions of our epoch into their works, they will perhaps succeed in creating the tales and myths of the technological era which we are still sorely missing.[35]

Actually a new type of fantastic literature including innovative fairy tales which address themselves to social problems has been in the making in different Western countries for over a decade, but this literary production by itself cannot offset the general tendency of the culture industry to mediate this literature as an ideological commodity. Any discussion of the fantastic or the marvellous in the arts and its use value for children, that is, any discussion of the way folk and fairy tales are used, must take into consideration the changing means by which we distribute and receive the works. Perhaps the most important change for folk and fairy tales has been brought about by the film, which has ostensibly assumed the role of the old story tellers, but its perspective robs the audience of autonomy and a sense of community. Thus, its social value, at least as it functions now, is dubious.

In this brief discussion of mass media, folklore, and fairy tale, we have seen how difficult it would be to trace the myriad ways the fairy tale is mediated in the culture industry. It is time now to confine our study to the case of the fairy tale as film. Even here, the analysis cannot pretend to be complete or exhaustive. My focus will be ideological, and the discussion of the films is intended to open up questions about the mediated fairy tale and the instrumentalization of fantasy. Since some of the generalizations about the fairy tale and film might seem exaggerated, it will be important not to lose sight of the socio-economic context in which culture is made in the West. Here the framework is the Hollywood culture industry which judges its products largely according to the standards of commercial success. Thus, no matter how culturally innovative, avant-garde, serious or relevant the fairy tale as film may be, it will generally not be distributed and promoted if it does not meet the commercial and normative standards of Hollywood and to a certain extent of the TV industry which has developed its own market for films. Any analysis of the fairy tale as film must consequently begin with a critical premise regarding the commercial exploitation of both the gifted artists who produce films and the mass audiences who seek satisfying pleasure from cultural products. This focus is crucial, but it can also become too one-dimensional. The messages of the fairy tales are not all completely rigged to trigger off consumer reflexes of the mass audience. As we know from the development of the literary fairy tale, there were writers who produced serious fairy tales within the commercial framework which were critical of the market itself and the public sphere. This is also the case with the fairy tale as film. Therefore, after discussing four films which rely heavily on the fairy tale, and after focusing largely on how they affirm a capitalist ideology, I want to explore their anti-capitalist and utopian elements. The films which I shall examine are *Snow White and the Seven Dwarfs*, *Wizards*, *Star Wars* and *Rocky*. As I have stated before, my analysis will be largely ideological and confined to the narrative structure and the motifs of folk and fairy tales which have been transformed into new fairy tales selling the American dream of a free and democratic society. In this sense, the films are hypes*. Hypnotic in form and content, they carry us off to a never-never land with remarkable and dazzling technical tricks and absorbing images which make us forget that we have our own unfulfilled dreams which are more important to project and fulfil than those the film imposes on our imagination. Each film under discussion represents a different and often unique method of utilizing the fairy tale: *Snow White and the Seven Dwarfs* is a direct animated adaptation of a Grimms' fairy tale created for young audiences and families. *Wizards* is an original animated fairy tale by Ralph Bakshi intended largely for adult audiences. *Star Wars* is a science fiction film which relies basically on a fairy-tale plot and motifs to satisfy the outer-space fantasies of a general audience. *Rocky* is a sports film which is unconsciously based on fairy tales for a sports-minded general audience. All have been box-office hits. All are popular mass-consumer products. Though there are other types of films which might be considered mass-mediated fairy tales, these four reveal some of the most interesting and dominant methods by which the fairy-tale

*(slang) short for hypodermics; artificial stimulants

structure and motifs have been appropriated by film-makers to project their own fantasies about social conditions in capitalist society. The fairy tale structure and motifs form the basis for each one of the cinematic stories: an adaptation of a well-known fairy tale; the creation of a swinging contemporary hip fairy tale; the projection of science fiction through the fairy tale; the realistic sports story as a guise for the fairy tale. Though apparently different and seemingly innovative, each one of these films as fairy tale contains similar ideological contradictions and patterns which demand greater study.

In their book about imperialist ideology in the Disney comic, Ariel Dorfman and Armand Mattelart make the significant observation that most of the plots in Donald Duck comics (and in many other Disney comics as well) involve a circular pattern of substitution. After rebelling against adult rule the children take over the authoritarian role of the male adult and his entire value system.[36] Nothing is learned. There is simply an exchange of power and rule. Dorfman and Mattelart assert that 'Disney did not invent this structure: it is rooted in the so-called popular tales and legends in which researchers have detected a central cyclical symmetry between father and son. The youngest in the family, for instance, or the little wizard or woodcutter, is subject to paternal authority, but possesses powers of retaliation and regulation, which are invariably linked to his ability to *generate ideas*, that is, cunning.'[37] This cunning involves knowing how to beat the next guy, or knowledge used for domination. Dorfman and Mattelart rely on the studies of Vladimir Propp[38] and Marc Soriano[39] to substantiate their contention. However, these studies tend to formalize the structural patterns of folk and fairy tales too rigidly and do not take into account significant variations in form and content as folk and fairy tales were developed in different historical periods by different cultures. Nevertheless, there *is* among the *Zaubermärchen* (the tales of wonder) gathered in the early nineteenth century a general structural tendency which reveals a feudal ideology: might makes right. The pattern of these tales does involve the rise of a protagonist who fulfils a mission and rectifies the abuse of power. In the process he or she becomes ruler, but the system remains the same as do the rules. This structure and content were broken by the bourgeois fairy tale in the nineteenth century which expressed a certain pluralism and variety in form and themes indicative of the *laissez-faire* ideology of liberal capitalism. What is interesting to note in the twentieth century is that the mass media have utilized folk *and* fairy tales to bring about a certain refeudalization of the structure similar to Habermas' observations about the re-feudalization of the bourgeois public sphere. To this extent, Mattelart and Dorfman have perceived a growing *contemporary* tendency toward total control over cultural productivity which manifests itself in the manner fairy tales are mass-mediated. The pattern of the contemporary fairy tales of the culture industry tends to be variations of the cyclical structure noted by Mattelart and Dorfman. Chaos and conflict are followed by the restoration of order which affirms the goodness of the existing system. Young heroes are initiated and socialized as the new vigorous leaders who incorporate the virtues of decency, integrity, courage, nobility, industry and justice. The rise of the hero, generally male, is equivalent to the social mobility stamped with the seal of good American corporate housekeeping. The utopian wishes of the masses are thereby formulated within the fantasy palaces of the cultural industry: their unfulfilled dreams and wishes are restructured and compensated by a commodity which temporarily gives them relief and blinds them to the social realities hindering the actual possibilities for self-realization from being articulated.

Snow White and the Seven Dwarfs, produced in 1936 as Walt Disney's first full-length animated feature, is most important because it became the prototype not only for all of Disney's other fairy tales but for most feature film adaptations of folk and fairy tales by other producers. It has also served in part as the basis for his fairy-tale-like insipid family films. The circular pattern is dominant: an ageing beautiful queen wants her stepdaughter killed because Snow White is fairer than she. However, the young princess is saved by a royal hunter and eventually protected by seven dwarfs in the forest. The queen learns of this and transforms herself into an old crone who sells Snow White a poison apple. The dwarfs pursue the queen and cause her death. Snow White is apparently dead and encased in a glass coffin. But then Prince Charming arrives on the scene to give Snow White a kiss, and she is restored to life and power and rides off singing with her prince.

As Richard Schickel has noted, the numerous changes made by Disney endowed the film with an entirely different

113

meaning from the Grimms' tale.[40] The tale involves a violent struggle over power with no holds barred, and it is told with lurid detail and powerful symbols which have deep psychological and social implications. The film saccharinized all these elements and actually switched the focus to the dwarfs who play a minor role in the tale. This refocusing in the mediation is significant, for it reveals the underlying ideological meaning of the film and images. The dwarfs are little workers, miners to be exact, and they sing and whistle while they work. Their names — Doc, Happy, Grumpy, Sneezy, Bashful, Sleepy, and Dopey —suggest the composite humours of a single individual. They represent the healthy instincts of a person. When he or she as viewer orders them properly, they can become a powerful force against the forces of evil. Maintaining order and the ordering of the dwarfs become the central themes of the film. Even Snow White, who becomes the dwarfs' surrogate mother, helps order their house to keep it nice and tidy. The images of the home and forest are all clean-cut, suggesting trimmed lawns of suburban America and symmetrical living as models. To know your place and do your job dutifully are the categorical imperatives of the film. Snow White is the virginal housewife who sings a song about 'some day my prince will come', for she needs a dashing male saviour to order herself and become whole, and the boys are the breadwinners who need a straight mom to keep them happy. Though the wicked queen — the force of disorder — dies, the social order is not changed but conserved and restored with youthful winning figures who will keep the realm and their minds spick and span.

In order to understand this structured cleansing process in the film more clearly, it is important to bear in mind that America was still in the throes of a depression in 1936. Work was difficult to find, and workers' discontent led to violent strikes and the rise of a strong socialist movement. Chaos, hunger, depravity were all common conditions to the masses. Government and industry sought all sorts of 'new deals' to coerce and pacify the dejected people and to discourage active opposition while maintaining the basic structure of the capitalist system. The image of America as one happy family pulling together to clean up the economic mess was important to disseminate if capitalism was to remain the dominant form of production in the society. Snow White as Miss America symbolizes the basic goodness of the American socio-economic system, and the dwarfs as workers order themselves nice and neat to defend this system. The need for security and a good home was basic to the dreams of the American people at this time, and Disney fed his audiences what they desired — but certainly not on their behalf. He reduced the wants and dreams of the American people to formulas which prescribed how to gain a measure of happiness by conforming to the standards of industry's work ethos and the constraining ideology of American conservatism. As Schickel has noted, Snow White signified the end of Disney's great experimentation and eclectic period and the beginning of his instrumental phase — a phase which led him to build a corporate empire based on the instrumentalization of his art and fantasy to affirm and beautify the dehumanization process of the culture industry. Schickel asserts that 'eclecticism might have served as a brake on "Disneyfication", that shameless process by which everything the studio touched, no matter how unique the vision of the original from which the studio worked, was reduced to limited terms Disney and his people could understand. Magic, mystery, individuality — most of all, individuality — were consistently destroyed when a literary work was passed through this machine that had been taught there was only one correct way to draw.'[41] The uniformity of structure, style and themes established in 1936 was further developed in Disney's next great animated feature *Cinderella* (1950), which reeks of sexism, sentimentality, and sterility, and can be traced in all his fairy-tale products. However, it would be false to assume that Disney himself consciously conspired to create his world and images to deceive the masses and strengthen the ties of monopoly capitalism. Disney's 'popular' culture reflects the socio-economic conditions of his times, and he was able to capsulate the needs of both the culture industry and the American people in his art work to conceive a synthetic image of what America came to mean for him. That this image became destructive to the individual imagination and the emancipation movement of oppressed groups is a reflection of how Disney himself had become victimized and deluded by the demands of the culture industry.

Obviously the measure of any culturally significant fairy tale will be the manner by which it distinguishes itself from and carries a critique of the average products of the culture industry. A work such as Ralph Bakshi's *Wizards* (1977) apparently does this at first glance, and yet, upon further examination, this original fairy-tale film thrives upon the same formulas Disney concocted to pander to the culture industry. Take the circular plot: the setting is the distant future. The world has become rustic, quaint and medieval again. Technology, an evil force, has been banished, and magic and superstition hold sway in the kingdom of Montagar. Avatar, a paunchy, clumsy wizard, symbolic of the imagination, rules the world with benevolence while his evil brother Blackwolf, who represents technology and has been fighting Avatar for hundreds of years, has discovered a new weapon that will help him gain control over the kingdom of Montagar. This weapon is a film projector with clippings of Nazis and Hitler, including the Führer's voice, which will inspire the beastly forces of Blackwolf to devastate the people of Montagar. Though Avatar, who has become lazy and indulgent, would prefer to stay in his romantic setting, he is impelled to fight his brother because the evil forces have begun to encroach on his powers of imagination. Accompanied by the chief of the elves, a young idealist, and Elinor, the voluptuous young daughter of the late president of Montagar, Avatar sets out on his mission to fight his brother. After numerous ups and downs and comic interludes, Avatar encounters his brother and mows him down with a slapstick dirty trick: he simply plugs him with a revolver, as if all one needs do to eliminate dictators is to shoot them down. Avatar is then reunited with the sexy Elinor, whom he will marry, and he installs the young chieftain of the elves who has faithfully served the powers of the imagination as the new ruler of the realm.

Bakshi's film appears to be a critique of the instrumentalization of fantasy by technological society, and yet, his defence of the fantasy is spurious since the utopian realm he pictures is a regressive projection of a feudal kingdom with hip, amusing but freakish characters who delight in imaginative antics of live and let live. And, even this Peter Pan world of infantile regression is not as idyllic as it seems. Sexism abounds in the portrayal of men lusting after sexually titillating women. Only men are warriors while women flitter about. Serious enemies such as Nazi lumpenproletariat are depicted as the evil holders of power. The one-dimensional portrayal of imagination = good and technology = bad casts a magic spell over the use and significance of technology today. Such obfuscation with regard to the control of technology and the purposes to which it is put merely contributes to a warped sense of the conflict in the world, as if the crucial battle were between the imagination and machines and not between the class which controls machines *and* the imagination and the large majority of people who form the working classes. As in Disney's film, nothing actually changes in *Wizards*. This is also true of Bakshi's film rendering of Tolkien's *The Lord of the Rings* (1978). Figures are created to be amusing for the sake of amusement. Technical innovation in the animation is concerned with aweing the audience by showing off the technical brilliance and cleverness of the film-maker. The narrative structure shows no reordering but a restoration and affirmation of Avatar's role. The young chieftain has been initiated into the rites of battle and will safeguard the regressive notions of escapism. This ending of a seeming counter-cultural film presents no real critique of the culture industry which thrives on escape as a commodity.

Perhaps the best of the more recent 'great escape' commodity productions of the culture industry is *Star Wars*. This film succeeds with audiences more than *Wizards* because it interweaves science fiction material with a fairy-tale plot and motifs. Instead of taking place 'once upon a time', the story takes place in 'another galaxy, another time', but the contemporary fairy-tale circular structure is familiar. Princess Leia Organa is captured by the evil forces of the Empire. Our young prince Luke Skywalker, who maintains his father's tradition of the Jedi Knights, guardians of justice in the galaxy, seeks to rescue the princess. Naturally, in fairy-tale tradition, Luke has his helpers: the fatherly adviser Ben Kenobi, a great warrior of the Old Republic, who knows the secrets of the mystical Force which holds the galaxy together; Han Solo, red-necked captain of the freighter *Millenium Falcon*, who provides muscle support for Luke; and Chewbacca, a Wookie or ape-like creature, who is characterized by his loyalty to the cause of Luke. These three, combined with two zany robots, form such a formidable team behind Luke that he is able to place his powers in the hands of the Force, free the princess, and blow up the dangerous space station of the Evil Empire. The Old Republic is restored, and Luke is honoured with a medal from Leia. 'As he stood awash in the cheers and shouts, Luke found that his mind was neither on his possible future with the Alliance nor on the chance of travelling adventurously with Han Solo and Chewbacca. Instead, unlikely as Solo had claimed it might be, he found his full attention occupied by the radiant Leia Organa. She noticed his unabashed stare, but this time she only smiled.'42

On one positive level — and I shall discuss this later — the film which was naturally made into a book to capitalize on the cinematic success can be interpreted as a science fiction fairy tale about the evils of totalitarianism. However, one must first pose the question about the Old Republic or the restoration of a social order that was supposedly magnificent but had become corrupted from within by power-hungry individuals and massive organs of commerce which aided the ambitious Senator Palpatine to become elected as President of the Republic. The most obvious symbol of the republican virtues is our snow-white princess Leia, clad always in white, who is pure, brave, honest, clean, and just the kind of doll you'd like to have your children play with or your son marry. Leia is Miss America, and it is obvious that the alliance or forces she represents are true-blooded Americans: they are clothed in the traditional American khaki uniforms and behave loosely and good naturedly in contrast to the members of the Empire who are clothed in dark olive resembling the uniforms of the Nazis or the Russians. Their manner is austere and authoritarian, and, of course, Lord Darth Vader, the dark force behind the throne, is clad in black. Both Luke and Han are also stereotyped portrayals of familiar American figures: Luke the idealist innocent who believes in the great American dream of justice and equality for all. Han the truck-driver cynic, who has seen the world and is out for number one but basically has a good heart. In contrast to *Wizards*, the fantasy blend of the film fuses the good humans and the good machines to form a utopia of a good republic which actually needs only a little patchwork to knock out the evil kinks in the system so that it will function again in the good old way it used to. Underlying this depiction of utopia in the film is an apology for American imperialism. Made in 1976, the film obviously endeavours to serve as a palliative for the discord which divided Americans in the late 1960s and early 1970s. It suggests that the system is all right, but that it can fall into evil hands at times, and this evil must then be subdued by the mystical force of democracy. In other words, the war against Vietnam, the Watergate scandals, the exposure of malpractice by the FBI, CIA, and local police forces were all aberrations which have nothing to do with the structure of the social order and economy. Essentially, the democratic system in America will function as long as the right people are in control like Luke, Princess

Leia and General Dodonna, who led the rebel forces. Yet, such illusions about democracy are forms of escapism preying upon the wish-fulfilment of American audiences who undoubtedly seek an end to the divisiveness and bitter conflicts in the US and who would like to believe once again that America is the land of their dreams. However, the audiences are the underdogs in the fight against the mass media which expertly exploit their humble daydreams to protect the vested interests of corporate capitalism.

The underdog can only realistically make it in America if he or she succumbs to the market conditions of the culture industry. Sylvester Stallone, the hero and writer of *Rocky*, states this rather bluntly: 'To tell you a little bit about myself, I'm not that much more exceptional than any other actor. I've always maintained that maybe I had something unusual, maybe I had something special that eventually I could sell, but the problem was finding someone who would buy that product — and that's exactly what it is: a product. If people think along heavily esoteric terms in which they are pure artists who won't ever sell out, they'll never make it because, unfortunately, the business revolves around the decimal point and the dollar sign; so you have to be artistic and commercial at the same time.'[43] The film *Rocky* as a fairy-tale success story glamorizes and supports Stallone's statement. The structure of the film is based on the folk-tale motif of the swineherd who becomes a prince, and, to a certain extent, on the fairy-tale motif of beauty and the beast. Here our lonely lower-class hero must show that he has the class of Prince Charming to oppose the commercial interests of the boxing world. He is a brute or beast whose nature becomes more noble as he meets his homely and homey princess who is also transformed into a beauty once she grants the beast a kiss. It is the power of their love plus the help of an old-time trainer and friends — the inevitable animal as friend is there, too — that help Rocky in his mission to oppose the forces of evil symbolized by black heavy-weight champion Apollo Creed wearing the American colours during the Bicentennial in Philadelphia. Implicit in the film's structure, then, is a contradiction: Rocky sets out to prove the commercial shallowness of the American dream, and yet, he substantiates this myth by becoming the great white hope who successfully proves that the underdogs have something special to them and that the system does allow them to make it to the top. The ending also plays

upon the racism of American audiences, for it is the white
Rocky who represents goodness and integrity versus the
black Apollo who represents evil and sham. Defeat is victory
in this tale. Rocky is acknowledged the winner when Apollo
whispers to him that he will not give him a rematch and when
Rocky answers, he does not want one. Like most humble,
modest Americans, all he wants most is his girl Adrian, his
pride, and love. Again the circular pattern of the fairy tale
has a hero rise to the top and affirm the possibility of achieving happiness within the system.

There is a temptation to make Rocky into a noble working-
class hero and celebrate him for a lack of other more positive
heroes in American films. Thus, Ira Shor exclaims: 'In a
society jaded at all levels, Rocky is both a moral jewel and
dinosaur. His old fashioned values include a sentimental love
for animals and a fondness for corny jokes. He has a good
word to say to street kids singing on the corner, but he
delivers a stern, paternal lecture to a friend's teenage sister
about getting a street rep as a whore. Rocky the male fossil
cringes at the word, because he doesn't like to talk dirty in
front of women. Stallone brilliantly creates a chivalric and
gentle Rocky. Watching him radiate in the seedy tenements,
we want him to make it. He gets his chance.'[44] But what is
this chance in actuality? A moment to make a buck and buy
into the respectable middle-class world in a seemingly digni-
fied way. And why do we want Rocky to win? It is not so
much because he is an anti-hero or counter-cultural hero, but
because he apologizes for the so-called jaded and sordid social
conditions in America which we must accept day-in and day-
out if we want to survive. Rocky makes us feel a bit more
comfortable for our lack of social conscience and for the
daily compromises we make to keep the system running
smoothly. As a cheap hood, Rocky not only actively accepts
crime, but he must learn to control his goodness so that it
does not appear too neurotic. Stunted in his thinking and
development as is Adrian, he cannot achieve any sense of
self-realization except through the boxing industry which he
knows is a hype. His acceptance of the hype — selling himself
and the fight as a seemingly authentic product — even with
his limited expectations and desire to retain his pride, is not
an act of self-realization but a passive recognition and acceptance that he will remain a commodity for the rest of his
life. It is exactly this condition which the culture industry
manipulates minds to accept. The illusion of a working-class

hero at the end of the film remains a deception because it does not speak to the working-class impulses to abandon a condition which requires such an illusion.

But is *Rocky* really a film without hope for the subjective self-realization of human beings? Are the other fairy-tale films totally under the magic spell of the culture industry? What is the meaning behind the late 1970s media wave of spectacular fairy-tale films such as *The Lord of the Rings, Superman* and *Watership Down*? In a discussion about the contradictions of utopian nostalgia with Adorno, Ernst Bloch stressed the positive side of fairy tales containing fantastic elements of social utopia which resist the strictures of instrumental rationalization.[45] In contrast to the philosophers of the Frankfurt School, Bloch endeavoured throughout his life to elaborate a philosophy based on the principle of hope. One of his primary interests was the exploration of common everyday cultural phenomena or what might be called popular culture including daydreams, fairy tales, dress, advertising, decoration and manners in order to identify their utopian potential for anticipating a better life on earth. In opposition to plain wishful thinking, Bloch maintained that there are concrete utopias which await their human fulfilment through the action of conscious individuals who learn through their conscious action how to take possession of these projections. These utopias have a political significance in that they do not affirm and strengthen the ruling classes in society but anticipate a new class and justify its emergence. Creative art is significant in that it helps induce what is not yet conscious (unfulfilled and repressed wishes, dreams and needs) to become conscious so that human beings can seize upon the projections of what is not yet conscious to realize their full potential. To Bloch's mind fairy tales are extremely important because their utopian elements are projections of human dissatisfaction with existing human conditions. The source of their attraction for the common people is their protest against repression:

> No matter how fantastic the fairy tale is, it is always clever in the manner by which it overcomes difficulties. Also, courage and slyness succeed in the fairy tale in a completely different way from life, and not only that: As Lenin says, it is always the existing revolutionary elements which pull together the given strands to spin a yarn. When the peasant was still bound

by serfdom, the poor young hero of the fairy tale conquered the king's daughter. When sophisticated Christianity trembled upon encountering witches and devils, the fairy-tale soldier deceived witches and devils from beginning to end. (Only the fairy tale emphasizes how 'dumb' the devil is.) The golden age is sought and mirrored where paradise was to be glimpsed in its depths. But the fairy tale does not let itself be imposed upon by the present owners of paradise. So, it is rebellious, a burned child and lucid. . . The fairy tale has been softly mocked for its mere wishing and fairy-like simple means of reaching a goal, and enlightened criticism has pointed this out as well. But this is not discouraging. In times of old, as the fairy tale about the Frog Prince begins, where wishing still helped — the fairy tale does not therefore pretend to be a substitute for doing. However, the clever hero of the fairy tale does practise the art of not allowing himself to be intimidated. The might of giants is painted as one with a hole which the weak individual can get through victoriously.[46]

Bloch's defence of the fairy tale is a defence of a popular culture that carries utopian elements which are those needs, wishes and dreams that have been repressed in the course of time through the instrumentalization of reason and authoritarian rule. Thus, they cannot appear in the course of time when they might flower, nor can they be adequately realized in the concrete social organization of life. The masses respond unconsciously to utopian signs out of need, and these are the signs which we must read, interpret and elaborate when we consider the great response of audiences to such fairy-tale films as *Snow White and the Seven Dwarfs*, *Wizards*, *Star Wars* and *Rocky*. People do not go to the cinema simply to be amused, distracted or waste money. They are also driven by utopian longings, and they respond to positive utopian elements contained in the fairy-tale structures of these films which provide them with some small amount of hope for a qualitatively better future. Though it is difficult to find a common utopian denominator underlying these four films, one could possibly talk about the anti-authoritarian or anti-totalitarian element which can be traced back to the utopian, revolutionary component of the original folk tales and to their original task of bringing people closer together so they can make their own history. In *Snow White and the Seven Dwarfs* the little people and the frail Snow White unite to overthrow the oppressive rule of the evil queen. In *Wizards* all the different ethnic groups who are portrayed as small and unconventional form an alliance to combat the Nazi forces of technology in the name of the free imagination. In *Star Wars* the believers in democracy and justice wage a victorious war against the corrupt power-hungry Titans of totalitarianism. In *Rocky* the downtrodden working class supports the underdog in a system loaded to exploit the little man's efforts to gain self-dignity. In each case the film as fairy tale projects the possibility of a better future with freedom for the imagination if there is unity in struggle against authoritarian rule. In each case, the underdog (i.e., the youngest son or daughter) serves as the symbol of the common people. As Bloch implies, there are holes in authoritarian systems through which little people can crawl and bring about its downfall. The project depends on keeping the imagination free to project the holes and alternatives on to the dominant repressive system.

In his discussion with Adorno, Bloch made an interesting remark: 'When I get up in the morning, my daily prayer is: grant me today my illusion, my daily illusion. Illusions have become necessary today, vital for life in a world that has been fully exposed by utopian conscience and utopian presentiment.'[47] In other words, Bloch argues that the culture industry has depleted the world to such an extent that the utopian vision cannot but help reveal the banal conditions of daily life. Therefore, we still need illusions of hope to keep us going in a direction which might enable us to counter the banal conditions. In a certain sense the genuine utopian illusion is paradoxical since it must contain a call to the common people to abandon their illusions about their condition which must also be a call to abandon a condition which requires illusions.

Given the extensive control and power of the culture industry over the mass production of aesthetic illusions and images in fairy tales, Bloch's defence of the fairy tale must be qualified as must his interpretation of the folk and fairy tales themselves. From the very beginning folk tales tended to be contradictory, containing utopian and conservative elements. What kept the utopian aspect alive was the context in which the tales were actively received and retold by the common people. It is the socio-historical context of the folk and fairy tale which Bloch fails to take into account in his positive analysis of the utopian elements in this genre. Today the audience for fairy tales, whether they be transmitted as a literary text, film, play, advertisement, or TV show, has become passive, and the narrative perspective and voice are generally guided by commercial interests. Despite

123

all the possible utopian images contained in the narrative structures of the films which certainly contain anti-capitalist tendencies, they cannot have a liberating effect because of the context in which they are embedded, the circular structure of cultural affirmation, and secondly because of the context in which they are transmitted, received and circulated, i.e., the culture industry. Still, Bloch's theory can help us see possibilities for seizing upon the utopian elements of popular culture and grounding them in our everyday life. The instrumentalization of reason and fantasy has not become totally totalitarian. The contradictions in the mediated fairy tales as films indicate precisely this.

Oskar Negt and Alexander Kluge have focused on these contradictions and have developed Bloch's theses in a psycho-sociological manner to suggest alternatives to the culture industry which they define more precisely as the consciousness industry. Here their analysis of the instrumentalization of fantasy is extremely important since it cuts through the pessimism of the older members of the Frankfurt School. Negt and Kluge argue that 'the commodity as sensual/trans-sensual thing becomes a means to transform useful things into products of the fantasy which are not only the object of consumption but also suggest a world-view. The object of the massive realization of this commodity is the consciousness. The consciousness industry takes advantage of the economical opportunity provided by the total development of commodity production for its special production. The motivating fantasies of human beings such as hopes, wishes, and needs are no longer set free, can no longer unfold according to coincidental interests but are concretely occupied by use values and by commodities. It is not advertising which manipulates in this case. It only seizes upon the opportunity. . . . Today all this assumes a material, direct and visible form. This commodity form ties together concrete motivating fantasies, needs, the psycho-dynamic structure of the individual and integrates them more or less freely in the utilization system. At this stage the question no longer concerns the mere limitation of the private sphere of the individual but rather the differentiated forms in which it is utilized as totality.'[48] To offset the instrumental purpose of the 'consciousness industry', Negt and Kluge have elaborated a radical theory which concentrates on the experience and interests of the working classes in order to gauge the potential for setting up a 'proletarian public sphere' in opposition to the bourgeois public sphere. Important here, in contrast to Habermas, is that Negt and Kluge's epistemological standpoint is more political and praxis-oriented and retains the notion of productive human beings capable of acting as subjects in determining their own interests. They expand the definition of the traditional working class to include service workers, oppressed groups, intellectuals and marginal strata. In this regard the adjective 'proletarian' (at least in English) is really inadequate or too limiting to express the qualitative distinction which Negt and Kluge want to make in developing a counter notion to the bourgeois public sphere. The word 'proletarian' binds their notion too closely to the industrial proletariat and orthodox Marxist categories of class.

Essentially Negt and Kluge project a *plebeian public sphere* constituted by various strata of people who *oppose* consciously and subconsciously the formation of policy in the bourgeois public sphere by creating alternative agencies to articulate and secure their interests. It is not so much the working class which defines the contours of the plebeian public sphere but the way labour is put to use by different classes of people to form counter modes and vehicles which will allow for greater fulfilment of their lives. Negt and Kluge enlarge the category of the public sphere which they define as the central element in the *organization of human experience*, i.e., the public sphere organizes human experience, mediating between the changing forms of capitalist production on the one hand and the cultural organization of human experience on the other. Thus, they posit a 'block of real life' which opposes the value system of capitalism and whose revolutionary potential cannot be destroyed by capitalism. Anthropologically this means that there are certain *blocks of authentic needs and wants* of human beings which are reflected in the use values produced by humans and which resist total commodification. The constitution of the plebeian public sphere is qualitatively informed by human experience in response to changing forms of production. Similar to Ernst Bloch's concept of 'concrete utopia', the plebeian public sphere emerges out of people's needs and experience, makes itself felt but has never achieved full development. Consequently, it is different from those public spheres such as unions established by workers to defend their interests. The plebeian public sphere is *not* an institution but a contradictory and non-linear production process which unites the fragmented experiences of social contradictions and

125

interests of 'plebeians' so that they can create the basis for a class consciousness which develops a praxis of change. One need only think about autonomous community initiatives to provide local services for exploited people in opposition to the institutional ones, or alternative shops, factories, restaurants, newspapers, communes, etc., to grasp the essence of the plebeian public sphere as a process.

> The interest of the producing class must be the driving force; a form of interaction must be created which can relate to specific interests in the realms of production for the entire society; and finally the inhibiting and destructive influences emanating from the declining bourgeois public sphere must not overpower the emerging plebeian public sphere. In all these points, the plebeian public sphere is nothing other than the form in which the plebeian interest itself develops.[49]

In revising Habermas' category of the public sphere, Negt and Kluge insist that there is no longer one unified public sphere, but that it has been transformed historically into new and multiple public spheres of production. The emphasis here is on production and there are three large areas in which these spheres have developed: 1) the sensual-demonstrative public spheres of factories, banks, urban centres and industrial zones; 2) the consciousness industry, including consumption and advertising; and 3) public relations carried on by corporations, associations, states and parties. As these spheres of production turn the basic conditions of human life into the object of production (what we might call the commodification of daily life), they engender their own contradictions in the socio-psychological constitution of human beings. Again, this can best be understood by postulating the notion of 'a block of real life', which contains a complex of contradictory tendencies and opposes the maximizing interests of capitalism. Thus, despite or because of the very commodification of daily life, new forces reflecting the potential discontent of the plebeian strata rise up and can be seen in the legitimation and motivation crises of capitalism, and these forces shape the plebeian public sphere which is the constitutive element of a 'highly complex process of organization that has as its goal the release and free development of the experience that remains locked within the basic conditions of plebeian life.'[50]

Negt and Kluge do not come up with specific strategies, prognoses, or schemes to solidify the emancipatory tendencies of the plebeian public sphere. The value of their analysis stems from their praxis-oriented approach to the problem of the culture industry and the instrumentalization of reason and fantasy. Unlike many of their predecessors in the Frankfurt School, they ground their concepts in the actual experience and interests of the fragmented plebeian strata and place great emphasis on the need to effect greater co-operation between the plebeian and professional strata, particularly in the area of mass media and education.

> In connection with the proletarian public sphere the question concerns a transformation of those forces of the intelligentsia which have experience in the production of authentic artistic and scientific works that places them in a position to bring about a cooperative arrangement between the intelligentsia and the material need of the masses. Without this transformation process which can only succeed in a collective manner, the raw material, that is, the experiences and fantasies in the masses, and the skill in the organization of experience as it has been accumulated historically in advanced sectors of the intelligentsia will remain separated from one another. Of course this transformation process designates only a first stage since the self-organization of the experience of the masses by the masses must in later stages replace the intellectual work which stems from the division of labour.[51]

This perception of the possibility for change informs Negt and Kluge's critique of the culture industry and sets the framework for emancipatory praxis. The first step toward resisting the debilitating effects of the culture industry and guarding the fantasy from instrumentalization must lead toward a counter public sphere which could lend force and expression to groups opposed to the systematic alienation that results from commodity production. One factor in mass media production which a radical movement might exploit is the very collective nature of the technological mass media. As Real has pointed out: 'Crucial to the potential of the newer media is their *collective structure*. As opposed to the individualism of writing and reading, the new media call forth collective efforts of social organization.'[52] The problem remains one of stimulating people actively to organize around their interests. Real argues that

> technology and the need are present to develop utopian possibilities beyond the limits of contemporary mass-mediated cultural

systems. Mass-mediated culture can be rendered more understandable and humanistic by increasing cultural studies and policy research, by continuing consumer activism and reform efforts, by reducing the role of private capital and profit, by reversing one-way authoritarian transmission, by decentralizing, by developing in the wake of structural revolution a cultural revolution that returns to top priority the full, collective humanity of persons, the value of life, and the appreciation and balanced development of the environment.[53]

Given the manner in which the fairy tale is locked into mass-mediated culture, its own structure and capacity to convey creative images of emancipation depend on what Real and Negt and Kluge call for, namely, a radical reordering of the public sphere. The fairy tale may contain utopian elements, but its need to become history will not be realized unless people learn how to depend on themselves. Here we return to Novalis, Benjamin and Horkheimer, but the return is not the traditional circle, for Novalis and Horkheimer broke with traditional and rational thinking to glean in the fairy tale what was lacking in actuality — the reappropriation of humankind's own productive and creative value by conscious human beings. This lack is still there, and the fairy tale, though mediated, still projects rays of hope that humankind may yet come into its own.

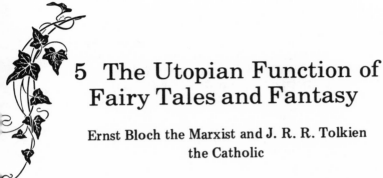

5 The Utopian Function of Fairy Tales and Fantasy

Ernst Bloch the Marxist and J. R. R. Tolkien the Catholic

It might seem somewhat incongruous if not risky to couple the names of Ernst Bloch and J.R.R. Tolkien. It is almost like taking two names in vain at the same time. But in the name of the fairy tale anything goes. And, as we know from the fairy tale, risks are more often rewarded than not. So what about these names?

Bloch, hardly known in the Western world except to erudite scholars and theologians, was a Marxist philosopher, who endeavoured to unravel the resilient latent qualities of humankind manifested in the struggle for a better world. He viewed these qualities as constituting a principle of hope and illuminating the possibility for human beings to change and become makers of their own history. He himself was an example of what he termed the upright posture (*der aufrechte Gang*) — a concept he used to describe the position human beings must assume if they are to stand tall, imbue history with the integrity, courage and compassion needed to resist forces of divisiveness and oppression. The essence of his philosophy is stated succinctly in this passage from *Das Prinzip Hoffnung (The Principle of Hope)*:

Humankind still lives in prehistory everywhere, indeed everything awaits the creation of the world as a genuine one. The real genesis is not at the beginning, but at the end, and it only begins when society and existence become radical, that is grasp themselves at the root. The root of history, however, is the human being, working, producing, reforming and surpassing the givens around him or her. If human beings have grasped themselves and what is theirs, without depersonalization and alienation, founded in real democracy, then something comes into being in the world that shines into everyone's childhood and where no one has yet been — home.[1]

Born in 1885 in Ludwigshafen, Germany, Bloch began very early to seize his own radical roots.² His study of philosophy was pursued against his father's will, and this opposition to patriarchal authoritarianism marked the path which his life would take and defined his political-philosophical project. When the First World War erupted, Block as a socialist pacifist went into exile in Switzerland where he wrote *Der Geist der Utopie (The Spirit of Utopia)*. When he returned to Germany, he become more committed to socialism and began formulating his views in the Marxist Hegelian tradition which was enjoying a renascence at that time. In 1933 he was forced to leave the country due to his strong anti-fascist position, and after stops in Switzerland, France, Austria and Czechoslovakia, he landed in Boston where he spent approximately a decade in the seclusion of Harvard's Widner Library elaborating his major philosophical and political premises. In 1948 he was hired by the University of Leipzig in East Germany as professor of philosophy, his first academic job at the tender age of 63. However, after witnessing and opposing the ossification of the socialist experiment in the German Democratic Republic, Bloch left that country to accept a post as professor at the University of Tübingen, West Germany, in 1961. There, too, he remained active in his protest against political repression and supported oppositional groups until his death in 1977. To the very end he spoke out in the name of socialism and in the spirit of a utopia which projected the possibilities for revolutionary change.

Bloch's active political life was in stark contrast to his English contemporary J. R. R. Tolkien, who preferred the pedestrian, conservative way. Ironically, Tolkien, who spent most of his life in Oxford as a professor of Anglo-Saxon and English literature and tended to shun publicity and politics, achieved world fame in the 1950s as author of *The Lord of the Rings*. His great passions were words, Catholicism and tradition, and his official biographer Humphrey Carpenter has presented an insightful picture of just how his conservatism expressed itself.

> Tolkien was, in modern jargon, 'right wing' in that he honoured his monarch and his country and did not believe in the rule of the people; but he opposed democracy simply because he believed that in the end his fellow-men would not benefit from it. He once wrote: 'I am not a "democrat", if only because humility and equality are spiritual principles corrupted by the attempt

to mechanize and formalize them, with the result that we get not universal smallness and humility, but universal greatness and pride, till some Orc gets hold of a ring of power — and then we get and are getting slavery!'³

Though conservative, Tolkien saw himself as a defender of the 'masses' surrounded on all sides by corruption and forces of progress which prevented them from seeking salvation in true religion. Strangely enough, his religion and conservatism provided the radical cutting edge of his romantic anti-capitalist position which still stamps his works today and constitutes part of their appeal.

Born in South Africa in 1892, Tolkien was raised in England after his father's death in 1896.⁴ His early schooling and religious training were greatly influenced by his mother who encouraged his interest in literature and supervised his conversion to Roman Catholicism which she underwent at the same time. Since most of the relatives of Mrs Tolkien opposed this conversion, she was deprived of both emotional and economic support while trying to make ends meet in the environs of Birmingham. Actually, such tribulations doubled her fortitude, and Tolkien and his younger brother learned the virtues of discipline, hard work, devotion and commitment from her. After the mother's death in 1904, Tolkien developed stronger ties to Catholicism and pursued his studies in a diligent way, eventually winning a scholarship to Oxford. As a young man, he displayed a unique interest in ancient languages and particularly sought the companionship of men in literary circles to share his insights and discoveries. Aside from a brief stint in the First World War which struck horror in him, he spent the rest of his years in the groves of academe and executed his duties loyally as professor, husband and father. There was very little excitement in Tolkien's pedestrian university world except for debates with Oxford colleagues and family tensions. He remained rooted in upper-class English tradition and his own mythological fantastic projections. His major social complaint was lodged against the desecration of the 'natural' world by technology. Otherwise, he affirmed the class hierarchy as good and ordained by God. A pious man, a pious life. He died in 1973, ironically celebrated more for his pagan fairy tales than for his 'catholic' view of the world.

Obviously Tolkien had very little in common with his contemporary Ernst Bloch. But the obvious here is misleading. Both Tolkien and Bloch employed the fairy tale to articulate deeply felt philosophies and to project utopian visions of better worlds which human beings are capable of realizing with their own powers. Certainly it could be argued that Tolkien's other world, his utopia, appears to be a romantic regression into a legendary past, an escape from the brutalities of modern-day conditions. Yet, Bloch, if he had ever written about Tolkien, might have been the first to point out that the return to the past is also part of the way to the future, that Tolkien unearths buried and repressed 'non-synchronic' elements of unfulfilled wishes and dreams which cannot be left unfulfilled if the potential of human beings to bring about a millennium on earth is to be achieved. Tolkien's search for a solid 'home' is what Bloch might designate as that which has not-yet-become but which we can sense in the anticipatory illusion (*Vor-Schein*) of certain works of art that employ fantasy to offset instrumental rationalization and call forth our authentic utopian impulses.

Both Bloch and Tolkien wrote key essays about the utopian function of the fairy tale and fantasy, and it will be worth our while to examine them in detail, for they might help us understand why the recent commodification of fantasy, that is, the fashionable trend to worship and consume the fantastic as art and commodity, contains a subversive element of revolutionary hope. Neither Bloch nor Tolkien were concerned with elaborating historically founded theories of the folk and fairy tale, and there are certain inconsistencies in their essays with which we must deal. Their primary interest lay in defending fantasy, and there are striking similarities in their quest since their battle was essentially against the same 'dragon of dehumanization'.

I

Bloch's voluminous writings are filled with references to folk and fairy tales. In fact, it would not be much of an exaggeration to say that his towering philosophical works rest on the foundation of the fairy tale. Consequently, any analysis of his longer detailed essays about fairy tales will involve an explanation of his basic notions of revolutionary aesthetics and philosophy. Significant here are two short studies: *Das Märchen geht selber in Zeit* (The Fairy Tale Moves on its Own in Time) and *Bessere Luftschlösser in Jahrmarkt und*

The Utopian Function of Fairy Tales and Fantasy

Zirkus, in Märchen und Kolportage (Better Castles in the Air in the Fair and Circus, in the Fairy Tale and Sensationalist Literature). Since this first essay is so short, I want to reproduce it here in its entirety and then comment on it with references to the other essay and Bloch's key philosophical ideas.

The Fairy Tale Moves on its Own in Time (1930)

Certainly good dreams can go too far. On the other hand, don't the simple fairy-tale dreams remain too far behind? Of course, the fairy-tale world, especially as a magical one, no longer belongs to the present. How can it mirror our wish-projections against a background that has long since disappeared? Or, to put it a better way: How can the fairy tale mirror our wish-projections other than in a totally obsolete way? Real kings no longer even exist. The atavistic and simultaneously feudal—transcendental world from which the fairy tale stems and to which it seems to be tied has most certainly vanished. However, the mirror of the fairy tale has not become opaque, and the manner of wish-fulfilment which peers forth from it is not entirely without a home. It all adds up to this: the fairy tale narrates a wish-fulfilment which is not bound by its own time and the apparel of its contents. In contrast to the saga which is always tied to a particular locale, the fairy tale remains unbound. Not only does the fairy tale remain as fresh as longing and love, but the demonically evil, which is abundant in the fairy tale, is still seen at work here in the present, and the happiness of 'once upon a time', which is even more abundant, still affects our visions of the future.

The young protagonist who sets out to find happiness is still around, strong as ever. And the dreamer, too, whose imagination is caught up with the girl of his dreams and with the distant secure home. One can also find the demons of old times who return in the present as economic ogres. The politics of the leading 200 families is fate. Thus, right in America, a country without feudal or transcendental tradition, Walt Disney's fairy-tale films revive elements of the old fairy tale without making them incomprehensible to the viewers. Quite the contrary. The favourably disposed viewers think about a great deal. They think about almost everything in their lives. They, too, want to fly. They, too, want to escape the ogre. They, too, want to transcend the clouds and have a place in the sun. Naturally, the fairy-tale world of America is more of a dreamed-up social life with the kings and saints of big business life. Yet, even if it is deceiving, the connection emanates partly from the fairy tale. The dream of the little employee or even — with different contents — of the average businessman is that of the sudden, the miraculous rise from the anonymous masses to visible happiness.

The lightning of gold radiates upon them in a fairy-tale-like way. The sun shines upon them from commanding heights. The name of the fairy-tale world is publicity (even if it is only for a day). The fairy-tale princess is Greta Garbo. Certainly, these are petty bourgeois wishes with very untrimmed, often adulterated fairy-tale material. However, this material has remained. And where does one ever really get out of the bourgeois style of living? Yet, there is a certain surrealistic charm in presenting old, fairy-tale materials in modern disguise (or, also, in divesting them of their apparel). It is precisely the unbound character of the fairy-tale which has floated through the times that allows for such developments, such new incarnations in the present, incarnations which not only occur in the form of economic ogres or film stars.

Cocteau's modernization of the great fairy tale of longing, Orpheus and Euyridice, is an example of this, an especially glaring one: Orpheus wears horn-rimmed glasses; Madame la Mort wears an ancient gold mask and a Parisian evening dress. The scene is a Parisian town house. A mirror becomes the entrance to the underworld. Everything is different from ancient times, and everything is retained, enlivened, nothing disturbed in its radiant`longing. The eroticism keeps old traits of the fairy tale even in depictions of much narrower and questionable kinds and knows what to make of Eurydice. Typical also in this respect (despite all the kitsch*) are two plays by Molnar, a dramatist, who knows how to use Fata Morgana in a refined if not a cunning manner, and who also understands her survival after disillusionment which is often dangerous and unwarranted. The first play is called* The Guardsman, *the second,* The Wolf. *Both deal with the genuine fairy-tale world of a petty bourgeois young woman of today, a world in which almost every part is false and nevertheless the whole is true. In* The Guardsman *the wife of an actor is disappointed by the everyday life with the man she formerly idolized, and she continues to dream of another kind of Lohengrin. But the actor, though somewhat unctuous in appearance, is kind and likes to undergo changes, and he fulfils her dream wish. He disguises himself as a chivalrous count in a sufficiently fabulous manner. A sublime game of love commences, sublime infidelity to her husband, sublime fidelity to the idea incarnated by him, and the disillusionment, partly sensed in advance, partly not sensed, and certainly not desired, is caused by the husband actor who reveals his true identity. This lands the petty bourgeois woman right back to the beginning, without a lesson learned, with a Chopin nocturne and dream which is unanswered and continues to move on. In* The Wolf, *the fairy-tale dream is even cloaked by technical stage devices in a real dream: it anticipates the party at which the wife of a lawyer is supposed to see her former lover. And it fills the four fairy-tale scenes for the dreamer: scenes in which the lover seeks to appear as a triumphant general, as brilliant diplomat, as famous artist, or also just as a humble servant who is gradually humiliated because*

134

of his broken heart and obliged to carry out the commands of his mistress. Again the disillusionment (none of the four is to be found in the original of the dream) does not cancel the idolatry of the fairy-tale projection. On the contrary, the fairy-tale prince continues to live, and the sobriety of reality pops up again only in the form of a crying fit. However, if one turns from here, that is, from the old story which remains eternally new, to the really new and newest history, to the fantastic changes of technology, then it is not surprising to see even here a place for forming fairy tales, i.e., for technological—magical utopias.

Jules Verne's Journey Around the World in Eighty Days *has by now become significantly shortened in reality, but* The Journey into the Middle of the Earth *and* The Journey to the Moon *and other creative narrations of a technological capacity or not-yet-capacity are still pure formations of fairy tales. What is significant about such kinds of 'modern fairy tales' is that it is reason itself which leads to the wish projections of the old fairy tale and serves them. Again what proves itself is a harmony with courage and cunning, as that earliest kind of enlightenment which already characterizes* Hansel and Gretel: *consider yourself as born free and entitled to be totally happy, dare to make use of your power of reasoning, look upon the outcome of things as friendly. These are the genuine maxims of fairy tales, and fortunately for us they appear not only in the past but in the now. Unfortunately we must equally contend with the smoke of witches and the blows of ogres habitually faced by the fairy-tale hero in the now. The fairy-tale hero is called upon to overcome our miserable situation, regretfully just in mere fairy tales. However, this takes place in such tales in which the unsubjugated often seems to be meant — tiny, colourful, yet unmistaken in aim.*[5]

Despite the profound insights contained in the above essay and in Bloch's other work *Better Castles in the Air*, there are misleading notions about the folk and fairy tale, and these must be clarified before we can evaluate his ideas about the utopian function of the fairy tale and fantasy. First of all, Bloch reduces the meanings of the oral folk tale and the literary fairy tale in an effort to find some kind of common denominator. Therefore, distinctions collapse so that the historical specificity of the folk tale and fairy tale becomes lost in socialist postulations and speculations about the power of *the* fairy tale. Yet, the alleged paradigmatic fairy tale as Bloch envisions it does not exist either in history or in present-day reality. In fact, Bloch often confuses myth and other fantastic literature with the fairy tale so that the latter category assumes a deceptive character of universality. Ultimately the tendency to universalize and idealize *the* fairy tale leads Bloch to gloss over the contradictions and historical essence of both folk and fairy tales. For instance, if we examine in depth the folk tales gathered by the Grimm Brothers, we learn that folk-tale maxims are not as emancipatory as Bloch leads us to believe. Such tales as *Cinderella, Little Red Riding Hood, King Thrushbeard,* and *Rapunzel* are decidedly biased against females who must either be put in their places or have their identity defined by males. The outcome is determined by the constraints of a conservative feudal ideology, and what Bloch continually glorifies as the striving for 'home' or 'a golden age' is actually, if we place the folk tale in a historical context, a reconstitution of society with the underdog merely replacing his or her former oppressor. In both his essays on the fairy tale, Bloch praises the cunning and courage of the narrative itself and the hero of the narrative for demonstrating how reason and talents can be used to overcome difficulties in the cause of true enlightenment. The power and strength of the poor and underprivileged become magnified with the result that the hope for a better future for small people is safeguarded. In certain instances, this may be true, but again folk tales, for instance, must first be understood as historically bound cultural expressions of different peoples. Thus, they exhibit not only the positive yearnings and wishes of the narrators and their audiences but also their contradictory drives. In the folk tales gathered by the Grimm Brothers, the male underdog is indeed cunning and courageous, but he is often only too willing to sacrifice autonomy or to compromise fantasy, cunning and courage just to succeed in society. In such works as *The Gallant Tailor, The White Snake, Faithful John* and *Puss 'n Boots* the goal of the protagonist concerns social status and recognition. The *change* in the tale does not involve a change in social conditions and relations. The protagonist simply improves his position in regard to material wealth and power.

But it is not only the folk tale which Bloch dehistoricizes and consequently misinterprets. The literary fairy tale, too, is subjected to vague generalities. The treatment of Cocteau, Molnar and Verne in *The Fairy Tale Moves on its Own* disregards the particular relationship of the individual authors to their societies and art and also neglects the conditions of reception. This is also true in *Better Castles in the Air* when Bloch discusses Hauff, Andersen, Keller, Meyrink, Stevenson and Kipling. Certainly there are fantastic elements resembling the colourful worlds of the fair and circus in the fairy tales of these authors, but these elements are divested of their historical sense when universalized by Bloch. For example, Hauff's protagonists are tied to a Swabian landscape and are caught in a conflict between pietistic beliefs and materialist strivings for a better life. The fantastic projection of a better life in Andersen is often representative of a contradictory urge to be accepted in the high society of Denmark and to expose the shallowness of this very same upper-class society. These are just two examples of how one would have to distinguish similar but different elements in fairy tales if one could accept the generalizations made by Bloch.

Where does this leave us? Perhaps it would be best simply to dismiss Bloch's ideas about folk and fairy tales as erroneous and suitable only for understanding his philosophy. However true this may be, we would be making a mistake, for Bloch sheds light on the utopian function of folk and fairy tales in a manner unsurpassed by contemporary commentators. His notions of folk and fairy tales become valid when we recognize their limitations and put them to use more discriminatingly than he actually does. That is, Bloch's ideas hold true for *certain* folk tales and *certain* fairy tales. This results from the fact that Bloch was not concerned with constructing a historical theory of the folk and fairy tale. At heart it is a general aesthetic theory which can help us understand the utopian function of popular *and* high culture. This is why he purposely blends the folk and fairy tale. In a significant essay about Bloch's aesthetics, Gert Ueding points out that

in contrast to Hegel, art for Bloch is not the reflection (*Widerschein*) of a metaphysically determined truth. Consequently, it is not to be regarded as something of the past which has a high point of determination. Rather it is an anticipatory—illusory (*vorscheinende*) formation of an achievement that has yet to come, and thus it is a *stimulant for revolutionary praxis.* 'Moreover, meaningful literature brings us an *accelerated current of action,* an elucidated daydream of the essential to the consciousness of the world. In addition, it wants to be changed. Among other things, the world correlate to the poetically suitable action is precisely the *tendency,* the world correlate to the poetically suitable daydream is precisely the *latency* of being. And it is very much in our day and age that the poetically exact dream does not die from truth, for truth is not the reflection of facts, but of processes. In the final analysis, it is the portrayal of tendency and latency of that which has not yet become and needs

137

an activator!' (Bloch) In that art as illusion and anticipatory—
illusion also reflects the *process*, just as it can anticipate the
totality of its goal in outline form, in that art as signifier with its
codes and symbols continually points beyond itself, its effect
upon the social reality is activating.[6]

In his discussions about art, Bloch constantly returns to
the folk tale in particular because he seeks to place his finger
on the driving utopian force which is constitutive in the best
of both folk *and* fairy tales, of both high and low art. As perhaps the oldest of all literary forms, the folk tale retains the
immediacy of the common people's perspective which has
always sought and indicated the possibilities for a better
world. Thus, the distinction between folk and fairy tale becomes negligible in Bloch's writings since he is primarily
concerned with tracing the manner in which the utopian
impulse of common people has been transmitted through
the fantasy, transformed and translated up to the present.
Therefore, we can accept his *universal category* of the fairy
tale if we recognize that he is addressing himself to the best
of the folk and fairy tales which have carried forth in manifold ways the utopian sensibility. As Bloch rightly asserts,
'the fairy tale narrates a wish-fulfilment which is not bound
only by its own time and the apparel of its contents'. What
makes the old folk tales and the new fairy tales vital is their
capacity to harbour unfulfilled wishes in figurative form and
project the possibility for their fulfilment. Bloch did not
believe that fairy tales were substitutes for action but indica-
tors. He developed a special category of *Vor-Schein* (anticipatory illusion) to explain how the fairy tale can mirror
processes through fantastic formations of the imagination,
processes which depend on humankind's use of reason to
carry through the wishes of fantasy. In a world in which
reason has to be used for irrational purposes, Bloch argues
that the world of the fairy tale contains a corrective: the
utopian perspective becomes a critical, figurative reflection
of everyday banality and subverts the arbitrary use of reason
that destroys and confines the capacity of people to move
on their own as autonomous makers of history. The critical
utopias of fairy tales do not outline a graphic plan of what
the future world will be like. Rather, their purpose is, as
Ueding suggests, 'to tear the affairs of human culture from
the superstructure and sort them out from that ideology
which legitimizes and glorifies a society with false con-

sciousness'.[7] This means that the fairy tale shows the necessity for restoring the concerns of society to where they belong — with the people, the little fellows who are imbued with the power to make decisions for themselves. When Bloch referred to the 'little fellows', he generally meant the lower-middle class, youth and marginal groups whom he considered pivotal for bringing about socialism. That is, their solidarity with the proletarian class was a necessary ingredient for revolutionary change. In the contemporary situation this classification of 'little fellows' would have to be enlarged in the Blochian sense to include large sectors of the changing middle classes whose needs and awareness have suffered from the ideological indoctrination and technological machinations of the capitalist consciousness industry. Even the proletarian class itself would now have to be seen as part of the little people due to their lack of autonomous class consciousness. The recovery of autonomy is crucial for building concrete utopias, and, according to Bloch, literature can contribute to a reawakening through a process of estrangement. In particular, the fantastic images and magic of the fairy tales can estrange the reader to everyday life and expectations if they are combined with dreams and wishes which lend them a new quality determined by the *Vor-Schein* of the tale which awakens a utopian consciousness that may have been repressed and needs articulation. At its best the fairy tale is always conscious of doing this. As Bloch time and again notes, the protagonist is the underdog, the youngest child, the most deprived, the most discontented. In fact, the fairy tale thrives not only on the hope and wish projection of its narrators and audiences but also on their dissatisfaction. Bloch places special emphasis on *dissatisfaction* as a condition which ignites the utopian drive. The fairy tale gives full expression to the dissatisfactions of average people, and this is why it remains such a powerful cultural force among them. Here is the connection to other seemingly popular and trivial forms of art such as circuses, fairs and sensationalist literature. Bloch has argued that socioeconomic developments bring about a certain non-synchronism in the lives of people, fractures in the relationship between being and consciousness.[8] For instance, the consciousness of a certain group or class does not flow directly from the conditions of its existence. A group of people may still think in terms of a previous time or behave according to thought patterns and traditions of a past society while living in the present. This is often the case when the social development does not fully work out the contradictions of the past society while moving forward and leaves groups and classes of people dissatisfied, uprooted, confused, etc. Consequently, they yearn legitimately for the fulfilment of their needs and wants which may have been overlooked in, let us say, the transition from feudalism to capitalism, or in the movement in late capitalism from manual forms of labour and simple mechanics to automation and complex technology. In each case, the needs and wishes of certain groups of people may have been bypassed too quickly in the change of the socio-economic structure, and they non-synchronously move forward while longing backward.

What some high-culture critics dismiss disdainfully as popular or commercial art contains a wealth of non-synchronous elements, some entirely regressive, some legitimate. By dismissing popular culture as appealing to the base instincts of the masses, these critics fail to perceive the utopian potential of such art which embodies the wish projections of ordinary people, and they fail to mediate between the aesthetic tastes of social classes thereby ignoring the value of popular culture. Bloch endeavoured to bridge this gap by pointing to the aesthetics of everyday life and popular culture as the realm which *anticipated* more strikingly and more immediately the possibilities for humankind to complete the project of gaining a home, i.e., creating a new society with unalienating work conditions. Here it is important to stress that Bloch's ideas on non-synchronism and the fairy tale were developed in the 1920s and 1930s in response to fascism and the reactionary, mobilization of the *petite bourgeoisie* in Germany. The historical dimensions of his theory were defined by his conscious effort to oppose and clarify totalitarian manipulation. This is also why he expressed so much interest in pivotal groups of 'little fellows'. To the degree that the domination of the masses (now including the middle classes) remains a given factor in the socio-economic order of things, Bloch's notions of non-synchronism and aesthetics of everyday life remain valid. The little fellow as the average consumer consumed by bureaucracies and corporations indicates the problematic nature of transforming society along socialist— humanist lines. Part of such a transformation depends on how one *traces* and *reads* the signs of what constitutes culture. As Bloch saw it, the fairy tale is the most vital artistic expression of ordinary people — their projection of how they want themselves to change and transform society. The fantastic form of the fairy tale carries a realistic lode of what is open-ended and fragmentary but can still be realized. It plays upon the imagination not to open it up to escape into a never-never land but to make greater contact with reality. The escape is estrangement or separation from a defeating situation which induces a feeling of possible liberation. In this sense, all the sensationalist popular literature of today must be studied with all its contradictions as literature which comes very close to the core of the dissatisfaction of 'little fellows'' lives and their need for emancipation. Consequently such literature must be taken more seriously than it has been.

Certainly Tolkien's works have been dealt with seriously. But they have not been examined for their radical thrust, and they certainly have not been related to Bloch's theories. This is the framework which I shall now use to discuss them. First I want to comment on Tolkien's own essay *On Fairy-Stories* and then show how such a work as *The Hobbit* contains more explosive power than one might imagine.

II

Tolkien's purpose in writing his essay *On Fairy-Stories* was threefold: he wanted to define them, trace their origins and discuss their function. The first two points are dealt with in cursory fashion, and, like Bloch, Tolkien misinterprets the meaning and origins of folk and fairy tales. He, too, reduces the categories of the folk and fairy tale so that they become indistinct, and he underestimates the value of historical— anthropological studies about the evolution of the folk tale. The result is a vague definition: 'A "fairy-story" is one which touches on or uses Faërie, whatever its main purpose may be: satire, adventure, morality, fantasy. Faërie itself may perhaps most nearly be translated by Magic — but it is a magic of a peculiar mood and power, at the furthest pole from the vulgar devices of the laborious, scientific magician.'[9] Faërie is also defined as the 'Perilous Realm, which cannot be laughed at or explained away.' It must be taken seriously, for 'the magic of Faërie is not an end in itself, its virtue is in its operations: among these are the satisfaction of certain primordial human desires. One of these desires is to survey the depths of space and time. Another is (as will be seen) to hold

communion with other living things' (p. 13). Such a definition of folk or fairy tales has no basis in history, nor does it
enable us to grasp the origins of the tales which have been
studied much more thoroughly by other scholars.[10] Nevertheless, Tolkien's comments are most significant for an
understanding of his own fairy tales. Like Bloch, he was
primarily concerned with the socio-psychological effect of
the tales as they are received by contemporary audiences.
Thus, his running together of folk and fairy tales into *one
genre* is acceptable as long as we bear in mind that he wants
to analyse how fairy tales and fantasy are esteemed and used
today. Here his humanistic and idealistic concerns are remarkably similar to those of Bloch, but before such parallels
are drawn, let us examine the latter portion of Tolkien's
essay which deals with the value and function of fairy tales
in the present.

According to Tolkien the worth of fairy tales depends on
their function which is connected to estrangement: 'They
open a door on Other Time, and if we pass through, though
only for a moment, we stand outside our own time, outside
Time itself, maybe' (p. 32). By entering the realm of Faërie,
Tolkien did not believe that we were entering a false or
make-believe world. The fairy tale is a sub-creation of truth.
If creation is the world and the creator God, then the artist
as sub-creator believes in his or her own creation which
transports us to another world from which we can γiew and
perhaps better grasp the primary forces acting upon us. Tolkien noted four factors which account for the magic power
of the fairy tale: fantasy, recovery, escape, consolation. Since
he attached special meanings to these terms, let us examine
them in more detail.

Essentially, Tolkien distinguishes imagination from fantasy.
The former is the mental power of making images, while
fantasy is a form of art which embraces the quality of strangeness and wonder derived in its expression from the image and
lends the image an inner consistency of reality. Fantasy is
thus the artistic *mediator* between imagination and the final
result, sub-creation. Tolkien stresses that fantastic images are
'images of things that are not only "not actually present",
but which are indeed not to be found in our primary world,
or are generally believed not to be found there' (p. 47). This
is its virtue — 'the arresting of strangeness'. Time and again
Tolkien argues that fantasy is a rational and natural human
activity, and he seeks to grasp its social essence. For him the

central desire and aspiration of human fantasy could be
stated as follows: 'it does not seek delusion nor bewitchment
and domination; it seeks shared enrichment, partners in
making and delight, not slaves' (p. 53). Clearly Tolkien is
writing a defence of fairy tales and fantasy, and he takes
issue with those traditionalists who have relegated the fairy
tale to the realm of children and the domain of trivial art.
In the process he subscribes to some heretical views of fairy
tales, and ironically his staunch conservatism in religious
matters is at the heart of his radical ideas. Tolkien hated
machines, industrialism, and 'progress' because they were
signs that the human being was being devalued and that
money was being worshipped as the almighty god. In opposition to this 'fallen primal' world which was turning away
from true religion, he sought ways through the sub-creation
of fairy tales to *recapture* that humane essence which was
becoming lost in the evolution of technology. Clearly, his
defence of fantasy had large socio-political ramifications,
much larger than he himself realized. To state his theory of
the fantasy in slightly different terms, we could say that
fantasy is human labour power, the mental exertion of
ordering images conceived by the mind for the purpose of
enjoyment, enlightenment and communion. Fantasy is
liberating and can be shared. As it takes the form of a fairy
tale, it provides three nurturing and civilizing qualities:
recovery, escape, consolation.

According to Tolkien, by moving to the past or another
world, the fairy tale enables readers to regain a clear view of
their situations. Recovery includes return and renewal of
health. The placing of objects from our everyday world in
a luminous, estranged setting compels us to perceive and
cherish them in a new way. The creative fantasy embodied
in the fairy tale can help us see new connections between
past and present. These connections must be made if we are
to move forward in time more in keeping with our subjective
concerns.

The move forward or the general movement in the fairy
tale is indeed an 'escape', and Tolkien persuasively argues
that escape is not cowardly but can be heroic: 'Why should
man be scorned if, finding himself in prison, he tries to get
out and go home?' (p. 60). Tolkien sees the world as a prison
and as irrational. Fantasy is a form of protest against irrational confinement and such rationalized man-made things as
'factories, or the machine-guns and bombs that appear to be

their most natural and inevitable, dare we say "inexorable" products' (p. 63). And the fairy tale also provides escape from 'hunger, thirst, poverty, pain, sorrow, injustice, death' (p. 65). This escape would not be positive if it kept us suspended from reality which some fantasy tales do. Yet, this is not the case, as Tolkien stresses, with the fairy tale which liberates us so we can accept its consolation.

Like Bloch's, Tolkien's philosophical understanding of the fairy tale is grounded in the notion of hope: 'The consolation of fairy-stories, the joy of the happy ending: or more correctly of the good catastrophe, the sudden joyous "turn" (for there is no true end to any fairy-tale): this joy, which is one of the things which fairy stories can produce supremely well, is not essentially "escapist", nor "fugitive". In its fairy-tale — or otherworld — setting, it is a sudden and miraculous grace: never to be counted on to recur. It does not deny the existence of *dyscatastrophe*, or sorrow and failure: the possibility of these is necessary to the joy of deliverance; it denies (in the face of much evidence, if you will) universal final defeat and in so far is *evangelium*, giving a fleeting glimpse of Joy, Joy beyond the walls of the world, poignant as grief' (p. 68). Though Tolkien endows the fairy tale with Christian faith, he is not orthodox. The great virtue of the fairy tale does not lie in its promise of a better world after death but 'a far-off gleam or echo of evangelium in the real world' (p. 71). Fantasy is imbued with an almost religious, mystical fervour: 'in Fantasy he [Man] may actually assist in the effoliation and multiple enrichment of creation. All tales may come true; and yet, at the last, redeemed, they may be as like and as unlike the forms that we give them as Man, finally redeemed, will be like and unlike the fallen that we know' (p. 73).

This religious glorification of fantasy is not strange, and Tolkien unconsciously places his finger on what is missing or being distorted in contemporary Western society. Fantasy as it takes form in the fairy tale serves as a redeemer of humankind. It sets free the wants and wishes of human beings and declares that the pursuit of their fulfilment is valid and can provide validation of the self. In so far as fantasy is not recognized in our everyday world as an *occupation* with needs to be taken seriously (just as the day-dreamer is generally mocked) Tolkien's religious devotion to fantasy assumes socio-political dimensions which must be further clarified.

The Utopian Function of Fairy Tales and Fantasy

If we accept the notion of fantasy as the operative medium of our labour power which endows our images with meaning derived from unfulfilled wishes and needs, then the form which it takes is a kind of revelation, whether this be regarded as high or low art. The psychical and physical energy which goes into synthesizing images of the imagination in a fantastic work of art is a power that is closely associated with magic, for this power of fantasy is propelled by imaginings of changed circumstances and conditions. The roots of the imagistic projections lie in the very matter of existence and being which calls for a satisfactory response and will continually demand this until the want is stilled, not repressed. Since reason cannot entirely articulate and fulfil our needs and has actually been instrumentalized to govern or curb them, imagination rises up in protest and invents strategems to undo the way the rational has been made irrational. Thus, if we understand our labour power in an expansive way as comprising the process of physically *and* mentally producing and reproducing conditions necessary for our sustenance, we can begin to see the socio-political meaning behind Tolkien's and Bloch's religious devotion to the fairy tale. Moreover, the stress on productive fantasy does not concern only the artist but the reader as well, for it provides the possibility for communion and consolation. As Anna K. Nardo has argued:

> Because the fictional role imposed on the reader of fantasy literature requires that he transcend the probable and the possible to play 'the game of the impossible,' he may experience a greater loosening of the boundaries between fantasy and fact than in realistic literature. . . . The reader of fantasy literature must, as Irwin claims, 'knowingly enter upon a conspiracy of intellectual subversiveness.' It is this play-belief in a story which occurs in a play-world, not necessarily faith in a shadow of the Christian story, that offers the reader of fantasy literature Consolation for his irrevocable finiteness. Although Tolkien argues that the Joy accompanying the 'Eucatastrophe' (happy ending) of much fantasy literature may be 'a far-off gleam or echo of *evangelium* in the real world,' we need not deny non-Christian fantasy the power of offering its readers Consolation. The play-belief necessary to join the game is belief enough.[11]

However, it can also be a search for belief or the disintegration of belief which impels author and reader to explore fantastic realms. For instance, in fairy tales the aesthetic rules of play and imaginative projections are always bounded by socio-political forces reflecting the religious and philosophical concerns of social classes or communities.

What draws Tolkien and Bloch together in their views on the fairy tale is a *secularization* of religion. At first glance this may seem untrue with regard to Tolkien, but it is noteworthy that his major works, *The Hobbit, The Lord of the Rings*, and *The Silmarillion* are devoid of Christian doctrine and that even his essay *On Fairy-Stories* alludes to the underlying Christian implications of fairy tales more in a secular sense, and this mainly in the epilogue. To put it another way, Tolkien was acutely aware, whether he stated this or not, that the essence of Christianity could only be conveyed to human beings in secularized form, given the changing referential framework of values in a capitalist world which has smashed the aura of the Judaeo-Christian tradition with crude utilitarian and rationalistic means for guaranteeing the sanctity of commodity production. Thus, fantasy is not only art for Tolkien, but *religion*, secularized religion, which is informed by a chiliastic perspective of a redeemed humanity. The reasons why Tolkien was forced to secularize most of his orthodox notions of Christianity can only be gleaned from the changing social conditions to which he responded out of protest. The failings of institutionalized religion, the rise of atheism and communism, the threats of war and fascism, the reification of values and human relations under capitalism — all these factors disturbed Tolkien, and it is quite clear that he created his mythological realm of the Middle Earth to demonstrate how human beings could 'recover' religion to offset the forces of inhumanity. The irony here is that Tolkien raises the small person, the Hobbit, to the position of God, that is, he stands at the centre of the universe and is the humanistic source of all creation. God is absent from the Middle Earth. The spiritual world manifests itself through the actions of the redeemed small person. And it is fantasy which liberates both the protagonist and the reader at the same time to seek redemption. Fantasy is at one and the same time the form and content of consolation.

Tolkien's unconscious secularization of religion brings him close to that Marxist viewpoint of religion most clearly associated with Bloch's philosophy of hope. Here it must be understood that Bloch never dismissed religion but carried forth its impulse dialectically to its most logical conclusion. The 'promises' of religion — the millennium, the better life, the life after death, paradise — have become rooted more and more in the potential of humankind to realize and concretize them on earth than through the powers of some transcendental being since human beings have historically evolved changing nature and themselves at the same time to gain more control over their own destinies. Sacrifice and self-sacrifice have become less meaningful due to technological developments, and human beings have increasingly sought immediate gratification of needs and wishes which cannot be provided by a transcendental being. This is also true of spiritual contentment which cannot be supplied by traditional and orthodox religions. This tendency toward immediate gratification of sensual and spiritual needs can lead and has led to strife, brutality, possessiveness, anarchy and dehumanization. Clearly these are only the negative tendencies in our polarized age. There are also positive aspects of immediate gratification, but both negative and positive point to a need to replace traditional religion by a faith which emanates from the Judaeo-Christian tradition and yet replaces it on a higher level. For Bloch religious faith and hope are not to be destroyed by socialism but will be placed in a materialist context which dispenses with the concept of a transcendental God only to redefine it as the supreme utopian problem.

> The true materialism, the dialectical one, while voiding the transcendence and reality of any divine hypostasis, does so without stripping the final qualitative contents of the process, the real utopia of a realm of freedom, of that which had been meant by an *ens perfectissimum*. Something attainable, something to be expected from the process, is not at all denied in dialectical materialism; a place for it is maintained, rather, and kept open as nowhere else. What this amounts to is that even in secularized form, and much more in utopian totality, the kingdom remains *a messianic frontal space without any theism*; indeed as increasingly demonstrated by every anthropologization of heaven from Prometheus down to the belief in a Messiah, it is only without theism that kingdom remains at all.[12]

The eschatological framework of Bloch's thought revolves around a paradox: God must be eliminated in order for humankind to be liberated and seize the essence of religion. Revelation comes when the atheist secularizes faith which becomes one of the motivating forces of the historical process. Secularized faith is 'the belief in a messianic kingdom of God without God. Therefore, far from being an enemy of religious utopianism, atheism is its premise: *without atheism there is no room for messianism*.'[13]

Bloch clearly imbues Marxism with the forceful messianic spirit of past religions which are appropriated and transformed by the deeds of humankind acting in and for itself. Only in this way can real history come into being. Pivotal for Bloch is Marx's assertion that 'a being can be said to be independent only when it stands on its own two feet, and it stands on its own feet only when it owes its *existence* only to itself. A human being, who lives by the grace of another, regards itself as a dependent being. But I live entirely by the grace of another when I am not only indebted to another for the sustenance of my life but when this other being has, beyond this, *created* my *life*. This being is the *source* of my life, and my existence necessarily has a purpose outside of itself, too, when it is not my own creation.'[14] This Marxist concept of the dialectics of existence (*Dasein*) points to the necessity of communality. Meaning cannot be achieved by a human being alone. The dependence on other beings must be acknowledged if the individual is to raise himself up and stride forward in an *upright posture* toward *home*, which, as we know, is the beginning of history, a realm without alienating conditions.

The importance of communality, fraternity and solidarity is striking in the writings of both Bloch and Tolkien as is the longing for a *true home*. The major difference between the two writers, who were eminently religious and idealistic, can be found in their respective positions toward capitalism. While both were anti-capitalist, Tolkien was more the reactionary romantic while Bloch was the progressive romantic. Tolkien placed the blame for the decadence and crass materialism of contemporary society on the *hubris* of human beings who sinned by seeking to change the world through machines and by using money to promote their own glory. Bloch clearly honoured the so-called hubris of human beings. He placed the blame for greed, exploitation, and waste on the capitalist system which he knew had to be superseded through the struggle of human beings to transform themselves into the more positive models they glimpsed in dreams and concrete utopias. He sought both to conserve the positive qualities of traditional religion and to replace the negative with illuminating ones which opened the path to a better world realizable in the here and now.

Perhaps, if we turn to a discussion of Tolkien's *The Hobbit* we can come to a better understanding of the similarities and dissimilarities between Bloch and Tolkien. Here I should like to do something unusual. Using Blochian categories, I shall explain the significance of such a work as *The Hobbit* while simultaneously criticizing its drawbacks. In the process I hope to make clear why such a fantastic fairy tale is a bestseller, not just because of the current vogue for fantasy today but because the very commodification of fantasy has brought with it *new sensual* longings which commodity production itself cannot fulfil. The very strength of the system is also its weakness, and fantasy, even as it is being instrumentalized, demands a sensual and spiritual fulfilment which runs contrary to the exploitative goals of capitalism.

III

The plot of *The Hobbit* follows the pattern of numerous folk and fairy tales. Bilbo Baggins, a small, unassuming, almost nondescript person, is chosen by a wizard named Gandalf for an adventure. He travels with thirteen rugged dwarfs and has numerous hair-raising encounters with trolls, goblins, wolves, and spiders, who represent the evil forces in the Middle Earth. After surviving these encounters, he helps the dwarfs regain their treasure-hoard from the dragon Smaug, who is killed by a great archer named Bard while attacking a nearby town of Men. Since the dwarfs want to keep the entire hoard for themselves, they must now contend with the elves and men who lay claim to some part of it. While they quarrel, the goblins and wild wolves appear and seek to annihilate them all. Thus, the battle of Five Armies takes place, and, while Bilbo plays safe by vanishing from sight thanks to his magic ring, the elves, dwarfs and men (aided by the eagles) defeat the forces of evil. Bilbo then returns home to his snug hobbit-hole, somewhat of a hero, but now regarded as not quite respectable and a little queer by other hobbits who generally never dare to undertake such dangerous adventures. While Bilbo learns from the wizard Gandalf that he has played a hand in helping fulfil a messianic prophesy, the wizard reminds him to keep things in their proper perspective: 'You don't really suppose, do you, that all of your adventures and escapes were managed by mere luck, just for your sole benefit? You are a very fine person, Mr. Baggins, and I am very fond of you; but you are only quite a little fellow in a wide world after all!'[15]

A little fellow to be sure, but a giant in potential and deeds. Like all 'little fellows' Bilbo possesses vital powers which can contribute to the defeat of oppressors and the making of a new world. These powers are within him and must be brought out through 'magic' (transformation) and shared communally to realize a common project with other beings. A hobbit is a forbear or descendant of all little-fellow heroes — David, Tom Thumb, the gallant tailor, the exploited daughter, the youngest son, Jack the giant killer, all those who do combat to right wrongs and create a just society. As Bloch stresses, these intrepid heroes show the holes in systems of domination through which small people can slip to liberate themselves and gain their ends. Their goals are socialist and utopian in nature in that they assert the potential for humanity to be on its own, not dependent on a system, on phantom gods. The individual moves into his or her own, undergoing a metamorphosis while gaining strength from the gifts of other beings. The building of the self and the other world is essentially a communal project.

In *The Hobbit* there is an important twist in the pattern at the beginning of the narrative, and this distinguishes it from most tales about 'little fellows'. Traditionally the little hero is courageous, initiates the adventure, and welcomes the chance to prove himself. Not Bilbo. He is perfectly content to rest in his pleasant hobbit-hole and must be prodded to go on an adventure. Tolkien's description of Bilbo (and all hobbits for that matter) is extremely significant, for it is quite clear that he is depicting elements of himself and the masses of 'nondescript' people in the world. Bilbo is an unlikely hero: fifty years old, portly, unambitious, a creature of routine, nothing attractive or alluring about him. In other words, Bilbo is the ideal passive consumer who would probably like to sit in front of his TV set, smoke a cigar, drink a beer, munch on chips, and have his fantasies played out for him on an electronic screen. But Bilbo, like all small people, has a spark within him which, when touched, can cause a chain reaction and explosion of his latent powers. 'Although he looked and behaved like a second edition of his solid and comfortable father,' Bilbo 'got something a bit queer in his makeup from the Took side, something that only awaited to come out' (p. 17). The Took side was his mother's family which was known to be adventurous, and indeed, we soon discover that there is something 'Tookish' about Bilbo. After a visit by Gandalf, the wizard, who is renowned for sending people on 'mad adventures', we know that trouble is brewing. Gandalf is preparing Bilbo for an adventure of his own. In fact, thirteen dwarfs, including their great king Thorin, invade Bilbo's home the next day to prevail upon him to join their struggle and help regain their gold and kingdom from the dragon Smaug. If we were to continue our analogy with the contented TV viewer, this would be comparable to the great coach of a football team jumping out of the TV screen and telling our viewer that he has been chosen to lead the team into the fray against the foe. At first startled and uncertain, our humble little viewer, who has always had fantasies about such an adventure, is persuaded to try his luck when thirteen members of the football team show up at his house the next day, overwhelm him, and simply assume that he will now play a vital role in their victory, for their great coach has promised that the 'idle viewer' is a slick operator who will make all the difference in the fight against the opposing team.

To return to the real story, that is, the fairy tale, the dwarfs (or our tried and tested football players) have some doubts about Bilbo's abilities. One dwarf says quite frankly: 'He looks more like a grocer than a burglar!' (p. 30). However, the wizard-coach gets angry and asserts: 'I have chosen Mr. Baggins and that ought to be enough for all of you. If I say he is a Burglar, a Burglar he is, or will be when the time comes. There is a lot more in him than you guess, and a deal more than he has any idea himself' (pp. 33-4). This initial situation set up by Tolkien is the key to comprehending the utopian project of the narrative. The protagonist is an insignificant fifty-year-old creature who resembles a harmless grocer rather than your typical dashing hero. He is passive, not inclined to take risks, thinks about 'out-of-pocket expenses, time required and remuneration' (p. 34). However, unbeknown to him, he has unusual powers which are waiting to be tapped. It is a question of the not-yet-having-become awaiting realization. In sum, Bilbo is described as a lower middle-class shopkeeper who has confined his dreams to a provincial realm and limited his own capacity to fulfil his human potential. He is one-sided until the Took side can be given equal rights.

Now who are the dwarfs? Why does Bilbo join forces with them? Who is the dragon? Why must he be overcome? The dwarfs are associated with miners and skilled workers. They are tough, somewhat crass, forthright, energetic and brave. The dragon is a parasite; or to put it in socio-political terms, he is the picture-image of the capitalist exploiter. Tolkien tells us that 'dragons steal gold and jewels, you know, from men and elves and dwarves, wherever they can find them; and they guard their plunder as long as they live (which is practically forever, unless they are killed), and never enjoy a brass-ring of it. Indeed they hardly know a good bit of work from a bad, though they usually have a good notion of the current market value; and they can't make a thing for themselves, not even mend a little loose scale of armour' (p. 35). The dragon lives off the hard work of small people and accumulates wealth without being able to appreciate its value. The dwarfs, expropriated, seek to reappropriate what is legitimately theirs. They *cannot* accomplish this alone but need and will continually need the help of hobbits, elves, men and other friendly creatures. Exactly why Bilbo the hobbit joins forces with them is unclear at first. In orthodox Marxist terms — and far be it from me to call Tolkien an orthodox Marxist, although there are unusual similarities between orthodox Catholics and orthodox Marxists — Bilbo's hesitation to join the dwarfs, i.e., the working class, is understandable since the lower middle class has always preferred to move upward and side with the ruling forces in society, namely the dragons, largely out of fear and social conditioning. Yet, the lower middle class can swing either way depending on how the unfulfilled wishes and needs may be satisfied by the praxis of the group or party they join. In this case, Bilbo is moved by the *song* of the dwarfs to *recover* what belonged to these hard-working, courageous creatures. He identifies with their cause and is swayed to give expression to his Tookish side.

The rest of the tale is predictable. The adventure begins in May, for it is the time of rebirth for Bilbo, who gradually sheds his provincial habits to learn about himself and the necessity for brotherhood in the struggle against the evil forces who take the shape of trolls, a Gollum, wolves and goblins. Tolkien makes it most clear at one point that these creatures are to be identified with the destructive agents of capitalism. In describing the goblins he says: 'Hammers, axes, swords, daggers, pickaxes, tongs, and also instruments of torture, they make very well, or get other people to make to their design, prisoners and slaves that have to work till they die for want of air and light. It is not unlikely that they invented some of the machines that have since troubled the world, especially the ingenious devices for killing large numbers of people at once, for wheels and engines and explosions always delighted them, and also not working with their own hands more than they could help' (p. 70).

In the initial encounters against trolls and goblins, Bilbo shows that he is no hero in the usual sense, for he is scared. He is just plain human and wonders why he ever left his hobbit-hole. However, soon thereafter he discovers the magic ring which has the power of making him invisible.[16] This discovery signifies the self-discovery of invisible latent powers which are gradually emerging in Bilbo's character as he faces challenge after challenge. As a symbol of transformation, the ring endows Bilbo with the power to perform in a way which he himself and the dwarfs never thought possible. In a sense the ring is a gift which represents the recovery of Bilbo's own gifts; it also suggests the circle of brotherhood, the commitment to a cause necessary to upend evil.[17] From this point on Bilbo's gifts will be put to use to help the dwarfs but also to deter their own avarice. During the long, gruelling adventures they come to trust and respect Bilbo. Yet, they have become so obsessed with regaining their treasure that they are unwilling to share it once Smaug the dragon is killed. The whole pursuit of money, even if it is wealth that legitimately belongs to the pursuers, is viewed by Tolkien as a corrupting process. The dwarfs are described as 'calculating folk with a great idea of the value of money' (p. 204). The dragon's rage is depicted as 'the sort of rage that is only seen when rich folk that have more than they can enjoy suddenly lose something that they have long had but have never before used or wanted' (p. 208). With the dragon's death, the dwarfs refuse to compensate the elves, men, and other creatures who directly and indirectly helped them defeat the monster. They become hoarders like the dragon, with the exception of Bilbo, who seeks to create harmony among the different groups. It is Bilbo, who presents the Arkenstone of Thrain to the men and elves so that they can have a better hand in bargaining for a share in the treasure and peace with the dwarfs. This act is a sacrifice on Bilbo's part and also shows that his participation in the adventure was not, even from the beginning, based on material motives but on a desire to give expression to his Tookish side — to become whole with himself and the world at large. This world at large — the Middle Earth — is menaced by dark forces which are equated with money, machines, exploitation, slavery, greed and irrationalism. Ironically, the power of the imagination provides the thread of reason which can restore peace and harmony to the world. This is the lesson of the final battle, and the dying Thorin, king of the dwarfs, acknowledges this when he blesses Bilbo: 'There is more in you of good than you know, child of the kindly West. Some courage and some wisdom, blended in measure. If more of us valued food and cheer and song above hoarded gold, it would be a merrier world' (p. 273).

There is a secure sense of *home* at the end of *The Hobbit*. Though Bilbo is considered somewhat strange by the other hobbits, he has *regained* his place in society with a more profound understanding of his powers and the knowledge of how to cope with the divisive forces in the world. He has also learned how to work with and trust other creatures and knows the necessity of brotherhood for maintaining peace. A small fellow at the beginning of the tale, he has won the respect of elves, dwarfs, men and a wizard. And this does not go to his head. Bilbo remains small. That is, he remains humble because of the vast self-confidence he has gained. He is now in touch with himself through the power of fantasy, and it is Tolkien's fantasy which allows us, too, to glimpse the possibilities of *home*.

Yet, there are certain disturbing features in the anticipatory illusion of home in Tolkien's work. The utopian perspective becomes practically myopic due to the author's regressive anti-capitalism. To begin with, Tolkien depicts a Middle Earth entirely without women.[18] It is almost as though the girls are relegated to the kitchen or house while the boys are sent out to mix it up, have fun, and return 'home' when all's over. But both the world outside and home remain barren here as long as the *presence* of women is denied. Though it may be appropriate to view the male Bilbo as a literary symbol for all genders of 'small folk', the one-sided male-oriented Middle Earth allows no room for establishing the place and function of women in reality or in fantasy. This is harmful to both female and male readers. (Let us not talk about Tolkien's own psychological problems in this arena.) The general impression one receives after reading *The Hobbit* is that all crucial problems of the world must be fought out and resolved by men. Women have no role to play except in reproduction, and even here, in the

Middle Earth, it appears as though men are self-productive. Fraternity exists unto itself and is not to be disturbed by females. Yet, the very absence of women destroys the forward look of his utopia, for Tolkien inadvertently promulgates notions about women which hark back to feudalism.

This is Tolkien's quandary. Essentially he wants to move forward toward a new humanism while moving backward. In certain instances of nonsynchronism, this may indeed be progressive in so far as capitalist progress has outstripped human subjectivity which feels plundered and cannot find adequate forms to express needs which have been left in the lurch. In this light, Tolkien is correct to step back into the past, for he wants to *restore* and *recapture* the humanist essence of the utopian project. We can define this as 'human beings coming into their own', 'the upright posture', 'home'. But, by stepping back into the past, Tolkien gets lodged there and has difficulty projecting a way back into the present and future. As in many folk tales which were widespread in feudalism, there is no change in social relations at the end of *The Hobbit* or in *The Lord of the Rings*. Essentially, the world is temporarily purged of evil, and Bilbo accepts his tiny place in the male-dominated hierarchy of the world with humility as does Frodo later on. Nothing against humility, but *home life* does not become endowed with a quality of freedom. What was magnificently expressed as the full creative powers in the adventures of Bilbo and Frodo retires in favour of the comfortable old life. It is the eternal recurrence of the old after the good new has been perceived and even partially realized.

Tolkien's strong Catholic views stand in the way of his utopianism and are decisive in making his secularization of religion contradictory. Evil comes from the arrogance, greed, sloth, pride and vanity of humankind. The seven deadly sins are at work in *The Hobbit* and *The Lord of the Rings*, and it is the virtuous Bilbo and Frodo, the innocents, who are set up as an example to *man*kind. They are seemingly enlightened at the end of their adventures, but the secret message is that there are forces greater than man in the world, and we must know our place, accept it, do our duty when we are called upon in the name of good, i.e., God. Harmony as ordained by higher forces must be restored. This is in contradiction to what Bloch praised in the ideal fairy tale: 'consider yourself as born free and entitled to be totally happy, dare to make use of your power of reasoning, look upon the outcome of things as friendly.' These maxims lose their cutting edge when Tolkien makes his hero a male who liberates himself to learn about humility. What Bloch admired most about the best of folk and fairy tales was their anti-authoritarian quality — the disregard for hierarchy, the ceaseless impulse to break out and realize the surging dreams of the imagination.

This is not to say that Tolkien, when all is said and done, was a reactionary. On the contrary, his works were much more progressive than even he himself realized. And this is the very reason why the comparison of Bloch with Tolkien is fruitful: the mixed messages of Tolkien's fantasy works can be made more clear when seen in the light of Bloch's philosophy. In particular, the positive value of their present popularity can be distinguished from their commodity value. Admittedly, it is extremely difficult to estimate the value of a bestseller such as *The Hobbit*, particularly when fantasy has become a vogue. In Tolkien's case the situation is compounded by a tremendous craze[19] which has transformed his fantasy world into a commercial industry closely resembling that of Walt Disney. For sale are artefacts resembling his creatures, posters, calendars, T-shirts, buttons, records, costumes, etc. There have been TV productions and a spectacular film by Ralph Bakshi based on Tolkien's works. The variety of Tolkieniana on the markets of the US and Great Britain is immense and is spreading to foreign countries. Correspondingly Tolkien clubs have also mushroomed in the last ten years. All this is obviously part of a fad, but a fad to be taken seriously. As C.N. Manlove has pointed out,

The trilogy came just when disillusion among the American young at the Vietnam war and the state of their own country was at a peak. Tolkien's fantasy offered an image of the kind of rural conservationist ideal or escape for which they were looking (it also could be seen as describing, through the overthrow of Sauron, the destruction of the U.S.). In this way *The Lord of the Rings* could be enlisted in support of passive resistance and idealism on the one hand and of draft-dodging and drugs on the other. A second factor may have been the perennial American longing for roots, a long tradition and a mythology: these things are the fibre of Tolkien's book, where every place and character is lodged at the tip of an enormous, growing stem of time. For the subsequent success of the book in Britain one can offer as possible reasons *(a)* Tolkien's being a British writer — his country at last claiming him for its own, *(b)* following the fashion, *(c)* the pastoral ideal held by youth (without the sense of crisis to sharpen it).[20]

Clearly when friends in a Tolkien club gather together to read the master's works, or when millions of people in the West continue to be drawn to this strange world, then this cannot be dismissed as trivial — as another sign of how the masses can be misled, deluded and mystified. Undeniably these elements are there, but I believe that it is more important to analyse the form of *community* and *communion* which Tolkien's fantasy offers his readers. Despite the imbalance, ambivalence, and stereotypes in Tolkien's contrived Manichean world, aptly dissected by Manlove[21], *The Hobbit* and *The Lord of the Rings* still manage to stimulate a sense of sharing, reverence, devotion and communion among Tolkien fans which cannot be found in the everyday relations of society itself. What is missing in reality is discovered by the fantasy which does not simply pacify the reader but reinforces the *need* to overcome the divisiveness and fragmentation of everyday life. In the particular case of *The Hobbit*, Bilbo demonstrates a way to reach out to his fellow creatures, presents a secularized religious communion which offers the hope to alienated individuals that imagination can pierce the administered walls of their existence and illuminate the path toward a utopia within humankind's grasp. Bloch saw this clearly:

So religious imagination cannot be dismissed *in toto* even after a successful disenchantment of the world image; it can be overcome only by a specific philosophical concept that will do justice to the ultimate intended substance of the imagination. For what was alive and is rising in the midst of all is this sighing, this conjuring, this preaching at the red dawn; and even amid the mythical nonsense that is so easy to note there lived and rises the unfinished question that has been burning only in religions, the question of the sense we cannot make out, of the meaning of life. It is the true realism that will be stirred by this question, one so far removed from mythical nonsense as to be responsible, rather, for every bit of sense. Needed, therefore — because of the particularly total pull of desire from this sphere — is a new *anthropology of religion*. And overdue — because of the particularly totally intended essence of perfection in this sphere — is a new *eschatology* of religion. Both without religion, but both with the corrected, unfinished problem of mankind's growing such enormous wings, such changing and at times incompatible wings, including some that adjoin obvious fool's paradises and yet keep tempting, attempting the uncommon sense — according to the human—social horizon.[22]

Clearly Bloch was pointing to something much more profound in his philosophical works than Tolkien could ever realize in his fantasy world. And it is important to keep in mind the crucial differences between Bloch the Marxist and Tolkien the Catholic. Bloch was essentially *a critic of utopias* who sought to grasp why humankind had failed thus far to overcome the obstacles confronting the concretization of utopia on this earth in the here and now. He harked back to the past only in so far as it might illuminate the future, and such terms as 'future', 'humanity', and 'utopia' were always closely tied to a socialist perspective. That is, Bloch's idealism was part of a religious faith that had its roots in a materialist anthropology, objective conditions of existence, and human needs and potentialities. For Bloch, the fairy tale was a kind of light beacon of socialism. In contrast, Tolkien was *a producer of utopias* who presented solutions and answers to the problems confronting humankind. He harked back to the past because he esteemed traditional religion and conservative forms of government. His perspective was definitely regressive but not totally reactionary, for his sympathies remained with the common people whom he regarded as exploited by capitalism and technology. For Tolkien, the fairy tale was artistic compensation and a healer of the injuries which human beings had to bear.

Though Tolkien provides answers to humankind's plight in the contemporary world, they are contradictory and need the critique of Bloch if we are to comprehend the utopian function of Tolkien's works of fantasy. The powerful interest expressed by people in the Western world in Tolkien's fantasy world is indicative of a need for a new eschatology of religion. Certainly this interest is also due to the commodification of Tolkien as well, and Tolkien is often simply consumed as just another marketable fanciful product. However, Bloch's notion of the 'religious imagination' suggests a more important motive for the high consumption of Tolkien. The religious imagination responds to the genuine utopian thrust in his works, and, whether one considers his fairy tales low or high art, serious fantasy or mere commercial entertainment, it must be recognized that he uncovers a social need of the religious imagination and points to the widening gap between a technologically constraining society and its alienated individuals in search of authentic community. Orthodox though Tolkien as a Catholic may be, he is radical as a sub-creator of utopia. His home may not be the concrete utopia of Bloch's socialist vision, but it is nevertheless an anticipatory illusion which houses some emancipatory impulses and provides hope that human beings can *still* come into their own.

6 On the Use and Abuse of Folk and Fairy Tales with Children

Bruno Bettelheim's Moralistic Magic Wand

Bruno Bettelheim was impelled to write his book *The Uses of Enchantment*[1] out of dissatisfaction 'with much of the literature intended to develop the child's mind and personality, because it fails to stimulate and nurture those resources he needs most in order to cope with his difficult inner problems'.[2] Therefore, he explored the great potential of folk tales as literary models for children since 'more can be learned from them about the inner problems of human beings, and of the right solutions to their predicaments in any society, than from any other type of story within a child's comprehension' (p. 5). This is, indeed, a grand statement on behalf of the folk tale's powers. However, despite his good intentions and moral concern in the welfare of children, Bettelheim's book disseminates false notions about the original intent of Freudian psychoanalytic theory and about the literary quality of folk tales and leaves the reader in a state of mystification. Not only is the manner in which Bettelheim would *impose* meaning onto child development through the therapeutic use of the folk tale authoritarian and unscientific,[3] but his stance is symptomatic of numerous humanitarian educators who perpetuate the diseases they desire to cure.

This is not to dismiss Bettelheim's book in its totality. Since folk and fairy tales have played and continue to play a significant role in the socialization process, a thorough study of Bettelheim's position is crucial for grasping whether the tales can be used more effectively in helping children (and adults) come into their own. A critical examination of his theory may ultimately lead to a fresh look at contemporary psychoanalytic views on internalization and new insights about the production and usage of folk and fairy tales.

The Use and Abuse of Folk and Fairy Tales with Children

Bettelheim's major thesis is a simple one: 'the form and structure of fairy tales suggest images to the child by which he can structure his daydreams and with them give better direction to his life' (p. 7). In other words, the folk tale liberates the child's subconscious so that he or she can work through conflicts and experiences which would otherwise be repressed and perhaps cause psychological disturbances. According to Bettelheim, folk tales present existential dilemmas in a clear-cut manner so that the child can easily grasp the underlying meanings of the conflicts. Most folk tales are an imaginative depiction of healthy human development and help children understand the motives behind their rebellion against parents and the fear of growing up. The conclusions of most folk tales portray the achievement of psychological independence, moral maturity and sexual confidence. Obviously, as Bettelheim admits, there are other approaches to folk tales. But, he maintains that it is primarily the psychological approach which uncovers the hidden meanings of the tales and their overwhelming importance for child development.

Given the immense volume of folk tales, Bettelheim limits his discussion to the better known tales. The book is divided into two parts. The first, fancifully entitled 'A Pocketful of Magic', focuses on a theoretical explication of his concepts, method and purpose. The second part, 'In Fairy Land', consists of 14 case studies of such different tales as *Snow White*, *Sleeping Beauty*, *Hansel and Gretel*, *Jack and the Beanstalk*, *Little Red Riding Hood*, *Cinderella*, etc. In the first part, Bettelheim asserts that adults should not explain the tales to children since that would destroy their 'magic'. However, adults should tell the tales because that shows approval of children's imaginative play. Children are allegedly drawn to folk tales because they symbolically depict the psychological problems which the children must work through *by themselves*. In doing this, a child supposedly attains a sense of his or her self. If we were to follow the logic of Bettelheim's argument, it is almost as though the folk tale could be considered a psychoanalyst in the manner in which it operates with a child. The tale by itself opens up unexplored realms of experience to children who learn to order their inner worlds by following the fantastic signposts of the tale and by identifying with the hero who becomes ruler of a kingdom, i.e. ruler of the self.

Characteristic of Bettelheim's orthodox Freudian approach

is the arbitrary way in which he makes excessive claims for the therapeutic power of the folk tale and then diagnoses the power to fit his strait-jacket theory about neurosis and the family. For instance, he unabashedly asserts that 'unlike any other form of literature, they [folk tales] direct the child to discover his identity and calling' (p. 24). Then he narrows the psychological meaning in a reductionist manner: 'the content of the chosen tale has nothing to do with the patient's external life but much to do with his inner problems, which seem incomprehensible and hence insolvable' (p. 25). Such flat assertions, common throughout the book, rest on shaky grounds. Bettelheim provides no documentation to prove that the folk tale is better than any other imaginative or non-fiction literature for helping children develop their character. Moreover, Bettelheim has a one-dimensional way of examining the relation of literature to the psyche. To suggest that the external life is isolated from the inner life and that there is a literature which primarily addresses itself to the inner problems of a reader completely eliminates the dialectical relationship between essence and appearance. Existence is divorced from the imagination, and a static realm is erected which resembles the laboratory of an orthodox Freudian mind that is bent on conducting experiments with what *ought* to be happening in the child's inner realm.

The categorical imperative used by Bettelheim constantly prevents him from achieving his purpose of uncovering the significance of folk tales for child development. Folk tales are said to personify and illustrate inner conflicts, and Bettelheim wants to demonstrate to his adult readers how a child views folk tales and reality so that they can be more enlightened in their dealings with children. This stance is in actual contradiction to his previous argument that children must be allowed freedom to interpret the tales and that adults must not impose interpretation. It is the authority, Bettelheim, who *claims to know* how children subconsciously view the tales and who imposes this psychoanalytic mode of interpreting tales on adults. In turn they ought to use his approach if they care for children. This moral argumentation has nothing to do with a more scientific explanation of the tales and how they can be used to aid children in their development. Everything remains in Bettelheim's own realm of reified Freudian formulas which restrain the possibilities for a vital interaction between the tale and the child and between the adult and the child.

This can immediately be seen when he presents his theoretical explanation of how folk tales clarify the meaning of conflicts for children and how they provide for resolution. Like many cultural censors of morality, Bettelheim believes that only literature which is harmonious and orderly should be fed to the delicate souls of children who should be sheltered from harsh reality. Thus, the folk tale is perfect. In contrast to myths, fables and legends, folk tales are allegedly optimistic because they allow for hope and the solution of problems. In addition, they involve a conflict between the reality and pleasure principles and show how a certain amount of pleasure can be retained while the demands of reality are respected (as in the example of the oldest pig in *The Three Little Pigs*). Indiscriminately using the discoveries of Piaget, who has demonstrated (among other things) that the child's thinking up till the ages of nine or ten is animistic, Bettelheim explains how the magic and fantastic images in the folk tale enable the child subjectively to come to terms with reality. The adventures in the folk tale allow for vicarious satisfaction of unfulfilled desires and subconscious drives (pp. 56-7) and permit the child to sublimate those desires and drives at a time when conscious recognition would shatter or shake the child's character structure which is not yet secure. The folk tale provides freedom for the child's imagination in that it deals at first with a problematic real situation which is then imaginatively transformed. The narrative breaks down spatial and temporal limits and leads the child into the self, but it also leads him or her back into reality. Bettelheim argues against true-to-life stories for child development because they impinge upon the imagination of the child and act repressively as would the rational interference of an adult. In contrast, the folk tale transforms reality in such a way that the child can cope with it. Like the symbols of the id, ego and superego, which Freud created as operative constructs, the folk-tale symbols represent separate entitites of the child's inner sanctum, and their representation in a folk tale (for a child) shows how order can be made out of chaos (p. 75). In particular, the folk tale demonstrates how each element (ego, id, superego) must be given its due and integrated if character structure is to develop without disturbance.

Many folk tales like *Brother and Sister* show how the animalistic (male/id) must be integrated with the spiritual component (female/ego, superego) to permit human qualities to blossom: 'Integration of the disparate aspects of our personality can be gained only after the asocial, destructive, and unjust have been done away with; and this cannot be achieved until we have reached full maturity, as symbolized by sister's giving birth to a child and developing mothering attitudes' (p. 83). At the bottom of all the chaos and conflict which children experience are parents, leading Bettelheim to make the following claim: 'Maybe if more of our adolescents had been brought up on fairy tales, they would (unconsciously) remain aware of the fact that their conflict is not with the adult world, or society, but really only with their parents' (pp. 98-9). In other words, the ambivalent attachments to one's parents are the roots of all evil and must be worked out by the child (particularly the Oedipal conflicts) if a well-integrated personality is to be achieved. Symbolically folk tales are the most clear and distinct representations of children's anxieties and unconscious drives, and therefore they can stimulate children to explore their imaginations for resolutions to the conflicts with their parents. They are like guidebooks for achieving true identity and a true state of independence. Thus now we know what becoming a ruler over a kingdom means, and Bettelheim can conclude his first part by advising adults again to take an active part in the telling of the tale but not to interpret it for the child. The participation will (like the psychiatrist) bring the child and parent closer together by magically restoring order to the child's mind.

This theory is fallacious on two levels, the psychoanalytic and the literary. Not only does Bettelheim misinterpret some of Freud's key notions about psychoanalysis, but he also twists the meanings of the literature to suit his peculiar theory of child development. The intended 'humanitarian' goals of his study are undermined by his rigid Freudian abstractions which prop up irrational and arbitrary forms of social behaviour whose norms and values children are supposed to adapt. The patterns of the folk tales allegedly foster ideal normative behaviour which children are to internalize; yet, some of these literary patterns like the forms of social behaviour are repressive constructs which violate the imagination of both children and adults alike. Let me clarify both charges against Bettelheim, his betrayal of the radical essence of Freudianism and his corruption of the literary meaning of the folk tale.

The critical task of Freud's psychoanalytic theory was to

demonstrate the manifold ways in which society made it impossible for the individual to achieve autonomy. His purpose was to expose the inner forces which hinder full development of the individual and cause psychic disturbances because of external pressures and conditions. His work in theory was to destroy illusions which society creates about the possibility of achieving autonomy and a happy life so that the individual could elaborate meaning out of the antagonistic relationship between self and society. As Russell Jacoby has demonstrated in his significant study *Social Amnesia: A Critique of Contemporary Psychology from Adler to Laing*, the basic radical thrust of Freudian theory has been forgotten and obfuscated. In particular, the orthodox Freudians have hampered the growth of Freudian theory by codifying the principles as absolute laws. Here it is important to make a distinction among orthodox Freudians as Jacoby does:

> Once the false opposition between orthodoxy and revisionism as that between obsolete dogma and contemporary insight is avoided, the notion of orthodoxy must be reformulated. To the point that the theories of Marx and Freud were critiques of bourgeois civilization, orthodoxy entailed loyalty to these critiques; more exactly, *dialectical* loyalty. Not repetition is called for but articulation and development of concepts; and within Marxism — and to a degree within psychoanalysis — precisely against an Official Orthodoxy only too happy to freeze concepts into formulas. . . . Freud and his students are clear enough as to what in psychoanalysis is to be preserved — not by thoughtless repetition but by reworking: the concepts of repression, sexuality, unconscious, Oedipal complex, infantile sexuality.[4]

Unfortunately, Jacoby does not elaborate his critique of official orthodoxy. He spends most of his time defending the dialectical orthodox Freudians. Yet, as a result of his work, it becomes eminently clear that Bettelheim *does not* have a dialectical relationship to Freudianism but has contributed to the banalization of Freudian theory by blandly applying its tenets without rethinking and reworking them in the light of social and scientific changes. Moreover, he has also picked up one of the worst traits of the neo- and post-Freudians — their moralizing. Aside from Bettelheim's mechanical repetition of Freud's thought, his postulates read like 'Sunday sermons'. 'The positive is promoted to drive out the negative. One strives to be cheery because it is a cheerless world. Since reflection on the latter is taboo,' Bettelheim 'seeks to make palatable the unswallowable: the lie that the isolated and abandoned individual can "become", "love", "be". Hence, the "how to" nature'[5] of his work. Bettelheim patches up his official orthodoxy with moral homilies about therapeutic self-help. He constantly asserts that the folk tale contains the answers to the good, happy life, implying that there is a social realm where individual autonomy can be reached. Yet, in *Civilization and Its Discontents*, Freud made clear just how repressive society was and how limited and varied the possibilities were to attain freedom and happiness.

> The liberty of the individual is not a benefit of culture. It was the greatest before any culture, though indeed it had little value at that time, because the individual was hardly in a position to defend it. Liberty has undergone restrictions through the evolution of civilization, and justice demands that these restrictions shall apply to all. . . . It is impossible to ignore the extent to which civilization is built on renunciation of instinctual gratifications, the degree to which the existence of civilization presupposes the non-gratification (suppression, repression or something else?) of powerful instinctual urgencies. This 'cultural privation' dominates the whole field of social relations between human beings; we know already that it is the cause of the antagonism against which all civilization has to fight.[6]

What is significant in Freud's work is that he located the cause for psychosis and all mental sicknesses in the historical and materialistic development of social conditions. He may have misconstrued some theories which were based on inconclusive and partial data, but the basis of his research for studying the relationship of the human psyche to civilization was dialectical and provided the fundamentals for a social science that could be altered as the social conditions changed. Bettelheim not only fails to develop Freud's far-reaching findings for application to the massive changes in society and the human psyche, but he actually eliminates the dialectic from Freud's method. He holds the family primarily responsible for the conflicts a child experiences, thus not locating it as *one of the mediating agencies* through which civilization causes repression. Even worse, he employs Freudian terminology like a puritanical parson encouraging parents to have faith in the almighty power of the folk tale which will lead children through the valley of fear into the kingdom of grace.

Gone is the dialectical antagonistic relationship between society and the individual. If anything, it is misplaced between child and family which shifts the real cause for repression and thus dilutes the dialectics. Bettelheim would have us believe that the child can voluntaristically work through internalized problems with the aid of a folk tale and become a well-adjusted, autonomous individual. Once familial conflicts are grasped and solved, happiness is just down the road. By assuming such a position, Bettelheim unwittingly becomes an apologist for a 'civilized' society noted for its abuse of children and its proclivity toward dehumanization. These negative tendencies of our contemporary society have been recorded not only by its critics but by its very own established news media which document the violation of human rights and violence of subjectivity every minute of every day.

Essentially Bettelheim's concern in children reflects a conservative Freudian notion of internalization and does not take into consideration the dire consequences which rational adjustment to the reality principle has for children. In contrast to Freud, for Bettelheim and other neo-Freudians,

> a theory of internalization is necessary which explains how the ego is formed through social interaction such that human beings come to comply with these laws rather than attempt to change them. Such a theory must recognize that internalization is a defense against unbearable reality, not a natural mode of constituting consciousness, necessitated by the opposition 'of the instincts. The idea of instincts has a role to play in the sense that the 'libido is the actual reality,' if we understand the libido as essentially object-seeking. Denial of this striving leads not only to illness but to compliance with authority, acceptance of helplessness. The way in which the striving for recognition is denied must be understood in the context of societal interaction rather than conceived as an eternal form of the ego.[7]

Instead of recognizing the power of society to deny autonomy, Bettelheim encourages an internalization which furthers the split between mind and body. The fantasy of the child is to be given free rein only if it finally succumbs to instrumental reason. No wonder that his book is largely male-orientated and fails to make careful distinctions between the sexes, ages and class backgrounds of children. Nor does he bother to consider that the theories derived from Freud have to be made more historical and scientific to account for sex, age and class differences. It is no longer valid to postulate theories of the imagination, penis envy, and Oedipal conflicts without reworking them and perhaps even dismissing them in the light of changing social conditions and normative behaviour.[8] Perhaps the greatest weakness of Bettelheim's book is his neglect of socio-linguistic studies and his own careless use of terminology which reflects just how faulty his theory of communication is. In one of the more important studies of this problem, *Class, Codes and Control*, Basil Bernstein has pointed out that

> as the child learns his speech or, in the terms used here, learns specific codes which regulate his verbal acts, he learns the requirements of his social structure. The experience of the child is transformed by the learning which is generated by his own apparently voluntary acts of speech. The social structure becomes the substratum of his experience essentially through the consequences of the linguistic process. From this point of view, every time the child speaks or listens the social structure of which he is a part is reinforced in him and his social identity is constrained. The social structure becomes the developing child's psychological reality by the shaping of his acts of speech. Underlying the general pattern of his speech are, it is held, critical sets of choices, preferences for some alternatives rather than others, which develop and are stabilized through time and which eventually come to play an important role in the regulation of intellectual, social and affective orientations.[9]

Bernstein discusses the ramifications of language for the psycho-social development of children, and he makes careful, empirically based distinctions between elaborated and restricted codes[10] used generally by middle-class and working-class children respectively. Since 'the mode of a language structure reflects a particular form of the structuring of feeling and so the very means of interaction and response to the environment,'[11] Bernstein investigates why working-class children respond differently and often negatively to the socialization process which has been developed to satisfy middle-class needs. In contrast, middle-class children adapt more readily and learn to use all sorts of codes to further their ends. The restricted code used by working-class children is not necessarily qualitatively poorer than the elaborated code of the middle-class child, but it is *different* and does reflect the more limited and authoritarian margins within which a working-class child is socialized. Thus, in a formal learning situation which is generally predicated on the elaborated code of the middle class, the 'I' of the working-class child is threatened. 'The attempt to substitute a different use of language and to change the order of communication creates critical problems for the working-class child as it is an attempt to change his basic system of perception, fundamentally the very means by which he has been socialized.'[12]

In Bettelheim's discussion of folk tales and their use with children, there is no regard for the differences between children and their particular relationships to language which influences their receptivity to the linguistic and aesthetic codes and patterns of literature. In fact, differences are virtually levelled out as if the education process were a democratizing experience and as if there were no codes, either in public or private language or in the folk tales themselves. This brings us to Bettelheim's misuse of the folk tale as an art form.

Though aware of the historical origins of the folk tale, Bettelheim fails to take into account that the symbols and patterns of the tales reflect specific forms of social behaviour and activity which often can be traced back as far as the Ice and Megalithic Ages. As August Nitschke has documented in his book *Soziale Ordnungen im Spiegel der Märchen*,[13] the contemporary psychological labels attached to the symbols and patterns of the tales are contradicted by the actual historical and archaeological findings. According to the data, the normative behaviour and labour processes of primitive peoples as depicted in the tales which they themselves cultivated cannot be explained by modern psychoanalytical theory. Properly speaking, any psychological approach to the folk tales would first have to investigate the socialization processes of primitive societies in a given historical era in order to provide an appropriate interpretation. Leaving aside the questionable methodology of the orthodox Freudians, who see penis envy and castration complexes everywhere in folk tales, and assuming that there is some validity to using folk tales therapeutically in educating children, one must still question the manner in which Bettelheim imposes meaning on the tales as well as his indiscriminate application of their meaning to children of all ages, sexes, and class backgrounds. As Nitschke demonstrates, the creative purpose and major themes of the folk tales did not concern harmony, but the depiction of changing social structures and alternative forms of behaviour so that new developments and connections between humans and things could be better grasped by the people. Central to most tales is the concept of power. Where does it reside? Who wields it? Why? How can it be better wielded? Many of the tales bespeak a primitive or feudal ideology of 'might makes right'. Depending on the historical epoch the tales portray either the possibilities for social participation or the reasons for social conflict. The immanent meaning of the tales has little to do with providing suitable direction for a contemporary child's life. From a contemporary perspective, the tales are filled with incidents of inexplicable abuse, maltreatment of women, negative images of minority groups, questionable sacrifices, and the exaltation of power.[14] Here I am only mentioning some of the more negative aspects of the tales which also contain positive features which will be discussed later. The point which I should like to make right now is that the psychological components and meanings can best be understood when first related to the contradictory developments of the historical period in which they originated.

To use the tales with children today as a means for therapeutic education demands first a historical understanding and secondly a careful delineation of the progressive and regressive ideological and psychological meanings of the tales. Here we are dealing with the entire question of reception. How does a child receive and perceive a given tale? It is necessary to ask whether a child actually knows what a king is. What does a king mean to a five-year-old, to an eight-year-old, to a girl or boy, to girls and boys of different races and class backgrounds? A prince who uses magical gifts which sometimes involve killing to become a king of a particular realm does not necessarily imply, as Bettelheim would have us believe, that the child (which child?) will psychologically comprehend this as a story about self-mastery. Could it not also serve to reinforce the aggressive instincts of a middle-class child to become more ego-centred, competitive and achievement-oriented? Could not the code be understood by a lower-class child so as to reinforce the arbitrary power of authoritarian figures and to accept a strict hierarchical world? What is obviously necessary in working with the impact of the tales on children is a method which takes into consideration the aesthetics of reception. Such a method would have to investigate the possibilities for comprehension by children in the light of the dialectical relationship of a specific audience to the tale at a given moment in history.

The Use and Abuse of Folk and Fairy Tales with Children

The ultimate weakness of Bettelheim's methodology can be seen in the second part of his book which contains his case studies of popular folk tales. Let us look at his exhaustive treatment of _Cinderella_ as an example of his approach. Bettelheim first discusses the various versions and cycles of the Cinderella story, in particular those of Basile and Perrault, and he diagnoses their major themes as those of sibling rivalry and the Oedipal complex. He then uses the basic plot of the Grimm version as the paradigmatic model for comprehending all the _Cinderella_ stories. Actually no matter what tale is touched by Bettelheim's orthodox Freudian wand, it is always transformed into a symbolic parable of self-realization and healthy sexuality. Here, as usual, Bettelheim is concerned with the hidden meanings which work wonders on children. _Cinderella_ teaches children about sibling rivalry and a young girl's endeavours to prove her worth. It is significant that Cinderella is given 'dirty' work to do since that reflects her own low self-esteem as well as the guilt she feels for desiring her father. Her thwarted Oedipal desires must be overcome if she is to prove her real worth and achieve complete sexuality. The hardships which Cinderella must endure are tests that involve the development of personality.

Using Erik Erikson's model of the human life cycle, Bettelheim talks about the 'phase-specific psychosocial crises' which an individual must go through in order to become the 'ideal human being'. In the case of Cinderella, she goes through five phases of the human life cycle to develop basic trust (the relationship with her original good mother), autonomy (acceptance of her role in the family), initiative (the planting of the twig), industry (her hard labours), and identity (her insistence that the prince see both her dirty and her beautiful side). Bettelheim is particularly penetrating on this last point.

> In the slipper ceremony, which signifies the betrothal of Cinderella and the prince, he selects her because in symbolic fashion she is the uncastrated woman who relieves him of his castration anxiety which would interfere with a happy marital relationship. She selects him because he appreciates her in her 'dirty' sexual aspects, lovingly accepts her vagina in the form of the slipper, and approves of her desire for a penis, symbolized by her tiny foot fitting within the slipper—vagina. . . . But as she slips her foot into the slipper, she asserts that she, too, will be active in their sexual relationship; she will do things, too. And she also gives the assurance that she is not and never was lacking in anything (p. 271).

171

It is quite clear that the virginal Cinderella is the most suitable for Prince Charming because her step-sisters in their act of self-mutilation reveal through the blood (menstrual bleeding) that they are sexually too aggressive and cause the prince anxiety. In sum, *Cinderella* as story 'guides the child from his greatest disappointments — oedipal disillusionment, castration anxiety, low opinion of others — toward developing his autonomy, becoming industrious, and gaining a positive identity of his own' (p. 276). After reading Bettelheim's concluding remarks, one wonders why such books as Dale Carnegie's *How to Win Friends and Influence People* and *How to Succeed in Business* are necessary when we have folk tales.

In contrast to Bettelheim's moral primer about folk tales, Nitschke has demonstrated that Cinderella originated toward the end of the Ice Age. The norms of behaviour and social activity depicted in *Cinderella* reveal that the tale revolves around a female who receives help and gifts from her dead mother, who continues living in the form of a tree, and from animals. Nitschke explains in some detail that the society which produced tales similar to *Cinderella* was one of hunting and grazing in which the woman was accorded the place of honour. Death was not feared, and women were sacrificed so that they could return to life in the form of a plant or animal to help their children develop. Life was seen in sequences and as eternal. Thus, a human being participated in his or her own time and, through transformation after death, there was a renewal of time. Most important is the function of the female. She was at the centre of this society and maintained it as nurturing element. *Cinderella* does not reflect society undergoing great changes in production but a maintenance of the hunting and grazing society. However, when compared to tales of the early Ice Age, it does show how human beings have taken over centre stage from animals, and the growing importance attached to the woman. Love and mutual self-respect are accomplished through the intercession of the mother.

Nitschke's explanation of the historical origins and meaning of *Cinderella* obviously cannot be grasped by children. But it does set the framework for a psychoanalytical approach which must first consider the people and their social behaviour if it wants to establish the psychological essence of a tale. The same thing holds true for the retelling of the tale today, but in a slightly different manner. And here the implications of the tale are remarkably different from what they were in the Ice Age. Instead of having a tale which does homage to women, we have a tale which is an insult to women. Here I want to concentrate on just one aspect of *Cinderella* to question the relevance Bettelheim bestows upon it. In the American society today where women have been in the vanguard of the equal rights movement, where female sexuality has undergone great changes, where the central agency of socialization of boys and girls has shifted from the family to the mass media, schools and the bureaucratic state,[15] a tale like *Cinderella* cannot (neither explicitly nor implicitly) guide children to order their inner worlds and to lead fuller, happier sexual lives. Though it is difficult to speculate how an individual child might react to *Cinderella*, certainly the adult reader and interpreter must ask the following questions: Why is the stepmother shown to be wicked and not the father? Why is Cinderella essentially passive? (How Bettelheim twists the meaning to see *Cinderella* as active is actually another one of his Freudian magic tricks.) Why do girls have to quarrel over a man? How do children react to a Cinderella who is industrious, dutiful, virginal and passive? Are all men handsome? Is marriage the end goal of life? Is it important to marry rich men? This small list of questions suggests that the ideological and psychological pattern and message of *Cinderella* do nothing more than reinforce sexist values and a Puritan ethos that serves a society which fosters competition and achievement for survival. Admittedly this is a harsh indictment of *Cinderella* as a tale. Certainly I do not want to make it responsible for the upkeep of the entire capitalist system. However, the critique of *Cinderella* is meant to show how suspect Bettelheim's theory and methodology are. There is something ultimately pathetic and insidious about Bettelheim's approach to folk tales. It is pathetic because he apparently wants to make a sincere contribution in fighting the dehumanization of life. It is insidious because his banal theory covers up the processes and social mediations which contribute most to the dehumanization. Fundamentally, his instructions on how to use the folk tales can only lead to their abuse. Our task is to explore the possibilities for their positive utilization with children.

There is no doubt but that folk tales are alluring, not only to children but to adults. Their imaginative conception of other worlds in which repressed dreams, needs and wishes might be fulfilled has long since motivated the common people to transmit and cultivate the tales in an oral tradition. As Johannes Merkel and Dieter Richter have demonstrated in their important study *Märchen, Phantasie und soziales Lernen*,[16] the folk tales were often censored and outlawed during the early phase of the bourgeoisie's rise to power because their fantastic components which encouraged imaginative play and free exploration were hostile to capitalist rationalization and the Protestant ethos. Once the bourgeoisie's power was firmly established, the tales were no longer considered immoral and dangerous, but their publication and distribution for children were actually encouraged toward the end of the nineteenth century. The tales took on a compensatory function for children and adults alike who experienced nothing but the frustration of their imaginations in society. Within the framework of a capitalist socioeconomic system the tales became a safety valve for adults and children and acted to pacify the discontents. Like other forms of fantastic literature — and it is significant that science fiction rises also at the end of the nineteenth century — the tales no longer served their original purpose of clarifying social and natural phenomena but became forms of refuge and escape in that they made up for what people could not realize in society. This does not mean that the radical content of the imaginative symbols in folk tales and other forms of fantastic literature have been completely distilled. As Herbert Marcuse has suggested, 'the truth value of imagination relates not only to the past but also to the future: the forms of freedom and happiness which it invokes claim to deliver the historical *reality*. In its refusal to accept as final the limitations imposed upon freedom and happiness by the reality principle, in its refusal to forget what *can be*, lies the critical function of phantasy.'[17] Still, the question remains as to how to make the artistic forms conceived by the imagination operative *in society*. In other words, how can the imagination and imaginative literature transcend compensation?

In essence, Bettelheim's book discusses the use of the folk tale to compensate for social repression. But folk tales and other fantastic literature can be used to suggest ways to *realize* greater pleasure and freedom in society. Let us take Oscar Wilde's literary fairy tale *The Selfish Giant* as an example. The plot is simple. It involves a giant who chases children out of his garden, erects a wall, and puts up a sign

'Trespassers will be Prosecuted!' Because he does this, spring and summer refuse to come to his garden, and he suffers from cold and loneliness. One day he notices through his window that the children had crept through a hole in the wall and had climbed up a tree. In that part of the garden inhabited by the children it suddenly turns spring, and the giant realizes how selfish he has been. After that he opens up his garden to all the children and learns to share in their happiness. Because of this he attains heaven upon his death.

I do not want to explore the different meanings of this tale in depth, for this would involve a consideration of Wilde's behaviour, socialist perspective and personal philosophy in light of the repression of Victorian society. My main concern is to touch upon the general meaning which, on both a literary and a psychological level, might have an impact on children today. The language and symbols of the tale are such that it is probably comprehensible to all children regardless of sex, race and background. The major theme involves collectivity versus individualism and the struggle over private property. The children band together and represent a principle of social interaction, sharing and joy while the giant obviously represents arbitrary power and greed. It is interesting that the tale depicts the alienation of the persecutor and how joy can only come through collectivity. Naturally it is possible to talk about the story in psychoanalytic terms; the fear of sexuality and parents, the id learning that there is a deeper pleasure to be attained by curbing its drive and participating in reality according to strictures of the super-ego. However, the message amounts to the same on an ideological and psychological level: the necessity for collective action and autonomous participation to attain pleasure, love and recognition. What is even more important is that we are dealing with a literary fairy tale which illustrates through the imagination an alternative manner of behaviour which *can be realized* in society. Wilde's tale is a valid critique of a society based on private property, a society which shuns children, and it provides hope that, if children stick together and use their initiative (*Hansel and Gretel* says this, too), they can convince their oppressors to change their ways. The children find a way into the giant's garden and show him the light, so to speak, and the process of overcoming his greed is depicted not as annihilation but a movement toward collective action. The focus is on intersubjective action which can nurture individual development.

There are numerous folk tales (*The Bremen Town Musicians, How Six Travelled Through the World*) and literary fairy tales which suggest means by which children can implement their imagination to promote collective action. I am not suggesting that it is only fantastic literature of this sort which should be used with children. In contrast to Bettelheim, I would argue that it is culturally repressive to dictate what forms of literature and types of tales are best suited for aiding a child's development. Folk tales, after all, were never conceived as tales for children, and there was never a special children's literature or culture until the late Middle Ages. Even now this distinction is somewhat arbitrary since children are exposed to all forms of art through the mass media, commercial outlets and institutions of socialization. Bettelheim's argument for the folk tale is apparently an argument for fantastic literature over realistic literature as the best mode for solving a child's inner problems. But, once we realize that literature in and by itself does not work automatically to solve psychological problems, that realistic literature is not inherently repressive, and that the evaluation of literature cannot be discussed without considering its production and reception, we draw nearer to a more sober approach to the use of folk and fairy tales for children.

One could perhaps talk about certain interesting experiments which have been undertaken in West Germany:[18] the rewriting of folk tales from a socialist perspective, the conceiving of contemporary fairy tales written by adults and children which expose social contradictions and oppression, the active telling of folk and fairy tales which allow for a critical dialectical relationship between adults and children as the tale is told and interpreted.[19] Such radical use of folk and fairy tales is significant in that it demonstrates ways in which the imagination can be used to operate in society so that children and adults gain a greater sense of forces acting upon them and begin relating to one another in non-repressive ways in their cultural work.[20]

The specific use of folk and fairy tales ultimately depends on the production and reception of the literature which is closely bound to the needs of the commodity market. Obviously, in American society it is near to impossible to control the Walt Disney industry and other conglomerates which mainly aim at making profit from the fantasy of children and adults. Educators sincerely interested in using fantastic or realistic literature to aid children in developing critical and imaginative capacities must first seek to alter the social organization of culture and work that is presently preventing self-realization and causing the disintegration of the individual. One cannot talk about the wounded child's psyche without talking about a social praxis which is geared toward ending the unfair speculation with lives that our socio-economic system endorses. Cultural work with children must begin from a critical perspective of the production and market conditions of literature, and this involves using fantastic and realistic literature to make children aware of their potentialities and also aware of the social contradictions which will frustrate their full development. Any other approach will lead to illusions and lies. Thus, a concrete humanitarian engagement on behalf of children means utilizing the existing literature of all kinds while also creating new, more emancipatory forms so that the fallacies and merits of the literature become apparent as well as the fallacies and merits of society. There is no need to resort to methods of censorship or enchantment as Bettelheim does. But there is a need to develop effective means of enlightenment so that the repressed dreams, wishes, and needs of children and adults alike can be realized in a mutually beneficial way in the fight against what Freud called 'cultural privation'.

Folk and fairy tales remain an essential force in our cultural heritage, but they are not static literary models to be internalized for therapeutic consumption. Their value depends on how we actively produce and receive them in forms of social interaction which lead toward the creation of greater individual autonomy. Only by grasping and changing the forms of social interaction and work shall we be able to make full use of the utopian and fantastic projections of folk and fairy tales. *Rumpelstiltskin* long ago demonstrated how we must seek the power to name the forces acting upon us if we want to be free and autonomous. But the *Rumpelstiltskin* folk tale did not and does not answer all the questions for us. It poses a predicament which we must continually confront and try to resolve anew. Writers of fairy tales have realized this, and at various times they have imagined alternatives to the *Rumpelstiltskin* folk tale which point in the direction of a new humanism. Though it may seem far-fetched to make this argument, the humanity of our culture does indeed depend on what we concretely make out of the following folk- and fairy-tale versions of

Rumpelstiltskin. The question still concerns breaking the magic spell.

> *Once upon a time there was a miller who was poor, but he had a beautiful daughter. Now it so happened that he came to speak with the king, and in order to make himself seem important, he said to the king: 'I have a daughter who can spin straw into gold.'*
>
> *The king replied: 'That is an art which pleases me! If your daughter is as talented as you say, then bring her to my castle tomorrow, and I'll put her to a test.'*
>
> *When the girl was brought to him, he led her into a room which was filled with straw. There he gave her a spinning-wheel and reel and said: 'Now get to work, and, if you do not spin this straw into gold by morning, then you must die.' Thereupon he locked the door himself, and she remained inside.*
>
> *The poor miller's daughter sat there and was close to her wits' end: she knew nothing about spinning straw into gold, and her fear grew greater and greater. She began to cry, and then suddenly the door opened and a little man entered and said:*
>
> *'Good evening, miss, why are you crying so much?'*
>
> *'Alas,' answered the girl, 'I'm supposed to spin straw into gold, and I don't know how.'*
>
> *The little man then asked: 'What will you give me if I spin it for you?'*
>
> *'My necklace,' the girl said.*
>
> *The little man took the necklace and sat himself down at the wheel and 'whizz, whizz, whizz,' three times round, the spool was full. Then he inserted another one, and 'whizz, whizz, whizz,' the second one was full. And so it went until morning. All the straw was spun and all the spools were filled with gold. The king showed up right at sunrise, and, when he saw the gold, he was surprised and pleased, but his heart grew even greedier. He locked the miller's daughter in another room which was even larger than the first one and ordered her to spin all the straw into gold if she valued her life. The girl did not know what to do and began to cry. Once again the door opened, and the little man appeared and asked: 'What will you give me if I spin the straw into gold for you?'*
>
> *'The ring from my finger,' answered the girl.*
>
> *The little man took the ring, began to work away at the wheel again, and by morning he had spun all the straw into shining gold. The king was extremely pleased by the sight, but his lust for gold was still not satisfied. So he had the miller's daughter brought into an even larger room filled with straw and said to her: 'You must spin all this into gold tonight. If you succeed, you shall become my wife.'*
>
> *Even though she's just a miller's daughter, he thought, I'll never find a richer woman in the world.*

When the girl was alone, the little man came again for a third time and asked: 'What will you give me if I spin the gold for you once more?'

'I have nothing left to give,' answered the girl.

'Then promise me your first child when you become queen.'

Who knows whether it will ever come to that, thought the miller's daughter. And, since she knew of no other way out of her predicament, she promised the little man what he demanded. In return the little man spun the straw into gold once again. And when the king came in the morning and found everything as he had wished, he called for a wedding, and the beautiful miller's daughter became a queen.

After a year she gave birth to a beautiful child. The little man had disappeared from her mind, but then suddenly he appeared in her room and said: 'Now give me what you promised.'

The queen was horrified and offered the little man all the treasures of the kingdom if he would let her keep her child, but the little man responded: 'No, something living is more important to me than all the treasures of the world.'

Then the queen began to grieve and weep so much that the little man felt sorry for her. 'I'll give you three days' time,' he said. 'If you can guess my name by the third day, you shall keep your child.'

The queen spent the entire night trying to recall all the names she had ever heard. She also sent a messenger out into the country to inquire high and low what other names there were. On the following day when the little man appeared, she began with Kaspar, Melchior, Balzer, and then repeated all the names she knew, one after the other. But to all of them the little man said: 'That's not my name.'

The second day she had her servants ask around in the neighbouring area what names people used, and she came up with the most unusual and strangest names when the little man appeared: 'Is your name Ribsofbeef or Muttonchops or Lacedleg?'

But he always answered: 'That's not my name.'

On the third day the messenger returned and reported: 'I couldn't find a single new name, but as I was climbing a high mountain at the edge of the forest where the fox and hare say good night to each other, I saw a small house and in front of the house was a fire and around the fire danced a ridiculous little man who was hopping on one leg and screeching:

Today I'll brew, tomorrow I'll bake.
Soon I'll have the queen's namesake.
Oh how hard it is to play my game,
for Rumpelstiltskin is my name!'

You can imagine how happy the queen was when she heard the name. And as soon as the little man entered and asked 'What's

*my name, your highness?' she responded first by guessing: 'Is
your name Kunz?'*

    'No.'

    'Is your name Heinz?'

    'No.'

    'Can your name be Rumpelstiltskin?'

    *'The devil told you, the devil told you!' the little man scream-
ed and stamped with his right foot so ferociously that it went
deep into the ground. Then he grabbed the other foot angrily
with both hands to pry himself from the ground, and he ripped
himself in two.*

— JACOB AND WILHELM GRIMM[21]

*After the miller has boasted that his daughter could spin straw
into gold, the king led the girl into a room filled with straw and
said: 'If you don't spin this straw into gold by tomorrow morning,
you must die.' Then he locked the door behind him. The poor
miller's daughter was scared and began to cry. Suddenly a little
man appeared and asked: 'What will you give me if I spin the
straw into gold for you?' The girl gave him her necklace. The
little man sat down at the spinning-wheel and 'whizz, whizz,
whizz,' three times the wheel went round, and soon the spool
was full and had to be replaced. And so it went until morning.
By then all the straw had been spun into gold.*

    *When the king saw this, he was pleased. He immediately
brought the miller's daughter to a larger room also filled with
straw and ordered her again to spin the straw into gold by
morning if she valued her life. And again the miller's daughter
cried until the little man appeared. This time she gave him the
ring from her finger. The little man began to make the wheel
whizz, and by morning all the straw was spun into gold.*

    *When the king saw the gold, he was overjoyed. But he was
still not satisfied. He led the miller's daughter into an even
larger room and said: 'If you spin this straw into gold by tomorrow, you shall become my wife.' When the girl was alone,
the little man appeared for the third time and asked: 'What
will you give me if I help you?' But the miller's daughter had
nothing to give away.*

    *'Then promise to give me your first child when you become
queen.'*

    This jolted her and finally made her open her eyes.

    *'You're crazy!' the miller's daughter yelled. 'I'll never marry
this horrible king. I'd never give my child away.'*

    *'I'm not going to spin. I'll never spin again!' the little man
screamed in rage. 'I've spun in vain!' The little man stamped
with his right foot so ferociously that it went deep into the
ground and jarred the door to the room open. Then the miller's
daughter ran out into the great wide world and was saved.*

— ROSEMARIE KÜNZLER[22]

The Use and Abuse of Folk and Fairy Tales with Children

In fairy tales, so people say, good always triumphs over evil, and in the end everything turns out well. But you don't have to believe what people say. You've got to think about things for yourself. For instance, about Rumpelstiltskin. I always felt sorry for him.

Just think about what happened to him. He helped the miller's daughter who was locked up in a room filled with straw and was supposed to spin the straw into gold only because her father was a liar and claimed that she could do this. Actually she couldn't do anything except cry and complain and give Rumpelstiltskin first a necklace and then a ring to thank him for having spun the straw into gold. Can you imagine — Rumpelstiltskin spins a whole room filled with straw into gold, and for this he receives a tiny ring. He could have spun himself a ring in ten minutes without any trouble!

And when the miller's daughter had nothing more to give away and still wanted Rumpelstiltskin to continue working for her because she wanted to become queen, she promised him her first child. A promise is a promise and almost as good as a gift — isn't that true? Well, not for a miller's daughter who then becomes queen. When the time came, she wanted to break the promise, and the nice Rumpelstiltskin even gave her a chance — she was supposed to guess his name. Then she could keep the child. Yet, the former miller's daughter and present queen didn't even make an honest effort to do this. She didn't go to a library and look up various names, nor did she even ask around — she sent out messengers who were supposed to find out Rumpelstiltskin's name. And this worked, too — but it has nothing to do with justice. She asked rather insidiously: 'Can your name be Rumpelstiltskin?' and the pegged Rumpelstiltskin became so furious that he ripped himself in two.

It is easy to imagine that all of this could have ended in a much better and much fairer way. This Rumpelstiltskin was a lonely wretch — the fairy tale refers to him as a 'ridiculous little man'; but when he spun gold, he wasn't ridiculous. For he was needed. What this little man accomplished in his work was worth a kingdom, and one can assume that Rumpelstiltskin knew that. But he wasn't happy because of this. He wanted to have something living, a friend, a human being, who laughed with him and was sad with him, who wished him a hearty appetite before each meal and asked him afterwards whether he enjoyed the meal. This is why Rumpelstiltskin wanted the royal child — so that he would not have to be alone.

Naturally no mother wants to give away her child. In this regard the queen's actions are understandable. But, if she had been a bit more sensible, a bit more just, and a bit more considerate to those who deserved this, then she would have said: 'I can't give you my child, for he belongs only to himself. But why don't you come live with us — with my child, with me and the king? We could do a lot of things together. You'll see how much fun we can have.' Then Rumpelstiltskin would have first turned pale and then blushed for joy. He would have climbed on a chair and would have given the queen a kiss on her cheek and the king a kiss on the crown — honour those who deserve to be honoured — and he would have sung a lullabye for the royal child to help him fall asleep, and a song to rouse him in the morning. And they would have been happy with each other until the end of their days.

But as the fairy tale now stands, that is not what I call justice.

— IRMELA BRENDER[23]

Notes

PREFACE

1. Ödön von Horváth, 'Das Märchen in unserer Zeit', from *Märchen Deutscher Dichter*, ed. Elisabeth Borchers, Insel Verlag, (Frankfurt am Main, 1972).
2. Josef Wittmann, 'Dornröschen' from *Neues vom Rumpelstilzschen*, ed. Hans-Joachim Gelberg, Beltz and Gelberg, (Weinheim, 1976).
3. Jochen Jung, 'Dornröschen' from *Bilderbogengeschichten, Märchen, Sagen, Abenteuer*, ed. Jochen Jung, Deutscher Taschenbuch Verlag, (Munich, 1976).
4. Vera Ferra-Mikurra, 'Dornröschen' from *Neues vom Rumpelstilzchen*, op. cit.
5. Erich Kästner, 'Das Märchen von der Vernunft' from *Märchen Deutscher Dichter*, op. cit.
6. Robert Wolfgang Schnell, 'Märchengeschichte' from ˋ *Märchen Deutscher Dichter*, op. cit.

1. ONCE THERE WAS A TIME

1. Horst Künnemann, *Märchen — Wozu?*, (Hamburg, 1978), p. 5. See also Renate Steinchen, 'Märchen: Eine Bestandsaufnahme', in *Kinder und Jugenditeratur*, ed. Margareta Gorschenek and Annamaria Rucktäschel (Munich, 1979).
2. For a discussion of the problem of nomenclature for traditional narrative forms, see William Bascom, 'The Forms of Folklore: Prose Narratives', *Journal of American Folklore*, 78 (1965), pp. 3-20, and Linda Dégh, 'Folk Narrative', in *Folklore and Folklife*, ed. Richard M. Dorson (Chicago, 1972), pp. 53-84. For the distinction between folk tale and fairy tale, see my essay 'Might Makes Right' in this volume which originally appeared as 'Breaking the Magic Spell: Politics and the Fairy Tale', in *New German Critique*, 6(1975), pp. 116-35.
3. 'Culture Industry Reconsidered', *New German Critique*, 6(1975), p. 12.

4. James W. Heisig, 'Bruno Bettelheim and the Fairy Tales', *Children's Literature*, 6(1977), p. 94.
5. Roger Sale, *Fairy Tales and After* (Cambridge, Mass., 1978), p. 26.
6. See 'The Work of Art in the Age of Mechanical Reproduction', in *Illuminations*, trans. Harry Zohn (New York, 1968).
7. See *Soziale Ordnungen im Spiegel der Marchen*, 2 vols. (Stuttgart, 1976).
8. *Die Wahrheit des Märchens* (Halle, 1954), p. 14.
9. *Märchen, Phantasie und soziales Lernen* (Berlin, 1974), p. 46.
10. Cf. Max Lüthi, *Shakespeares Dramen*, 2nd ed. (Berlin, 1966) and Robert Weimann, *Shakespeare und die Tradition des Volkstheaters* (Berlin, 1967).
11. See the 'Nachwort' by Klaus Hammer to the edition *Französische Feenmärchen des 18. Jahrhunderts* (Berlin, 1974). Also useful is Gontheir-Louis Fink, *Naissance et Apogée du Conte Merveilleux en Allemagne 1740-1800* (Paris, 1966), pp. 11-73.
12. See Roger Sale's comments in *Fairy Tales and After*, op. cit., pp. 54-63.
13. For more information on the history of *Beauty and the Beast*, see Iona and Peter Opie, *The Classic Fairy Tales* (London, 1974), pp. 137-8.
14. 'Authority and the Family Revisited: or, A World Without Fathers?', *New German Critique*, 13 (1978), p. 36.
15. ibid., p. 36.
16. Oskar Negt and Alexander Kluge, *Erfahrung und Öffentlichkeit. Zur Organisationsanalyse von bürgerlicher und proletarischer Öffentlichkeit* (Frankfurt am Main, 1973), pp. 72-3.
17. These lists were taken from Joseph J. Arpad, 'Between Folklore and Literature: Popular Culture as Anomaly', *Journal of Popular Culture*, 9 (1975), p. 404.
18. New York, 1969.
19. Univ. of Bowling Green Press, 1972, p. 26. The situation in England was similar to that in Germany. See Richter and Merkel, *Märchen, Phantasie und soziales Lernen*, op. cit., pp. 58-103.
20. Kotzin, *Dickens and the Fairy Tale*, op. cit., p. 28.
21. See Melchior Schedler, *Kindertheater* (Frankfurt am Main, 1972), pp. 43-71.
22. *Folklore and Fakelore* (Cambridge, Mass., 1976), pp. 61-2.
23. *The Mind Managers* (Boston, 1973), p. 5.

2. MIGHT MAKES RIGHT

1. For a good discussion of the different approaches, see Mathilde Hain, 'Die Volkserzählung: Ein Forschungsbericht über die letzten Jahrzehnte (etwa 1945-70)', *Deutsche Vierteljahrsschrift*, 45 (May 1971), pp. 243-74, and Richard M. Dorson, 'Foreword,' *Folktales of Germany*, ed. Kurt Ranke (Chicago, 1966), pp. v-xxv.
2. See *The Folktale* (New York, 1946). The Finnish School's work is

Notes

best represented by Antti Aarne. See the essay 'Ursprung der Märchen', in *Wege der Märchenforschung*, ed. Felix Karlinger (Darmstadt, 1973), pp. 42-60. This excellent collection of essays contains short pieces by representatives of different schools such as Reuschel, Leyen, Panzer, de Boor, von Sydow, Röhrich, Lüthi, K. Ranke and Pop.

3. A good example of this type of work is Otto Brinkmann, *Das Erzählen in einer Dorfgemeinschaft* (Münster, 1931).
4. See Gottfried Henssen, ed., *Mecklenburger Erzählen . . . aus der Sammlung Richard Wossidlos* (Berlin, 1958) and Reinhold Bünker, *Schwänke, Sagen und Märchen heanzischer Mundart* (Leipzig, 1906).
5. There is an excellent collection of essays covering the different approaches: Wilhelm Laiblin, ed., *Märchenforschung und Tiefenpsychologie* (Darmstadt, 1969). See also Paulo de Carvalho-Neto, *Folklore and Psychoanalysis* (Coral Gables, 1972).
6. *Morphology of the Folktale*, 2nd rev. ed., Indiana University (Bloomington, 1968). Propp has modified his views in his essay 'Les transformations des contes fantastiques', *Théorie de la littérature*, trans. and ed. Tzvetan Todorov (Paris, 1965), pp. 234-61.
7. See *Das europäische Volksmärchen*, 2nd rev. ed. (Bern, 1960). *Märchen*, 3rd rev. ed. (Stuttgart, 1968) and the English version of *Es war einmal* (Göttingen, 1962), which is translated as *Once Upon a Time* (New York, 1970).
8. *Märchen, Erzähler und Erzählgemeinschaft* (Berlin, 1962). There is also a good survey of folk-tale scholarship in the chapter 'Ueberblick über die Ergebnisse der bisherigen Märchenforschung', pp. 47-65. This book was revised to a certain extent and translated under the title *Folktales and Society* (Bloomington, 1969).
9. Iona and Peter Opie, *The Classic Fairy Tales* (London, 1974), p. 11.
10. 3rd rev. ed. (Oxford, 1955), p. 670.
11. Opie and Opie, *The Classic Fairy Tales*, op. cit., pp. 14-15.
12. Degh, *Folktales and Society*, op. cit., pp. 65-6.
13. Dieter Richter and Johannes Merkel, *Märchen, Phantasie und soziales Lernen* (Berlin, 1974), pp. 22-3.
14. ibid., p. 22.
15. See W. H. Bruford, *Germany in the Eighteenth Century: The Social Background of the Literary Revival* (Cambridge, 1965), pp. 291-327, and Klaus Epstein, *The Genesis of German Conservatism* (Princeton, 1966), pp. 29-83.
16. *Die Verbürgerlichung der deutschen Kunst, Literatur und Musik im 18. Jahrhundert* (Frankfurt am Main, 1972), pp. 288-99.
17. Dégh, *Folktales and Society*, op. cit., p. 66.
18. See the introductory chapters to Richard Benz, *Märchendichtung der Romantiker* (Gotha, 1908), and Dégh, *Folktales and Society*, op. cit., pp. 65-8.
19. See Richter and Merkel, *Märchen, Phantasie und soziales Lernen*

185

op. cit., pp. 20-22.

20. See Epstein, *The Genesis of German Conservatism*, op. cit., pp. 38-41.

21. *Märchen, Phantasie und soziales Lernen*, op. cit., p. 18.

22. For the debate about the function of fantastic elements in fairy and folk tales, particularly among Marxists, see Christa Bürger, 'Die soziale Funktion volkstümlicher Erzählformen — Sage und Märchen', *Projekt Deutschunterricht 1*, ed. Heinz Ide (Stuttgart, 1971), pp. 26-56; Martin Freiberger, 'Wirklichkeit und kindliche Phantasie', *kürbiskern*, 1 (1974), pp. 51-67; Elvira Högemann-Ledwohn, 'Warum nicht auch die alten Märchen!', *kürbiskern*, 1 (1974), pp. 70-73; Bernd Wollenweber, 'Märchen und Sprichwort', *Projekt Deutschunterricht 6*, ed. Heinz Ide (Stuttgart, 1974), pp. 12-92. See also Wilfried Gottschalch's review of the Richter and Merkel book, 'Kinderunterhaltung: Phantasie und Märchen', in *Ästhetik und Kommunikation*, 20 (June 1975), pp. 85-7.

23. For the most comprehensive discussion of the folk tale's style and form, see Lüthi's *Das europäische Volksmärchen*, op. cit.

24. ibid.

25. Michel Butor, 'On Fairy Tales', *European Literary Theory and Practice*, ed. Vernon W. Gras (New York, 1973), p. 352.

26. See Wilhelm Schoof, *Zur Entstehungsgeschichte der Grimmschen Märchen* (Hamburg, 1959). The most important study dealing with the stylization of the folk tales by the Brothers Grimm is Heinz Röllecke's *Die älteste Märchensammlung der Brüder Grimm* (Cologny-Geneva, 1975). He compares the original handwritten manuscript of 1810, which was discovered in the Ölenberg monastery (Alsace) and published in 1927, with the first published volume of 1812. Through his close philological study it becomes clear how the Brothers Grimms' point of view practically shaped the collected folk tales into literary fairy tales.

27. *Kinder- und Hausmärchen* (Munich, 1963), p. 387. The German title of the tale is *Sechse kommen durch die ganze Welt*.

28. Cf. B. Wollenweber, 'Märchen und Sprichwort', pp. 24-8.

29. See 'Les transformations des contes fantastiques', *Théorie de la littérature*, pp. 234-61.

30. Dégh, *Folktales and Society*, op. cit., p. 65.

31. See Hans Mayer, 'Vergebliche Renaissance: Das "Märchen" bei Goethe und Gerhart Hauptmann', *Von Lessing bis Thomas Mann* (Pfullingen, 1959), pp. 356-82.

32. Munich, 1965.

33. Hans J. Haferkorn, 'Zur Entstehung der bürgerlichliterarischen Intelligenz und des Schriftstellers in Deutschland zwischen 1750 und 1800', in *Deutsches Bürgertum und literarische Intelligenz*, ed. Bernd Lutz (Stuttgart, 1974), p. 114.

34. E. T. A. Hoffmann, *Fantasie und Nachtstücke*, ed. Walter Müller-Seidel (Munich, 1960), p. 179, 'A Tale from the New Times'.

35. See *Oeuvres Complètes*, ed. Yves Gerard Le Dantec (Paris, 1961), pp. 323-462.

Notes

36. Cf. *Die Zerstörung der Vernunft* (Neuwied, 1962) and *Skizze einer Geschichte der neueren deutschen Literatur* (Neuwied, 1964).

3. THE ROMANTIC FAIRY TALE IN GERMANY

1. In order to make a clear-cut distinction between the *Volksmärchen* and the *Kunstmärchen*, I shall continue to use the terms 'folk tale' and 'fairy tale' respectively as they were elaborated in Chapter 2, 'Might Makes Right — The Politics of Folk and Fairy Tales'.

2. For some of the more significant general studies, see Hermann Todsen, 'Über die Entwicklung des romantischen Kunstmärchens', Diss. Berlin, 1906; Richard Benz, *Märchen-Dichtung der Romantiker* (Gotha, 1908); Rudolf Buchmann, *Helden und Mächte des romantischen Kunstmärchens* (Leipzig, 1910); Mimi Ida Jehle, 'Das deutsche Kunstmärchen von der Romantik bis zum Naturalismus', *University of Illinois Bulletin*, 32(1935); Marianne Thalmann, *Das Märchen und die Moderne* (Stuttgart, 1961); Hans Steffen, 'Märchendichtung in Aufklärung und Romantik', *Formkräfte der deutschen Dichtung vom Barock bis zur Gegenwart*, ed. Hans Steffen (Göttingen, 1963), pp. 100-23; Hugo Moser, 'Sage und Märchen in der deutschen Romantik', in *Die deutsche Romantik*, ed. Hans Steffen (Göttingen, 1967), pp. 253-76; James Trainer, 'The Märchen', *The Romantic Period in Germany*, ed. Siegbert Prawer (London, 1970), pp. 97-120, Jens Tismar, *Kunstmärchen* (Stuttgart, 1977). Tismar's book contains a more detailed bibliographical compilation with excellent annotation.

3. The most exhaustive treatment of the fairy tale's antecedents has been Gonthier-Louis Fink's *Naissance et Apogée du Conte Merveilleux en Allemagne 1740-1800*, Annales Littéraires de l'Université de Besançon, Vol. 80 (Paris, 1966). Despite the remarkable analysis of the parallels between the French *conte de fées* and the German fairy tale, Fink studies this development only as part of a literary tradition and does not consider the relationship of the fairy tale to socio-economic developments.

4. One of the deeper plunges along these lines is Anniela Jaffé's 'Bilder und Symbole aus E. T. A. Hoffmann's Märchen "Der goldene Topf"', *Gestaltungen des Unbewussten*, ed. C. G. Jung (Zurich, 1950), pp. 239-616. This exhaustive and exhausting Jungian study is twice as long as Hoffmann's original tale.

5. Published in two volumes. Band 1: *Das frühe Europa* (Stuttgart, 1976); Band 2: *Stabile Verhaltensweisen der Völker in unserer Zeit* (Stuttgart, 1977).

6. *Telos*, 15(1973), pp. 47-74.

7. *Narziss an der Quelle: Das romantische Kunstmärchen* (Wiesbaden, 1977).

8. For more thorough studies of the French fairy tales and their

literary development, see Fink's *Naissance et Apogée du conte Merveilleux en Allemagne 1740-1800*, op. cit., and Hermann Hubert Wetzel's *Märchen in den französischen Novellensammlungen der Renaissance* (Berlin, 1974).

9. *Narziss and der Quelle*, op. cit., p. 12.
10. See Mathilde Hain, 'Die Volkserzählung: Ein Forschungsbericht über die letzten Jahrzehnte (etwa 1945-1970)', *Deutsche Vierteljahrsschrift*, 45(1971), pp. 243-74; and Richard M. Dorson, 'Foreword', *Folktales of Germany*, ed. Kurt Ranke (Chicago, 1966), pp. v-xxv.
11. A. Nitschke, *Soziale Ordnungen im Spiegel der Märchen*, II, p. 19. Hereafter all page references will be made in the text.
12. See Helmut Böhme, *Prolegomena zu einer Sozial und Wirtschaftgeschichte Deutschlands im 19. und 20. Jahrhundert* (Frankfurt am Main, 1968), and Henri Brunschwig, *Enlightenment and Romanticism in Eighteenth-Century Prussia* (Chicago, 1974).
13. Cf. Chapter 2, 'Might Makes Right' in this volume, and Linda Dégh, *Erzähler und Erzählgemeinschaft* (Berlin, 1962).
14. Volker Klotz, 'Weltordnung im Märchen', *Neue Rundschau*, 81 (1970), pp. 73-91; Max Lüthi, *Das Volksmärchen als Dichtung* (Düsseldorf, 1975). For some other important works by Lüthi, see: *Das europäische Volksmärchen, Form und Wesen* (Bern, 1947); *Volksmärchen und Volkssage* (Bern, 1961); *Märchen* (Stuttgart, 1962); *Es war einmal . . . Vom Wesen des Volksmärchens* (Göttingen, 1962), which has been translated into English as *Once Upon a Time: On the Nature of Fairy Tales*, trans. Lee Chadeayne and Paul Gottwald (New York, 1970).
15. Klotz, 'Weltordnung im Märchen', op. cit., pp. 85-6.
16. Lüthi, *Däs Volksmärchen als Dichtung*, op. cit., p. 49.
17. ibid., pp. 177-8.
18. *Werke und Briefe*, ed. Alfred Kelletat (Munich, 1962), p. 505.
19. Tismar, *Kunstmärchen*, op. cit., p. 31.
20. 'Ursprünge und Stellung der Romantik', *Weimarer Beiträge*, 2 (1975), pp. 42-3.
21. Cf. G. P. Gooch, *Germany and the French Revolution* (1920); reprint, New York, 1966), pp. 230-316.
22. Cf. J. J. Heiner, 'Das "goldene Zeitalter" in der deutschen Romantik. Zur sozialpsychologischen Funktion eines Topos', *Zeitschrift für deutsche Philologie*, 91(1972), pp. 206-34. Also interesting for its historical presentation of the literary development of this topos is Hans-Joachim Mähl's *Die Idee des goldenen Zeitalters im Werk des Novalis: Studien zur Wesenbestimmung der frühromantischen Utopie und zu ihren ideengeschichtlichen Voraussetzungen* (Heidelberg, 1965).
23. *Enlightenment and Romanticism in Eighteenth-Century Prussia*, op. cit. Though he concentrates largely on Prussia, his remarks have great validity for the entire romantic movement.
24. ibid., pp. 244-5.
25. 'Is the Novel Problematic?', *Telos*, 15(1973), p. 48. Hereafter all

Notes

page references will be cited in the text.

26. See Rudolf Vierhaus, 'Ständewesen und Staatsverwaltung in Deutschland im späten 18. Jahrhundert', *Dauer und Wandel der Geschichte*, ed. Rudolf Vierhaus and Manfred Botzenhart (Münster, 1966), pp. 337-60, and Günter Birtsch, 'Zur sozialen und politischen Rolle des deutschen, vornehmlich preussischen Adels am Ende des 18. Jahrunderts', *Der Adel vor der Revolution*, ed. Rudolf Vierhaus (Göttingen, 1971), pp. 77-95.

27. For a discussion of the meaning of the public sphere, see Jürgen Habermas, *Strukturwandel der Öffentlichkeit* (Berlin, 1962), and 'The Public Sphere', *New German Critique* 3(1974), pp. 49-55. See also Peter Hohendahl's 'Introduction to Habermas', *The Public Sphere*', in the same issue of *New German Critique*, pp. 45-48.

28. *Prolegomena zu einer Sozial und Wirtschaftsgeschichte Deutschlands im 19. und 20. Jahrhundert*, op. cit., p. 23.

29. Cf. Brunschwig, *Enlightenment and Romanticism in Eighteenth-Century Prussia*, op. cit., pp. 223-45.

30. See E. J. Hobsbawm, *The Age of Revolution 1789-1848* (New York, 1964), p. 308: 'The real problem was that of the artist cut off from a recognizable function, patron or public and left to cast his soul as a commodity upon a blind market, to be bought or not; or to work within a system of patronage which would generally have been economically untenable even if the French Revolution had not established its human indignity. The artist therefore stood alone, shouting into the night, uncertain of even an echo. It was only natural that he should turn himself into the genius, who created only what was within him, regardless of the world and in defiance of a public whose only right was to accept him on his own terms or not at all.'

31. For informative studies of this situation, see W. H. Bruford, *Germany in the Eighteenth Century: The Social Background of the Literary Revival* (London, 1935); Hans J. Haferkorn, 'Zur Entstehung der bürgerlichliterarischen Intelligenz des Schriftstellers in Deutschland zwischen 1750 und 1800', in *Literaturwissenschaft und Sozialwissenschaften 3: Deutsches Bürgertum und literarische Intelligenz 1750-1800*, ed. Bernd Lutz (Stuttgart, 1974), pp. 113-276.

32. 'Das "goldene Zeitalter" in der deutschen Romantik', op. cit., pp. 211-12.

33. *Eros and Civilization* (New York, 1962), pp. 132-3.

34. ibid., pp. 82-3.

35. Cf. my analysis of this situation, 'W. H. Wackenroder: In Defense of His Romanticism', *Germanic Review* (1969), pp. 247-58, and Mary Hurst Schubert's critical introduction to her translation, Wilhelm Heinrich Wackenroder's *Confessions and Fantasies* (University Park, Penn., 1971), pp. 3-75.

36. W. H. Wackenroder, *Werke und Briefe* (Heidelberg, 1967), p. 387.

37. ibid., p. 405.

38. ibid., p. 404.

39. *Enlightenment and Romanticism in Eighteenth-Century Prussia*, op. cit., pp. 227-8.
40. The best study of his life which examines Novalis as a progressive thinker and writer is Gerhard Schulz, *Novalis* (Reinbek bei Hamburg, 1969). See also Richard Faber's *Novalis: Die Phantasie an die Macht* (Stuttgart, 1970), which links Novalis' ideas to those of Ernst Bloch and Walter Benjamin and tendencies of contemporary revolutionary movements.
41. Novalis, *Werke und Briefe* (Munich, 1962), p. 508.
42. ibid., p. 506.
43. ibid., p. 271.
44. ibid., p. 519.
45. ibid., p. 266.
46. *Weiblicher Lebenszusammenhang: Von der Beschränktheit der Strategien und der Unangemessenheit der Wünsche* (Frankfurt am Main, 1976), pp. 162-3.
47. Ludwig Tieck, *Schriften*, Vol. 4 (Berlin, 1828), p. 219.
48. Novalis, *Werke und Briefe*, op. cit., p. 502. 'The art of estranging in a pleasant manner, making an object unfamiliar and yet familiar and attractive, that is romantic poetics.'
49. This is described fully in Johannes P. Keur, *Ludwig Tieck, Dichter einer Krise* (Heidelberg, 1977), pp. 65-125. See also Marianne Thalmann, *Der romantische Weltmann aus Berlin* (Bern, 1955).
50. For an excellent analysis of Tieck's design in reversing motifs, see Marianne Thalmann, *Das Märchen und die Moderne* (Stuttgart, 1961), pp. 35-58.
51. For a complete study of Brentano's life and a discussion of other works about him, see Werner Hoffmann, *Clemens Brentano* (Bern, 1966). Wolfgang Frühwald's essay 'Clemens Brentano', in *Deutsche Dichter der Romantik*, ed. Benno von Wiese (Berlin, 1971), pp. 280-309, is also helpful.
52. Clemens Brentano, *Briefe*, ed. F. Seebass (Nuremberg, 1951), II, p. 7.
53. For a good account of his life and also a penetrating study of *Peter Schlemihl*, see Warner Feudel, *Adelbert von Chamisso* (Leipzig, 1971).
54. E. T. A. Hoffmann, *Späte Werke*, ed. Walter Müller-Seidel (Munich, 1965), p. 94.
55. ibid., p. 16.
56. ibid., p. 17.
57. ibid., pp. 75-6.
58. Though somewhat outdated in its over-all approach to the romantic period, Harvey Hewett-Taylor's biography is still one of the most comprehensive for demonstrating the seriousness of Hoffmann's artistic endeavours. See *Hoffmann: Author of the Tales* (Princeton, 1948).
59. *Morphology of the Folktale*, 2nd rev. ed. (Bloomington, 1968).

Notes

4. THE INSTRUMENTALIZATION OF FANTASY

1. Novalis, *Werke und Briefe*, ed. Alfred Kelletat (Munich, 1962), p. 506.
2. 'The Storyteller', in *Illuminations*, trans. Harry Zohn (New York, 1968), p. 101.
3. ibid., p. 102.
4. Heinrich Regius, *Dämmerung: Notzien in Deutschland* (Zurich, 1934), p. 102. This citation is from a 1972 reprint of the original which was published by Edition Max.
5. *Dialectic of Enlightenment* (New York, 1969), pp. 126-7.
6. ibid., p. 137.
7. For a discussion of the Frankfurt School's work in this area, see the chapter entitled 'Aesthetic Theory and the Critique of Mass Culture', in Martin Jay, *The Dialectical Imagination: A History of the Frankfurt School and the Institute of Social Research, 1923-1950* (Boston, 1973), pp. 173-218.
8. Marcuse, *One-Dimensional Man* (Boston, 1964), p. 154.
9. 'Technology and Science as "Ideology"', in *Toward a Rational Society* (Boston, 1970), p. 92.
10. See *Strukturwandel der Öffentlichkeit* (Berlin, 1962), pp. 157-98.
11. 'Technology and Science as "Ideology"', op. cit., p. 103.
12. ibid., pp. 118-19.
13. See Wolfgang Fritz Haug, *Kritik der Warenästhetik* (Frankfurt am Main, 1971).
14. See Oskar Negt and Alexander Kluge, *Öffentlichkeit und Erfahrung: Zur Organisationsanalyse von bürgerlicher und proletarischer Öffentlichkeit* (Frankfurt am Main, 1972).
15. *Legitimation Crisis* (Boston, 1975), p. 117.
16. See *The Consciousness Industry* (New York, 1974).
17. See *The Long Revolution*, rev. ed. (New York, 1961) and *Television: Technology and Cultural Form* (New York, 1975). Williams does not borrow directly from the Frankfurt School, but his work derives from many of the same critical promises.
18. See *False Promises* (New York, 1973).
19. See *Captains of Consciousness* (New York, 1977).
20. See Herbert I. Schiller, *The Mind Managers* (Boston, 1973) and Michael R. Real, *Mass-Mediated Culture* (Englewood Cliffs, N. J., 1977).
21. Real, *Mass-Mediated Culture*, op. cit., p. xi.
22. ibid., p. 14.
23. ibid., p. 14.
24. *Ideology and the Imagination* (London, 1975), pp. 203-4.
25. ibid., p. 209.
26. *The Milwaukee Journal* (November 10, 1977), part 2, p. 7.
27. Englewood Cliffs, N. J., 1972.
28. Tom Burns, 'Folklore in the Mass Media: Television', *Folklore Forum*, 2 (1969), pp. 99-106. Priscilla Denby, 'Folklore in the Mass

Media', *Folklore Forum*, 4 (1971), pp. 113-23.
29. Burns, 'Folklore in the Mass Media: Television', op. cit., pp. 98-9.
30. Denby, 'Folklore in the Mass Media', op. cit., p. 121. For further comments on this problem, see the chapter 'Das Märchen und die Medien' in Werner Psaar and Manfred Klein, *Wer hat Angst vor der bösen Geiss?* (Braunschweig, 1976), pp. 163-210.
31. See *How Can Children's Literature Meet the Needs of Modern Children: Fairy Tale and Poetry Today*, Arbeitskreis für Jugendliteratur (Munich, 1977), pp. 23-31, and 62-5.
32. ibid., p. 28.
33. ibid., p. 28.
34. ibid., pp. 62-3.
35. ibid., p. 31.
36. *How to Read Donald Duck* (New York, 1975), p. 46.
37. ibid., p. 53.
38. *Morphology of the Folktale*, 2nd rev. ed., Indiana University (Bloomington, 1968).
39. *Les Contes de Perrault: culture savante et traditions populaires* (Paris, 1968).
40. *The Disney Version* (New York, 1969), p. 182.
41. ibid., p. 190.
42. George Lucas, *Star Wars* (New York, 1976), pp. 219-20.
43. *The Official Rocky Scrapbook* (New York, 1977), p. 9.
44. 'Rocky: Two Faces of the American Dream', *Jump Cut*, 14 (1977), p. 1.
45. Rainer Traub and Harald Wieser, eds., *Gespräche mit Ernst Bloch* (Frankfurt am Main, 1975), pp. 59-77.
46. Ernst Bloch, *Ästhetik des Vor-Scheins I*, ed. Gert Ueding (Frankfurt am Main, 1974), pp. 73-5.
47. *Gespräche mit Ernst Bloch*, p. 73.
48. *Öffentlichkeit und Erfahrung*; op. cit., p. 287.
49. ibid., p. 163.
50. ibid., p. 60.
51. ibid., p. 294.
52. *Mass-Mediated Culture*, op. cit., p. 267.
53. ibid., p. 268.

5. THE UTOPIAN FUNCTION OF FAIRY TALES AND FANTASY

1. On Karl Marx (New York, 1971), pp. 44-5. Taken from Bloch's *Das Prinzip Hoffnung*. I have altered the translation slightly.
2. For biographical information on Bloch see Erhard Bahr, *Ernst Bloch* (Berlin, 1974); David Gross, 'Ernst Bloch: The Dialectics of Hope', in *The Unknown Dimension*, eds. Dick Howard and Karl Klare (New York, 1972), pp. 107-30; Douglas Kellner and Harry O'Hara, 'Utopia and Marxism in Ernst Bloch', *New German Critique*, 9(Fall, 1976), pp. 11-34; Silvia Markun, *Ernst Bloch* (Reinbek

Notes

bei Hamburg, 1977).

3. *Tolkien*, (Boston, 1977), p. 128.
4. Aside from Carpenter's important biography, see Daniel Grotta-Kursa, *J. R. R. Tolkien, Architect of Middle Earth* (New York, 1976) for another good interpretation of his life.
5. Ernst Bloch, *Die Kunst, Schiller zu sprechen* (Frankfurt am Main, 1969), pp. 10-14.
6. Ernst Bloch, *Ästhetik des Vor-Scheins 1*, ed. Gert Ueding (Frankfurt am Main, 1976), p. 22.
7. ibid., p. 9.
8. See 'Non-synchronism and the Obligation to Its Dialectics', *New German Critique*, 11(Spring 1977), pp. 22-38. Also important is Anson Rabinbach's analysis of nonsynchronism in the same issue of *New German Critique*, 'Ernst Bloch's *Heritage of our Times* and the Theory of Fascism', pp. 5-21.
9. *The Tolkien Reader* (New York, 1966), p. 10. Hereafter all page references to this essay will be in the text. This essay was first delivered as a lecture at St Andrews on March 8, 1939. Tolkien revised the lecture during the early 1960s, and it was published in 1964.
10. The scholarly works on folk and fairy tales are too numerous to list in their entirety. Two of the best on the folk tale are Stith Thompson, *The Folktale* (New York, 1946) and Max Lüthi, *Märchen*, 3rd rev. ed. (Stuttgart, 1968). For an introduction to the literary fairy tale, see Jens Tismar, *Das Kunstmärchen* (Stuttgart, 1977).
11. 'Fantasy Literature and Play: An Approach to Reader Response', *The Centennial Review*, 2 (1978), p. 207.
12. *Man On His Own: Essays in the Philosophy of Religion*, trans. E. B. Ashton (New York, 1971), p. 161. This essay is taken from *Das Prinzip Hoffnung*.
13. ibid., p. 162. For a thorough discussion of Bloch's notions on religion, see Gerard Raulet, 'Critique of Religion and Religion as Critique: The Secularized Hope of Ernst Bloch'; *New German Critique*, 9 (1976), pp. 71-85.
14. Karl Marx, *Die Frühschriften*, ed. Siegfried Landshut (Stuttgart, 1968), p. 246.
15. *The Hobbit* (New York, 1966), pp. 286-7. Hereafter all page references to the book will be in the text.
16. Though it is difficult to ascertain to what extent Tolkien was influenced by Richard Wagner's *Ring* tetralogy, the parallels are uncanny. In fact, if one were to do a study of Tolkien and Wagner on the basis of their romantic anti-capitalism, the similarities between the two might even be seen to be more striking. Some spade work has been done by William Blissett, 'The Despots of the Rings', *South Atlantic Quarterly*, 58 (1959), pp. 448-56, and Lin Carter, *Tolkien: A Look Behind 'The Lord of the Rings'* (New York, 1969), chs. 8-16.

17. The meaning of the ring changes dramatically in *The Lord of the Rings*, and its signification becomes greater. The power of the ring depends on the moral integrity of the ring-bearer, and Frodo exemplifies the greatness of the little fellow, the humanitarian guardian of civilization.
18. The picture of the Middle Earth becomes more varied and complex in *The Lord of the Rings*, but it remains essentially a conservative male world, and the value of women is determined by the manner in which they are prized and praised by men.
19. See Lin Carter's comments in his introduction to *Tolkien: A Look Behind 'The Lord of the Rings'*, op. cit., pp. 1-6.
20. *Modern Fantasy* (London, 1975), p. 157.
21. ibid., pp. 158-206.
22. *Man On His Own*; (New York, 1971), pp. 164-5.

6. THE USE AND ABUSE OF FOLK AND FAIRY TALES WITH CHILDREN

1. New York, 1974. Throughout his book, Bettelheim uses the term fairy tale to indicate folk tale or *Volksmärchen*. Occasionally he will make a distinction between a folk fairy tale and a literary fairy tale (*Kunstmärchen*), but more often than not he uses the term fairy tale indiscriminately. I shall employ the term folk tale when referring to the literature he discusses because it is largely of this variety.
2. *The Uses of Enchantment*, op. cit., p. 4. Hereafter the page references to this book will be cited in the text.
3. Cf. the excellent critique of Bettelheim's book in this regard, James W. Heisig, 'Bruno Bettelheim and the Fairy Tales', *Children's Literature*, 6(1977), pp. 93-115.
4. *Social Amnesia: A Critique of Contemporary Psychology from Adler to Laing* (Boston, 1975), pp. 12-13.
5. ibid., p. 50.
6. *Civilisation and Its Discontents*, trans. Joan Riviere, 5th ed. (London, 1951), pp. 60, 63.
7. Jessica Benhamin, 'The End of Internalization: Adorno's Social Psychology' *Telos*, 32(1977), p. 63.
8. Compare the excellent discussion of the debates around these topics in Patrick C. Lee and Robert Sussman Stewart, *Sex Differences: Cultural and Developmental Dimensions* (New York, 1976), pp. 13-32. See especially, William H. Gillespie's article 'Woman and Her Discontents: A Reassessment of Freud's view on Female Sexuality', pp. 133-150. See also Ulrike Prokop, *Weiblicher Zusammenhang. Von der Strategie und der Unangemessenheit der Wünsche* (Frankfurt am Main, 1976).
9. *Class Codes and Control: Theoretical Studies Towards a Sociology of Language* (New York, 1975), p. 124.

Notes

10. ibid., pp. 76-94.
11. ibid., p. 26.
12. ibid., p. 35.
13. *Band 1: Das frühe Europa*, (Stuttgart, 1976).
14. Cf. Robert Moore, 'From Rags to Witches: Stereotypes and Anti-Humanism in Fairy Tales', *Interracial Books for Children Bulletin*, 7(1975), pp. 1-3. Moore's major thesis is that fairy tales are dangerous material for children since they present stereotypes which are based on racist and sexist ideologies. The only positive way to relate fairy tales to children is to expose the destructive nature of the tales. Moore goes to the opposite extreme of Bettelheim, and thus, like Bettelheim, he distorts the meaning of the tales and their possibilities for positive use with children.
15. Cf. Lee and Stewart, *Sex Differences*, op. cit., pp. 15-22.
16. Berlin, 1974.
17. *Eros and Civilization* (New York, 1962), p. 135.
18. Cf. my article 'Down with Heidi, Down with Struwwelpeter, Three Cheers for the Revolution: Towards a New Socialist Children's Literature in West Germany', *Children's Literature*, 5(1976), pp. 162-79.
19. Aside from the radical reutilization of fairy tales, there have been other interesting experiments in West Germany along the lines of Bettelheim's work. However, the educators do not make the extraordinary claims Bettelheim makes. See Felicitas Betz, *Märchen als Schlüssel zur Welt* (Munich, 1977) and Gisela Erberlein, *Autogenes Training mit Märchen — Ein Ratgeber für Eltern und Kinder* (Düsseldorf, 1976).
20. See Lena Foellbach, *Es war einmal kein König: Spiele für Kinder nach Märchen aus aller Welt* (Berlin, 1977). While Foellbach's experiments are far from being radical, they indicate a way in which one can rewrite fairy tales as plays with children and activate their consciousness of social interaction. Such work has been conducted in East Germany and in the West as well and provides the basis for the reinvigoration of the folk and fairy-tale tradition.
21. This version of *Rumpelstiltskin* was taken from: *Kinder- und Hausmärchen gesammelt durch die Brüder Grimm*, vol. 1 (Frankfurt am Main, 1974), pp. 318-21.
22. Rosemarie Künzler, 'Rumpelstilzchen', in *Neues vom Rumpelstilzchen*, ed. Hans-Joachim Gelberg (Weinheim, 1976), pp. 26-8.
23. Irmela Brender, 'Das Rumpelstilzchen hat mir immer leid getan', in *Neues vom Rumpelstilzchen*, op. cit., pp. 198-200.

Index

Index

199